YOU MADE THAT DESSERT?

YOU MADE THAT DESSERT?

CREATE FABULOUS TREATS, EVEN IF YOU CAN BARELY BOIL WATER

BETH LIPTON

FOOD EDITOR FOR all you MAGAZINE

Guilford, Connecticut

Photos by Mark Russell

Library of Congress Cataloging-in-Publication Data

You made that dessert? : create fabulous treats, even if you can barely boil water / Beth Lipton, food editor at All you magazine.
    p. cm.
  Includes index.
  ISBN 978-0-7627-5008-5
  1. Desserts. I. Lipton, Beth. II. All you magazine.
  TX773.Y693 2009
  641.8'6—dc22

                                                              2009013875

Printed in China

10 9 8 7 6 5 4 3 2 1

For Mark, my best friend and the love of my life

CONTENTS

Introduction : viii

Before You Start Baking, Read This! : x

Cookies and Bars : xii

Cakes : 30

Custards and Puddings : 82

Pies and Fruit Desserts : 104

Candies : 150

Sauces and Frostings : 158

Emergency Desserts (Don't Panic!) : 171

The Tools : 174

The Ingredients : 179

The Lingo : 185

The How-Tos : 187

Acknowledgments : 193

Metric Conversion Tables : 195

Index : 196

INTRODUCTION

One afternoon when I was about thirteen, my friend Suki invited me to her house and offered to make us a snack. We were so busy giggling about boys that I wasn't paying attention to what she was doing—until I smelled the smoke. She was making pasta . . . without any water in the pot.

Fast forward to a few years ago. This time, my friend Philice—who had a meticulously renovated kitchen and nothing in the fridge but soy sauce, take-out ketchup packets, and Crystal Light lemonade—decided to make her fiancé's favorite pie for his birthday. His mom gave her the recipe, and promised that it was so simple, even a novice baker could make it. Philice, a sophisticated, educated, all-around fabulous woman, panicked when the recipe instructed her to "fold" two elements together. "I had no idea what that meant," she confessed to me later.

Finally, an acquaintance told me recently that she had lived in her apartment for nine years before she ever turned the oven on: "My new boyfriend offered to come over and cook dinner for me, and I realized I didn't even know if the oven worked."

Do any of these women remind you of yourself? If so, then you've picked up the right book.

Maybe you've heard people say that cooking is easy, but baking is hard because it's so precise. I think that's exactly the reason to start with baking—it is precise, so if you follow the directions, you'll be successful, and no guesswork.

Here is my pledge to you: You can open to any page in this book and make any of these desserts, today—without running all over town looking for exotic foods or fancy kitchen equipment. All you need is a few basic ingredients, a little bit of time, and a sense of adventure. Remember, it's just food—have fun trying out something new in the kitchen, and amaze whoever is lucky enough to taste the end result with your culinary skills. You'll be able to shrug and say, "Oh this? It was easy," even if you've never done more than make microwave popcorn.

The most important thing I hope you get from this book, aside from the admiration of your friends and loved ones for your previously hidden talent for baking, is enjoyment in the kitchen. This isn't life or death—it's dessert!—so please, try to relax and have a good time.

BEFORE YOU START BAKING, READ THIS!

Here are some tips before you get going, important things to remember whenever you set out to bake.

1. Read the whole recipe before you start! Read it before you even shop for ingredients. This is a good habit for baking or cooking anything, whether it's from this book or another source. The last thing you want is to get partway through making something only to find out that you need an ingredient or tool that you don't have, or that what you're making has to be refrigerated for 3 hours but you need it in 10 minutes. Read the whole thing first, start to finish—I promise it will save you time, money, and aggravation.

2. Get everything prepped before you begin. The French call this *mise en place*, meaning everything in its place. It may not seem easier, but believe me, having all of your ingredients and tools on the counter (or at the front of the fridge, if they need to stay cold) and measured out before you begin is very important. Not only will it make the whole process run more smoothly, but you run less risk of leaving something out (yes, I've learned this from personal experience!).

3. Prep your oven. Unless the recipe tells you otherwise, place a rack in the center rung of the oven. Preheat 10 to 15 minutes before you're ready to bake, to make sure the oven is primed and ready when it's time to put your item in there. If you're using more than one rack at a time—to bake two sheets of cookies, for example—place the racks in the top and bottom third of the oven, not all the way at the top or all the way at the bottom. Halfway through baking time, switch the two sheets, so the one that was on the higher rack moves to the lower rack and vice versa. When you do that, also switch the sheets front to back as well.

4. Test early. If the recipe gives a range for baking time, begin checking it at the earlier time. In other words, if the recipe says, "Bake for 35 to 40 minutes," start checking at 35 minutes.

5. Read the whole recipe before you start! Seriously, it's so important that I wanted to say it twice. So many baking efforts go wrong because of this. Don't let it happen to you!

Cookies and Bars

FUDGE BROWNIES 1

S'MORES BARS 2

TOBLERONE BROWNIES 4

COFFEE–CHOCOLATE CHIP BLONDIES 5

COOKIES-AND-CREAM CHEESECAKE BARS 6

GINGERSNAPS 7

HELLO DOLLIES 9

ORANGE–SCENTED CHOCOLATE CHIP
  COOKIES 10

PECAN PIE BARS 11

SALTY–SWEET CARAMEL NUT BARS 13

MOM'S MEXICAN WEDDING COOKIES 14

RASPBERRY JAM BARS 16

SESAME-OAT-PECAN COOKIES 17

CAPPUCCINO BISCOTTI 18

ROSEMARY BISCOTTI 20

PEANUT BUTTER COOKIES 21

PEANUT BUTTER AND JELLY BARS 22

CINNAMON–HAZELNUT SHORTBREAD 24

PISTACHIO–CRANBERRY BARS 26

CRANBERRY CORNMEAL COOKIES 27

CURRANT SCONES 28

"KITCHEN SINK" OATMEAL COOKIES 29

FUDGE BROWNIES

Prep time: 20 minutes ⏲ Baking time: 30 to 35 minutes ✋ Makes 24

There are bazillions of brownie recipes, many claiming to be "the best" or "the ultimate."
I won't claim that, but these dense, fudgy brownies always elicit groans of pleasure and requests
for the recipe. You won't taste the espresso—it just gives these brownies a little something extra.
They also freeze well, so make extras and keep them for "emergencies."

INGREDIENTS:

Cooking spray
4 ounces unsweetened chocolate
4 ounces semisweet chocolate
16 tablespoons (2 sticks) unsalted
    butter, cut into pieces
1¼ cups (5.4 ounces) all-purpose flour
1 teaspoon baking powder
1 teaspoon salt
2 teaspoons instant espresso powder
1 tablespoon vanilla extract
4 large eggs, at room temperature
2 cups (14 ounces) sugar
1¾ cups chopped walnuts (optional)

TOOLS:

Dry measuring cups
Measuring spoons
Cutting board
Chef's knife
9 x 13-inch baking pan
Saucepan
Fork
Flexible spatula
Large bowl
2 small bowls
Small cup
Whisk
Wire cooling rack

❶ Preheat the oven to 375°F. Line a 9 x 13-inch pan with foil, leaving a 2-inch overhang on two sides; mist lightly with cooking spray.

❷ On a cutting board, using a sharp chef's knife, chop both chocolates. Combine the chocolates and butter in a saucepan and place over your stove's lowest heat setting. Cook, stirring constantly with a flexible spatula, until the chocolate mixture is melted and smooth. Remove from the heat, pour into a large bowl, and let cool for 5 minutes.

❸ In a small bowl, combine the flour, baking powder, and salt; stir with a fork to mix well. In a small cup, dissolve the instant espresso powder in the vanilla extract, then stir it into the chocolate mixture. Use a whisk to beat the eggs and sugar together, then beat them into the chocolate mixture until well combined. Add the flour mixture; stir with the flexible spatula until all of the ingredients are well incorporated. Stir in the nuts (if using).

❹ Scrape the batter into the lined pan and spread with the flexible spatula until it's in an even layer. Bake for 30 to 35 minutes, until just set. Let the brownies cool in the pan on a wire rack.

❺ To slice, use the foil overhang to remove the brownies and place on a large cutting board. Use a chef's knife to cut them into 24 pieces, wiping off the knife between cuts, then carefully remove the foil.

(See photo, page 3)

S'MORES BARS

Prep time: 20 minutes ⏱ Bake time: 30 minutes ⏱ Chilling time: 1 hour ✋ Makes 24

The campfire treat comes indoors with these yummy bars. I really like the nuts in these, because they go well with the graham crackers and cut the sweetness a bit— but they're good without them, too.

INGREDIENTS:

Cooking spray
2½ cups (10.6 ounces) all-purpose flour
1½ cups graham cracker crumbs (from a box, or about 15 graham cracker sheets crushed in a food processor)
1½ teaspoons baking powder
½ teaspoon salt
16 tablespoons (2 sticks) unsalted butter, at room temperature
1 cup (8.4 ounces) packed dark brown sugar
2 large eggs
2 teaspoons vanilla extract
2 cups miniature marshmallows
2 cups chocolate chips
1 cup chopped walnuts (optional)

TOOLS:

Dry measuring cups
Measuring spoons
9 x 13-inch baking pan
Medium bowl
Fork
Large bowl
Electric mixer
Flexible spatula
Wire cooling rack

❶ Preheat the oven to 350°F. Line a 9 x 13-inch baking pan with foil, leaving a 2-inch overhang on two sides; lightly mist the foil with cooking spray.

❷ In a medium bowl, combine the flour, graham cracker crumbs, baking powder, and salt; stir with a fork to mix well. In a large bowl, with an electric mixer on medium speed, beat the butter and brown sugar until light and fluffy, about 2 minutes. Scrape down the sides and bottom of the bowl with a flexible spatula, then beat in the eggs and vanilla. Don't worry if the mixture looks curdled—just beat it for another minute or two.

❸ Add the flour mixture to the butter mixture and beat on low speed (or mix by hand with a wooden spoon or flexible spatula) until the mixtures are fully combined and a dough forms. Using your fingers, press about two-thirds of the dough evenly into the bottom of the pan. (If you find the dough is sticky, lightly dampen your hands before pressing on the dough.)

❹ Sprinkle the marshmallows, chocolate chips, and walnuts (if using) over the dough. Pull out clumps of the remaining dough and scatter them over the chocolate chips and marshmallows. Don't worry about covering the top completely. Using lightly dampened hands, gently press down on the top layer of dough to adhere it to the chips-and-marshmallows layer. Bake for 30 minutes, until the top layer of dough is golden and any marshmallows peeking out are lightly toasted. Let cool on a wire rack until room temperature, then refrigerate for 1 hour before cutting into bars.

From top: Cookies-and-Cream Cheesecake Bars, Coffee–Chocolate Chip Blondies, Fudge Brownies, and S'mores Bars

TOBLERONE BROWNIES

Prep time: 25 minutes ⏲ Baking time: 25 to 30 minutes 🖐 Makes 16

Toblerone is a delicious confection made with good-quality chocolate and a honey-almond nougat. Unlike American chocolate bars with nougat, such as Milky Way, in Toblerone the nougat is blended into the chocolate, so instead of different layers, it's one cohesive hunk. Even if you prefer milk or white chocolate for eating, use bittersweet Toblerone in this recipe.

INGREDIENTS:

Cooking spray
1 3–3.5-ounce bar semisweet chocolate
 or 6 ounces semisweet chocolate
 chips
2 3.5-ounce bars bittersweet Toblerone
8 tablespoon (1 stick) unsalted butter
2/3 cup (2.8 ounces) all-purpose flour
½ teaspoon baking powder
¼ teaspoon salt
2 large eggs
¾ cup (5.25 ounces) sugar
1 teaspoon vanilla extract
½ cup chopped walnuts (optional)

TOOLS:

Dry measuring cups
Measuring spoons
Cutting board
Chef's knife
Flexible spatula
Whisk
8-inch square baking pan
Fork
Saucepan
Large bowl
Small bowl
Medium bowl
Wire cooling rack

❶ Preheat the oven to 350°F. Line an 8-inch square baking pan with foil, leaving a 2-inch overhang on two sides. Mist with cooking spray.

❷ On a cutting board, using a sharp chef's knife, chop the semisweet chocolate into chunks just larger than chocolate chips. Set the chopped chocolate aside. Using the same knife and cutting board, chop both Toblerone bars into pieces about the same size as chocolate chips (the shape of the pieces doesn't matter). Place the chopped Toblerone bars in a saucepan. Using the same knife and cutting board, cut the butter into about 8 pieces and place it in the same pan with the chopped Toblerone.

❸ Place the pan with the Toblerone and butter on the stove over the lowest possible heat setting. Using a flexible spatula, stir the chocolate and butter mixture constantly, taking care to scrape the bottom and sides of pan to keep the chocolate from scorching. Continue stirring over the lowest heat until the chocolate and butter are melted and the mixture is smooth, about 5 minutes. Remove the pan from the heat, pour the mixture into a medium bowl, and set aside.

❹ Measure the flour, baking powder, and salt into a small bowl; stir with a fork to combine. In a large bowl, using a wire whisk, beat the eggs, sugar, and vanilla for about 2 to 3 minutes, until well combined and slightly thickened. Using the flexible spatula, stir the Toblerone-butter mixture into the egg mixture. Stir in the flour mixture until well combined, then stir in the chopped chocolate and walnuts (if using).

❺ Pour the batter into the prepared pan, spread it evenly with the flexible spatula, and bake for 25 to 30 minutes, until the sides look slightly dry and the center is set. Place the baking pan on a wire rack to cool. When cool, use the foil overhang to lift the brownies onto a cutting board to cut into bars.

(See photo, page 25)

You Made That Dessert?

COFFEE–CHOCOLATE CHIP BLONDIES

Prep time: 25 minutes ⏱ Baking time: 25 to 30 minutes ✋ Makes 24

Although I love brownies and anything chocolate, I may just like blondies more. Luckily, with this recipe, you don't have to choose between a blondie and chocolate—these rich bars incorporate both, plus a deep coffee flavor that gives them a grownup quality.

INGREDIENTS:

Cooking spray

1½ cups (6.4 ounces) all-purpose flour

1 teaspoon baking powder

½ teaspoon salt

12 tablespoons (1½ sticks) unsalted butter

1¼ cups (10.5 ounces) packed dark brown sugar

2 large eggs, at room temperature

2 tablespoons instant espresso powder

1 tablespoon vanilla extract

1 cup chopped walnuts

1¼ cups semisweet chocolate chips

TOOLS:

9 x 13-inch baking pan

3 small bowls

Large bowl

Dry measuring cups

Measuring spoons

Fork

Saucepan

Flexible spatula

Whisk

Wire cooling rack

❶ Preheat the oven to 350°F. Line a 9 x 13-inch baking pan with foil, leaving a 2-inch overhang on two sides; lightly mist the foil with cooking spray.

❷ In a small bowl, combine the flour, baking powder, and salt; stir with a fork to mix. In a saucepan, warm the butter and the brown sugar over low heat, stirring with a flexible spatula, until the butter has melted and the butter and sugar are well combined.

❸ Pour the butter-sugar mixture into a large bowl and let cool for about 5 minutes (test the temperature with your finger—it should feel warm but not hot). Meanwhile, lightly beat the eggs in a small bowl with a whisk, just to mix the yolks and whites. In a small bowl or cup, dissolve the instant espresso in the vanilla.

❹ When the butter-sugar mixture has cooled, beat in the eggs with the whisk, then beat in the espresso-vanilla mixture. Add the flour mixture and stir with a flexible spatula or wooden spoon. Scrape down the bottom of the bowl to be sure all the dry ingredients are mixed in. Stir in the chopped nuts and chocolate chips.

❺ Scrape the batter into the baking pan and spread it evenly with a flexible spatula. Bake for 25 to 30 minutes, until just golden brown and set in the center. Transfer the pan to a wire rack to cool. Let cool completely.

❻ For the neatest cuts, place the pan in the refrigerator for 20 minutes before slicing. To slice, use the foil overhang to remove the blondies and place on a large cutting board. Use a chef's knife to cut 24 pieces, wiping off the knife between cuts, then carefully remove foil.

(See photo, page 3)

COOKIES-AND-CREAM CHEESECAKE BARS

Prep time: 30 minutes ⏱ Baking time: 40 minutes ⏱ Chilling time: 3 hours ✋ Makes 24

If you like Oreos (who doesn't?) and cheesecake, you'll love these bars, which feature an easy Oreo crust and lots of chopped Oreos in the creamy filling. After you slice these bars, put them in flattened-out paper cupcake liners to make them easier to handle—or serve them on plates with forks.

INGREDIENTS:

Crust:

1 1-pound package Oreo cookies
4 tablespoons (½ stick) unsalted butter, melted

Filling:

3 8-ounce packages cream cheese, at room temperature
¾ cup (5.25 ounces) sugar
¾ cup sour cream, at room temperature
1 teaspoon vanilla extract
½ teaspoon salt
3 large eggs, at room temperature

TOOLS:

Dry measuring cups
Measuring spoons
9 x 13-inch baking pan
Food processor
2 large bowls
Flexible spatula
Wire cooling rack
Electric mixer
Chef's knife

❶ Preheat the oven to 325°F. Line a 9 x 13-inch pan with foil, leaving a 2-inch overhang on two sides.

❷ Make the crust: Place 28 Oreos in a food processor and process until finely ground. Pour into a large bowl, add the melted butter, and stir with a flexible spatula until all crumbs are moistened. Place the cookie-crumb mixture in the lined pan and, using your fingers, press the mixture firmly and evenly into the bottom. Bake 10 minutes, then remove to a wire cooling rack (leave the oven on) while you make the filling. Snap the remaining Oreos in half, put them in the food processor, and turn on and off quickly a few times, just until the cookies are roughly chopped.

❸ Make the filling: In a large bowl, using an electric mixer on medium speed, beat the cream cheese and sugar until well blended, about 2 minutes. Scrape down the sides and bottom of the bowl with a flexible spatula and beat again until uniform. Beat in the sour cream, vanilla, and salt. Scrape down the bowl and mix again. Add the eggs, one at a time, beating well after each. After beating in the last egg, scrape down the sides and bottom of the bowl and beat one more time, to make sure the mixture is fully combined. Stir in the chopped Oreos with the same spatula.

❹ Pour the cream cheese mixture over the baked cookie crust, smooth the top with the spatula, and bake for 40 minutes, until the filling is set around the edges but still slightly wobbly in the center when you gently shake the pan. Remove the pan to a wire rack to cool to room temperature, about 1 hour. When cool, cover it with foil and refrigerate until well chilled, at least 3 hours.

❺ To cut, use the foil overhang to lift the cheesecake out of the pan and place on a large cutting board. Use a sharp chef's knife to cut the cheesecake into bars, rinsing off the knife with hot water and wiping it dry between each cut.

(See photo, page 3)

GINGERSNAPS

Prep time: 30 minutes ⏱ Baking time: 30 minutes total 🖐 Makes 3 dozen cookies

I love gingersnaps on a cold day, especially with a cup of hot apple cider.
A little bit of black pepper brings out the spice in these goodies.

INGREDIENTS:

2 cups (8.5 ounces) all-purpose flour

2 teaspoons baking soda

½ teaspoon salt

1 tablespoon plus 2 teaspoons ground
  ginger

1½ teaspoons cinnamon

¼ teaspoon ground cloves

¼ teaspoon black pepper

12 tablespoons (1½ sticks) unsalted
  butter, at room temperature

1½ cups (10.5 ounces) sugar

1 large egg, at room temperature

¼ cup molasses

½ teaspoon vanilla extract

TOOLS:

Dry measuring cups

Measuring spoons

Liquid measuring cup

3 rimmed baking sheets (see Note)

2 small bowls

Large bowl

Fork

Electric mixer

Flexible spatula

Drinking glass with flat bottom

Wire cooling rack

Small ice cream scoop or 2 teaspoons

Spatula

Note: If you only have one or two baking
  sheets, that's okay; you can bake the
  cookies in batches

❶ Preheat the oven to 350°F. Line three rimmed baking sheets with parchment paper. In a small bowl, mix the flour, baking soda, salt, ginger, cinnamon, cloves, and pepper, and stir with a fork to combine.

❷ In a large bowl, using an electric mixer at medium speed, beat together the butter and 1 cup sugar until light and fluffy, about 2 minutes. Stop the mixer and add the egg, molasses, and vanilla, then beat until combined. Stop the mixer and scrape down the sides and bottom of the bowl with a flexible spatula. Beat again until the mixture is uniform. (The mixture may look curdled and separated at first, but don't worry; as you beat it, it will come together and turn a pale brown.)

❸ Stop the mixer and add the flour mixture. Use a flexible spatula or wooden spoon to mix the dry ingredients into the butter mixture until a dough forms. Scrape down the sides and bottom of the bowl and stir well so that all of the dry ingredients are fully incorporated.

❹ Place the remaining ½ cup sugar in a small bowl. Use a small ice cream scoop or two teaspoons to scoop out pieces of dough and roll them, one at a time, in your palms to form balls that are about 1½ inches wide. One at a time, roll the balls in the sugar until they're coated, then place the dough balls 2 inches apart on the baking sheets (don't crowd them—they will spread a lot). Use the bottom of a glass to lightly press the balls into discs.

❺ Bake the cookies for 10 to 11 minutes, until lightly browned. Let them cool on the pans on wire racks for 5 minutes, then use a spatula to remove the gingersnaps and place them directly on the wire racks to cool completely.

(See photo, page 8)

HELLO DOLLIES

Prep time: 10 minutes ⏱ Baking time: 25 to 30 minutes 🖐 Makes 24

Some people call these classic treats "magic cookie bars," but when I was growing up we called them Hello Dollies. The only thing I changed from how my mom made these is to add a bit of salt to the crust—it was my friend Jayna Maleri's idea, and once I had them her way I never went back.

INGREDIENTS:

Cooking spray
7 tablespoons unsalted butter
1½ cups graham cracker crumbs (from a box, or about 15 graham cracker sheets crushed in a food processor)
1¼ teaspoons salt
1 cup chopped walnuts
1½ cups semisweet chocolate chips
1¼ cups sweetened flake coconut
1 14-ounce can sweetened condensed milk

TOOLS:

Saucepan
Dry measuring cups
Measuring spoons
Medium bowl
Fork
9 x 13-inch baking pan
Wire cooling rack

❶ Preheat the oven to 375°F. Line a 9 x 13-inch baking pan with foil, leaving a 2-inch overhang on two sides; lightly mist with cooking spray. Melt the butter in a saucepan over low heat. In a medium bowl, using a fork, mix the butter, graham cracker crumbs, and salt until the crumbs are completely moistened. Press the crumb mixture into the baking pan, pressing down evenly with your fingers to form a crust.

❷ Sprinkle the nuts evenly over the crumbs, then sprinkle on the chocolate chips and the coconut. Drizzle the condensed milk evenly over the top.

❸ Bake for 25 to 30 minutes, until the top turns a light golden brown. Let cool on a wire rack for at least 20 minutes before cutting into bars.

Good to know! You can buy graham cracker crumbs in most supermarkets. But if you can't find them, simply crush the graham crackers in a food processor. Or, if you don't have a food processor, place the crackers in a large ziplock bag, seal the bag tightly, and beat the crackers with a rolling pin or skillet until they're crushed. Turn the bag over a few times so that you crush all of the crackers.

From top left: Orange-Scented
Chocolate Chip Cookies, "Kitchen Sink"
Oatmeal Cookies, Gingersnaps, and
Hello Dollies

ORANGE-SCENTED CHOCOLATE CHIP COOKIES

Prep time: 25 minutes ⏱ Baking time: 12 to 15 minutes (per batch) ✋ Makes 36

Nothing says "comfort food" like good, old-fashioned chocolate chip cookies. These make a great holiday gift wrapped in a festive tin, a lovely treat for your book club, or a fun dinner-party dessert served with vanilla ice cream.

INGREDIENTS:

2¹/₃ cups (9.9 ounces) all-purpose flour

1 teaspoon baking soda

1 teaspoon salt

16 tablespoons (2 sticks) unsalted butter, softened

½ cup (3.5 ounces) sugar

1 cup (8.4 ounces) packed dark brown sugar

Zest of 1 medium orange, grated

1 tablespoon vanilla extract

2 large eggs

10-ounce bag semisweet chocolate chunks or chips

1 cup chopped nuts (optional)

TOOLS:

Large bowl

Small bowl

Coffee cup or small bowl

Fork

Electric mixer

Dry measuring cups

Measuring spoons

Rasp grater

Flexible spatula

Small ice cream scoop or two teaspoons

Wire cooling rack

2 baking sheets

wooden spoon

❶ Preheat the oven to 350°F. In a small bowl, combine the flour, baking soda, and salt; stir with a fork to mix.

❷ In a large bowl, with an electric mixer on medium speed, beat the butter, sugar, brown sugar, and orange zest until light and fluffy, about 2 minutes. Beat in the vanilla extract, then beat in the eggs. Scrape down the sides of the bowl with a flexible spatula, then beat again until uniform.

❸ Add half of the flour mixture to the butter mixture and beat with the mixer on low speed, or stir well with a wooden spoon to combine. Repeat with the other half of the flour mixture. Stir in the chocolate chips and nuts with a wooden spoon (the batter will be very thick).

❹ Line 2 large baking sheets with parchment paper. Using a small ice cream scoop or two teaspoons, scoop out balls of dough and place them about an inch apart on the cookie sheets (you'll only fit about two-thirds of the batter).

❺ Bake the cookies for about 12 to 15 minutes, until they just look dry on top. Remove the cookie sheets from the oven and place on a wire rack for 2 minutes, then gently remove the cookies and place them directly on the rack to cool. You can use the same sheets of parchment to bake the remaining batches of cookies.

(See photo, page 8)

Good to know! I like walnuts in this cookie, but pecans or hazelnuts work well too.

Cookies are the ultimate make-ahead dessert. I like to make the dough, scoop out the cookies, and freeze them on a cookie sheet, then place the frozen cookie dough balls in ziplock bags and stick the bags back in the freezer. The dough will keep for several months in the freezer. They'll take a little longer to bake if the dough is frozen, about 15 to 17 minutes.

PECAN PIE BARS

Prep time: 20 minutes ⏱ Baking time: 40 to 45 minutes ✋ Makes 24 bars

I was almost finished with the recipes for this book when I ran into an actor pal named Ray
at a mutual friend's party. He was appalled that I didn't have a pecan pie on my list,
so I quickly moved things around to include these bars. I hope Ray likes them!

INGREDIENTS:

Cooking spray

Crust:

2 cups (8.5 ounces) all-purpose flour

½ cup (3.5 ounces) sugar

¼ teaspoon salt

12 tablespoons (1½ sticks) unsalted
　　butter, cold, cut into 24 pieces

Filling:

3 large eggs

¼ cup honey

¾ cup (6.3 ounces) packed dark brown
　　sugar

3 tablespoons unsalted butter, melted

2 teaspoons vanilla extract

1 tablespoon bourbon (optional)

¼ teaspoon salt

2½ cups chopped pecans

TOOLS:

Dry measuring cups

Measuring spoons

Liquid measuring cup

9 x 13-inch baking pan

Food processor

Wire cooling rack

Large bowl

Whisk

Flexible spatula

Wire cooling rack

Chef's knife

❶ Preheat the oven to 350°F. Line a 9 x 13-inch baking pan with foil, leaving a 2-inch overhang on two sides. Lightly mist the foil with cooking spray.

❷ Make the crust: In a food processor, combine the flour, sugar, and salt; use quick on-and-off turns to combine them well (this is called "pulsing"). Add the butter and pulse until all the ingredients are combined and the mixture resembles coarse sand. Pour into the prepared baking pan and press down evenly with your fingers or the bottom of a glass. Bake for 20 minutes, until the edges are golden. Remove the pan from the oven and place on a wire rack.

❸ Make the filling: Break the eggs into a large bowl and beat with a whisk just until the yolks and whites are combined. Add the honey, brown sugar, butter, vanilla, bourbon (if using), and salt; beat with a whisk just to combine. Stir in the nuts with a flexible spatula. Scrape the mixture over the crust and spread carefully but evenly. Bake for 20 to 25 minutes, until the filling is set. Let it cool completely on a wire rack.

❹ When the bars have cooled, use the foil overhang to pull them out of the pan, and place on a cutting board. Using a sharp chef's knife, cut into 24 bars.

(See photo, page 12)

SALTY-SWEET CARAMEL NUT BARS

Prep time: 15 minutes ⏱ Baking time: 40 to 45 minutes ⏱ Chilling time: 2 hours ✋ Makes 12 to 16 bars

The combination of salty and sweet has been trendy for a while now, and with good reason—both flavors dance well together on your tongue. If you enjoy salted butter caramels, you'll love these bars. Drizzle them with melted semisweet chocolate if you want to go all-out decadent.

INGREDIENTS:

Cooking spray

Crust:

5 tablespoons unsalted butter, at room temperature

2 tablespoons sugar

¾ cup (3.2 ounces) all-purpose flour

Pinch of salt

1 tablespoon heavy cream

Filling:

1 cup salted mixed nuts

6 tablespoons unsalted butter, at room temperature

¼ cup (2.1 ounces) packed dark brown sugar

¼ cup honey

2 tablespoons heavy cream

TOOLS:

Dry measuring cups

Measuring spoons

Liquid measuring cup

8-inch square baking pan

Large bowl

Electric mixer

Wire cooling rack

Cutting board

Chef's knife

Paring knife

Saucepan

Whisk

Fork

Pecan Pie Bars and Salty-Sweet Caramel Nut Bars

❶ Preheat the oven to 350°F. Line an 8-inch square baking pan with foil, leaving a 2-inch overhang on two sides; mist it lightly with cooking spray.

❷ Make the crust: In a large bowl, using an electric mixer, beat the butter and sugar until light and fluffy, about 1 minute. Add the flour, salt, and cream, and mix until a dough begins to form. The dough may be sticky. Rub a little bit of flour onto your fingers and use them to press the dough evenly into the baking pan, forming the crust. Poke the crust all over with a fork. Bake for 20 to 25 minutes, until the crust begins to turn light golden brown. Remove from the oven and place on a wire rack. Leave the oven on.

❸ Make the filling: On a cutting board using a chef's knife, chop the nuts roughly. Don't make them very small, just chop them a little bit to break them up. With a paring knife, cut the 6 tablespoons butter into several pieces and place it in a saucepan. Add the brown sugar and honey. Cook the mixture over medium-high heat, stirring constantly with a whisk, until the butter melts, the brown sugar dissolves, and the mixture comes to a boil. Stop whisking and let the mixture bubble for 1 minute. Stir in the chopped nuts. Remove the nut mixture from the heat and stir in the cream with the whisk.

❹ Spread the nut mixture over the crust and bake for 20 minutes, until the caramel bubbles. Place the pan back on the wire rack and let it cool for 2 hours. (Don't touch it until it's cool—the caramel is extremely hot.) When it has cooled, cover the pan with foil and refrigerate for 2 hours.

❺ Use the foil overhang to lift the bars out of the pan and place on a cutting board. Carefully remove the foil and cut into 12 to 16 bars.

MOM'S MEXICAN WEDDING COOKIES

Prep time: 15 minutes ⏱ Baking time: 23 to 26 minutes ✋ Makes about 38

As the name suggests, this is my mother's recipe. Why a little Jewish lady from New York
has a great recipe for Mexican wedding cookies is a mystery—but hey, why question
a good thing? These melt-in-your-mouth cookies freeze remarkably well.
After you've thawed them, re-roll them in confectioners' sugar to freshen them up.

INGREDIENTS:

16 tablespoons (2 sticks) unsalted
    butter, at room temperature
¼ cup (1.75 ounces) sugar
2 teaspoons vanilla extract
½ teaspoon salt
2 cups (8.5 ounces) all-purpose flour
1 cup finely chopped walnuts or pecans
1¼ cups (5 ounces) confectioners' sugar

TOOLS:

Dry measuring cups
Measuring spoons
2 baking sheets
Large bowl
Medium bowl
Electric mixer
Small ice cream scoop or two teaspoons
Wire cooling racks

❶ Preheat the oven to 325°F. Line two baking sheets with parchment paper.

❷ In a large bowl, with an electric mixer on medium speed, beat the butter and sugar until light and fluffy, about 2 minutes. Beat in the vanilla and salt. With the mixer on low speed, beat in about one-third of the flour until almost mixed in. Beat in another third, then the remaining flour, each time beating until the dry and wet ingredients are almost combined. Beat in the chopped nuts.

❸ Using a small ice cream scoop or two teaspoons, form the dough into pieces and roll them in your palms into 1½-inch balls. (Using an ice cream scoop will ensure even-sized balls.) Place the dough balls 1 inch apart on lined baking sheets. Bake 23 to 26 minutes, until cookies are very light golden. Place the baking sheets on wire racks and let cool for 30 minutes. Meanwhile, place the confectioners' sugar in a medium bowl. When the cookies have cooled completely, roll them a few at a time in the confectioners' sugar, tossing them with your hands until they're coated.

From top: Raspberry Jam Bars,
Mom's Mexican Wedding Cookies,
and Sesame-Oat-Pecan Cookies

RASPBERRY JAM BARS

Prep time: 15 minutes ⏱ Baking time: 35 to 40 minutes 🖐 Makes 16

This is a super-simple recipe that yields a pretty, yummy bar cookie. Use a small,
round cookie cutter instead of a knife to make little tarts, if you like.
Feel free to swap jams, too—strawberry or blackberry would be equally good.

INGREDIENTS:

1 cup (4.25 ounces) all-purpose flour
¼ teaspoon baking soda
Pinch of salt
8 tablespoons (1 stick) unsalted butter,
    at room temperature
½ cup (4.2 ounces) packed dark brown
    sugar
½ teaspoon vanilla or almond extract
½ cup quick-cooking oats (do not use
    instant)
½ cup sliced almonds
½ cup seedless raspberry jam

TOOLS:

Dry measuring cups
Measuring spoons
8-inch square baking pan
Small bowl
Fork
Large bowl
Electric mixer
Wooden spoon or flexible spatula
Wire cooling rack
Chef's knife or cookie cutter

❶ Preheat the oven to 350°F. Line an 8-inch square baking pan
with foil, leaving a 2-inch overhang on two sides. In a small bowl
mix the flour, baking soda, and salt; stir with a fork.

❷ In a large bowl, with an electric mixer on medium-high speed,
beat the butter and sugar until light and fluffy, about 2 minutes.
Mix in the vanilla. Using a wooden spoon or flexible spatula, stir
in the flour mixture, then the oats and almonds.

❸ Measure ½ cup of the mixture and set it aside. Using your
fingers, press the remaining dough evenly into the bottom of
the pan. Spread the jam over the dough, leaving a ¼-inch border
around the edges. Sprinkle the reserved dough in small clumps
all over the jam. Bake 35 to 40 minutes, until the dough is golden
brown and the jam is lightly bubbling. Remove the pan to a wire
rack and let cool.

❹ Use the foil overhang to pull the bars out of the pan. Place
them on a cutting board and carefully remove the foil. Use a sharp
chef's knife to cut into 16 bars, or use a small round cookie cutter
to make mini-tartlets.

(See photo, page 15)

SESAME-OAT-PECAN COOKIES

Prep time: 20 minutes ⏱ Baking time: 10 to 12 minutes (per batch) 🖐 Makes 40

I grew up eating halvah and other sesame-based sweets, thanks to a part of my family that's Middle Eastern. If you like those treats—or you've enjoyed tahini in savory dishes like hummus—give these crunchy cookies a try. They also happen to be dairy and gluten free, so they're good for people with lactose intolerance and gluten allergies.

INGREDIENTS:

½ cup quick-cooking oats (do not use instant)
½ cup chopped pecans
1 teaspoon baking soda
1 teaspoon cinnamon
Pinch of salt
1 cup sesame tahini, stirred
1 cup (7 ounces) sugar
⅓ cup honey
1 large egg, at room temperature
1 teaspoon vanilla extract

TOOLS:

Dry measuring cups
Measuring spoons
Liquid measuring cup
2 rimmed baking sheets
Food processor
Large bowl
Electric mixer
Small ice cream scoop or two teaspoons
Wire cooling racks

❶ Preheat the oven to 350°F. Line two rimmed baking sheets with parchment (if you only have one sheet, you can bake the cookies in batches).

❷ Place the oats and pecans in a food processor and turn it on and off in quick bursts six or seven times, until the oats and nuts are partially ground (this is called "pulsing"). You may still have some whole oat flakes; that's okay. Add the baking soda, cinnamon, and salt and pulse two or three more times, just to combine.

❸ In a large bowl, using an electric mixer, beat together the tahini, sugar, honey, egg, and vanilla until well combined, about 2 minutes. Stop the mixer, add the oat mixture, and beat again until the oat mixture is fully incorporated and moistened. Using two teaspoons or a small ice-cream scoop, gather up 2-teaspoon-size balls of dough and place about 2 inches apart on the cookie sheets. The dough will be sticky, so have a glass of warm water nearby. Dampen your ice cream scoop or spoons every two or three times you scoop the dough—that will help to keep the dough from sticking.

❹ Bake the cookies for 10 to 12 minutes, until they're slightly puffy and spread and are light golden. The cookies will flatten as they cool. Let them cool on the baking sheets on wire racks for at least 5 minutes, then use a spatula to take them off the sheets and place them directly on the wire racks to cool completely.

(See photo, page 15)

Get the Scoop People really will say, "You made those?" when you present a batch of gorgeous, perfectly uniform, bakery-quality cookies. The secret weapon for this is the ice cream scoop. I recommend getting one that holds about 1½ tablespoons of dough and has a squeezable handle that easily releases the dough (OXO makes a nice, sturdy one with a soft grip—the medium size is 1½ tablespoons). After scooping up a cookie's worth of dough, press the scoop against the side of the bowl to flatten what will be the bottom of the cookie, and scrape off any excess dough with your fingers. (If you cook, you can also use this tool to make lovely-looking meatballs.) Of course, no one in his right mind would turn down homespun-looking cookies, so if you prefer not to get a scoop, simply spoon out the dough by heaping teaspoon- or tablespoonfuls, and use another spoon to scoop the dough from the first spoon into a ball on the cookie sheet.

CAPPUCCINO BISCOTTI

Prep time: 30 minutes ⏱ Baking time: 50 to 55 minutes ✋ Makes 24

Biscotti take a bit more effort to make than other types of cookies, since you bake them in a log, then slice them, then toast them in the oven again—but I think they're worth it. These would make a great holiday gift, wrapped in cellophane and placed in a pretty mug.

INGREDIENTS:

2½ cups (10.6 ounces) all-purpose flour
1 tablespoon cinnamon
2 teaspoons baking powder
¼ teaspoon salt
3 tablespoons instant espresso powder
2 tablespoons hot tap water
8 tablespoons unsalted butter, softened
1 cup (7 ounces) sugar
2 large eggs
2 teaspoons vanilla extract
½ cup miniature chocolate chips
½ cup chopped hazelnuts

TOOLS:

Dry measuring cups
Measuring spoons
Baking sheet
Fork
Small bowl
Small cup
Large bowl
Electric mixer
Flexible spatula
Cutting board
Serrated knife
Wire cooling rack

❶ Preheat the oven to 350°F. Line a baking sheet with parchment. In a small bowl, combine the flour, cinnamon, baking powder, and salt; stir with a fork to mix well. In a small cup, dissolve the instant espresso in hot water.

❷ In a large bowl, using an electric mixer on medium-high speed, beat the butter and sugar until light and fluffy, about 2 minutes. Add the eggs one at a time, beating well after each addition. Stop the mixer and scrape down the sides and bottom of the bowl with a flexible spatula. Beat in the espresso mixture and the vanilla, then scrape down the bowl again. Add the flour mixture to the butter mixture and stir with the flexible spatula until the dough just comes together; this will take about a minute. Stir in the chocolate chips and hazelnuts until just incorporated.

❸ Divide the dough in half (it doesn't have to be exact, but try to get the two pieces as close to even as you can), and place them both on the lined baking sheet. Shape both pieces into long, narrow logs, about 10 inches long by 3 inches wide, leaving some space between them, as they will spread a bit. Bake for 30 to 35 minutes, or until light golden brown and firm to the touch. Place the baking sheet on a wire rack to cool for about 5 to 10 minutes. Reduce the oven temperature to 300°F.

❹ When the logs are cool enough to handle, place one on a cutting board. Using a serrated knife, carefully slice it on a slight diagonal into about 12 ¾-inch-thick slices. Lay the slices flat on the baking sheet (you can place them right up against each other; they won't spread anymore). Repeat with the other loaf. Bake the biscotti for 10 minutes, then take the baking sheet out of the oven (leave the oven on) and turn each cookie over. Return the baking sheet to the oven and bake 10 minutes longer, until the biscotti are dry and crisp. Remove them from the baking sheet onto a wire rack and let cool.

Cappuccino Biscotti and Rosemary Biscotti

ROSEMARY BISCOTTI

Prep time: 15 minutes ⏱ Baking time: 1 hour, 10 minutes ✋ Makes 40 biscotti

Rosemary is not a common ingredient in baking, but it should be. When you serve these crunchy biscotti, people might have trouble placing what the flavor is (but they'll love it!). These are delicious dunked into hot tea.

INGREDIENTS:

2 cups (8.5 ounces) all-purpose flour

1 teaspoon baking powder

¾ cup (5.25 ounces) sugar

1/8 teaspoon salt

1 tablespoon plus 2 teaspoons chopped fresh rosemary

3 large eggs, at room temperature

2 teaspoon vanilla extract

TOOLS:

Dry measuring cups

Measuring spoons

Baking sheet

Large bowl

Small bowl

Fork

Whisk

Cutting board

Serrated knife

Wire cooling racks

❶ Preheat the oven to 300°F and line a baking sheet with parchment paper. In a large bowl, combine the flour, baking powder, sugar, salt, and rosemary. Stir with a fork to mix well.

❷ In a small bowl, with a whisk, lightly beat the eggs and vanilla extract. Slowly whisk the egg mixture into the flour mixture, beating until a dough forms. The dough will be very sticky—don't be afraid to put down the whisk and finish mixing with your hands. Divide the dough in half (it doesn't have to be exact, but try to get the two pieces as close to even as you can).

❸ Sprinkle a bit of flour onto your countertop and rub some on your hands. Form the two pieces of dough into logs that are about 10 inches long and 2 inches wide. Place the logs on the baking sheet, spacing them apart (they will spread a bit while baking). Bake for 40 minutes, until the logs are lightly browned and feel firm to the touch. Remove the baking sheet and place it on a wire rack to cool for about 10 minutes.

❹ When the logs are just cool enough to handle, transfer one to a cutting board. Using a serrated knife, slice the log on a slight diagonal into about 20 pieces. Place them on the baking sheet (you can use the same piece of parchment and place them right up against each other; they won't spread anymore). Repeat with the second log. Bake for 10 to 12 minutes. Remove the baking sheet from the oven, flip over all the cookies, and bake for another 10 to 12 minutes, until the biscotti are firm and toasted. Remove the sheet from the oven and place the biscotti on wire racks to cool.

(See photo, page 19)

Good to know! You can store these in an airtight container at room temperature for up to 4 days.

PEANUT BUTTER COOKIES

Prep time: 15 minutes ⏱ Baking time: 6 to 7 minutes per batch ✋ Makes 36

Peanut butter cookies are a cookie-jar classic. If you want to make them even more special,
melt some chocolate and spread about ½ teaspoon on the bottom of half of a cookie,
then press the bottom of another cookie on top for a chocolate–peanut butter sandwich cookie.
Don't forget the milk!

INGREDIENTS:

1¼ cups (5.4 ounces) all-purpose flour
¾ teaspoon baking soda
½ teaspoon salt
4 tablespoons (½ stick) unsalted butter,
    at room temperature
¾ cup creamy peanut butter (don't use
    "natural")
¾ cup (6.3 ounces) packed dark brown
    sugar
1 large egg
1 teaspoon vanilla extract
1/3 cup (2.3 ounces) sugar

TOOLS:

Dry measuring cups
Measuring spoons
2 baking sheets
2 small bowls
Fork
Large bowl
Electric mixer
Flexible spatula
Small ice cream scoop or two teaspoons
Wire cooling rack

Good to know! Be sure to use regular creamy peanut butter, not one that says "natural" on the label, and not one that's freshly ground in the store.

You can add 2/3 cup chocolate chips to these, and make them even more decadent.

❶ Preheat the oven to 375°F and place racks in the top and bottom thirds of the oven. Line two baking sheets with parchment paper.

❷ In a small bowl, combine flour, baking soda, and salt; stir with a fork to mix. In a large bowl, with an electric mixer on medium-high speed, beat the butter, peanut butter, and brown sugar until light and fluffy, about 2 minutes. Stop the mixer and scrape down the sides and bottom of the bowl with a flexible spatula. Add the egg and vanilla and beat with the electric mixer just until combined.

❸ Scrape down the sides of the bowl again and beat the peanut butter mixture again until uniform. Stir in the flour mixture with your flexible spatula. Scrape the bottom of the bowl to be sure all of the flour mixture is mixed in. Place the sugar in a small bowl.

❹ Using a small ice cream scoop or two teaspoons, scoop up about 2 teaspoons' worth of dough, and gently roll it between your palms. Roll the ball of dough around gently in the bowl of white sugar until it's lightly coated, then place it on one of the baking sheets. Repeat with the remaining dough, spacing the dough balls about 1½ inches apart on the baking sheets. When all the dough is rolled into balls, rolled in the sugar, and placed on the baking sheets, take a fork and dip it in the remaining sugar. Press it into one of the dough balls to flatten it, then press again to make a criss-cross pattern. Repeat with the remaining dough balls, dipping the fork in the sugar before beginning with a new dough ball.

❺ Place the baking sheets in the oven and set the timer for 3 minutes. When the time is up, switch the baking sheets so that the one that was on the bottom moves to the top and vice versa. Bake for another 3 to 4 minutes. Remove the baking sheets to wire racks to cool for 5 minutes, then use a spatula to take the cookies off the sheets and place them directly on the wire racks to finish cooling. Repeat with any remaining dough.

(See photo, page 23)

PEANUT BUTTER AND JELLY BARS

Prep time: 20 minutes ⏱ Baking time: 20 to 25 minutes ✋ Makes 24

Everyone's favorite sandwich becomes a delicious dessert in these easy bar cookies.
They're great for kids—but you'll be hard-pressed to find a PB&J–loving adult who
will turn them down. I recommend strawberry jam or grape jelly, but feel free to use
whatever flavor you like best in your sandwiches.

INGREDIENTS:

2 cups (8.5 ounces) all-purpose flour
½ teaspoon baking soda
½ teaspoon salt
8 tablespoons (1 stick) unsalted butter,
　softened
¾ cup creamy peanut butter (don't use
　"natural")
½ cup (4.2 ounces) packed dark brown
　sugar
½ cup (3.5 ounces) sugar
1 large egg, at room temperature
1 teaspoon vanilla extract
1 cup quick-cooking oats (do not use
　instant)
½ cup peanut butter chips (optional)
1 cup strawberry jam or grape jelly

TOOLS:

Dry measuring cups
Measuring spoons
9 x 13-inch baking pan
Small bowl
Large bowl
Fork
Electric mixer
Flexible spatula
Tablespoon
Wire cooling rack
Spoon or offset spatula
Chef's knife

❶ Preheat the oven to 350°F and line a 9 x 13-inch pan with foil,
leaving a 2-inch overhang on two sides.

❷ In a small bowl, combine the flour, baking soda, and salt; stir
with a fork to mix well. In a large bowl, using an electric mixer on
medium speed, beat the butter, peanut butter, brown sugar, and
sugar until fluffy and light, about 2 to 3 minutes. Beat in the egg
and vanilla. Stop the mixer and scrape down the sides and bottom
of the bowl with a flexible spatula, then beat again until uniform.
Add the flour mixture, oats, and peanut butter chips (if using) and
beat on low speed just until combined and crumbly.

❸ Remove 1 cup of the mixture and set it aside. Press the remaining
mixture into the bottom of the pan, using your fingers to press the
mixture into an even layer.

❹ Spoon the jelly on top, spreading it with the back of a spoon
or an offset spatula. Crumble the reserved cup of peanut butter
mixture on top of the jelly, dropping clumps of dough all over the
jelly layer.

❺ Bake the bars for 20 to 25 minutes, until light golden brown
and firm. Remove the pan to a wire rack to cool completely. To
cut them, use the foil overhang to pull the bars out of the pan.
Carefully peel off the foil and place the bars on a cutting board.
Cut with a sharp chef's knife.

From top: Peanut Butter and Banana Bread,
Peanut Butter Cookies, and Peanut Butter
and Jelly Bars

CINNAMON-HAZELNUT SHORTBREAD

Prep time: 10 minutes ⏱ Baking time: 25 to 30 minutes 🖐 Makes 16 cookies

These buttery, not-very-sweet, nutty shortbreads are definitely cookies for grownups. They're great to bring in a tin as a holiday gift, because the hostess can serve them or sock them away for herself—they keep well in an airtight container for several days. Some folks like their shortbread thin and crispy—these are for people who prefer a thicker, softer variety.

INGREDIENTS:

2 cups (8.5 ounces) all-purpose flour
½ teaspoon salt
1½ teaspoon cinnamon
16 tablespoons (2 sticks) unsalted butter, softened
½ cup (4.2 ounces) packed dark brown sugar
½ cup finely chopped hazelnuts

TOOLS:

Dry measuring cups
Measuring spoons
Small bowl
Fork
Electric mixer
Wooden spoon
9-inch square baking pan
Wire cooling rack
Paring knife
Small offset spatula

❶ Preheat the oven to 325°F. In a small bowl, combine the flour, salt, and cinnamon; mix well with a fork.

❷ Using an electric mixer on medium speed, mix the butter and brown sugar until light and fluffy, about 2 minutes. Using a wooden spoon, stir the flour mixture into the butter mixture, stirring until just combined (the mixture will be dry). Stir in the hazelnuts.

❸ Using your fingers, press the dough into an ungreased 9-inch square baking pan. Be sure the batter is evenly distributed. (You can use the bottom of a glass to help press the dough evenly in the pan.) Bake for 25 to 30 minutes, until golden. Place the pan on a wire rack to cool.

❹ While the shortbread is still hot and in the pan, use a sharp paring knife to cut into 16 squares—don't cut all the way through; at this point you're just marking where you're going to cut later (this is called "scoring"), which will make the shortbread easier to cut later. Leave the shortbread in the pan until it's completely cool, then cut all the way through along your score marks, and use a small offset spatula to remove the shortbread from the pan.

Cinnamon-Hazelnut Shortbread, Pistachio-Cranberry Bars, and Toblerone Brownies

PISTACHIO-CRANBERRY BARS

Prep time: 20 minutes ⏱ Baking time: 25 to 30 minutes ⏱ Chilling time: 30 minutes ✋ Makes 24

The red and green hues in these festive bars make them perfect for a holiday cookie tray.
Be sure to use salted pistachios—they provide balance to the
sweet fruit and condensed milk.

INGREDIENTS:
Cooking spray
Crust:
1½ cups (6.4 ounces) all-purpose flour
½ cup (2 ounces) confectioners' sugar
¼ teaspoon salt
12 tablespoons (1½ sticks) unsalted
    butter, chilled, cut into 12 pieces
Filling:
14-ounce can sweetened condensed milk
1 large egg, at room temperature
1½ teaspoons vanilla extract
Zest of 1 small lemon (about
    2 tablespoons)
1 cup shelled salted pistachio nuts,
    chopped
1½ cups dried cranberries

TOOLS:
Dry measuring cups
Measuring spoons
Rasp grater
9 x 13-inch baking pan
Food processor
Wire cooling rack
Large bowl
Whisk
Flexible spatula
Cutting board
Chef's knife

❶ Preheat the oven to 350°F. Line a 9 x 13-inch baking pan with foil, leaving a 2-inch overhang on two sides; lightly mist the foil with cooking spray.

❷ Make the crust: Combine the flour, confectioners' sugar, and salt in the bowl of a food processor. Turn the processor on and off quickly a few times to mix the dry ingredients (this is called "pulsing"). Add the butter pieces and pulse a few times, until the butter is broken up into tiny pieces and is incorporated into the flour mixture (the whole thing should look like coarse sand). Dump the mixture into the baking pan and press with your fingers or the bottom of a glass so the crust is evenly patted into the pan. Refrigerate while making the filling.

❸ Make the filling: In a large bowl, whisk together the condensed milk, egg, vanilla, and lemon zest until well blended. Stir in the nuts and dried cranberries with a flexible spatula. Pour the mixture on top of the crust. Carefully spread the filling evenly over the crust with the flexible spatula.

❹ Bake for 25 to 30 minutes, or until the filling is a light golden brown and firm. Let cool in the pan on a wire rack. When cool, refrigerate for at least 30 minutes before cutting. Use the foil overhang to pull the bars out of the pan, and place on a cutting board. Using a sharp chef's knife, cut into 24 bars.

(See photo, page 25)

Good to know! When making the crust, you don't have to use a food processor. If you have a pastry blender, use that: Put the flour mixture in a large bowl and scatter the butter pieces over it. Press down on the butter with the pastry blender so it gets combined with the dry ingredients. Keep pressing and mixing until it is well combined and looks like coarse sand (this is called "cutting in"; see page 185). You can also do it with your fingers—just crush the butter pieces between your fingers, incorporating the flour mixture as you mush the butter into smaller pieces.

CRANBERRY CORNMEAL COOKIES

Prep time: 20 minutes 🕐 Baking time: 13 to 15 minutes ✋ Makes about 48

I've been making different versions of this cookie for years, and this is one of my favorites. The cornmeal gives the cookies a distinct texture, the cranberries add tartness and color, the white chocolate lends a delicate sweetness, and the almonds bring it all together.

INGREDIENTS:

1½ cups (6.4 ounces) all-purpose flour
½ cup cornmeal
1 teaspoon baking powder
½ teaspoon salt
12 tablespoons (1½ sticks) unsalted butter, softened
¾ cup (5.25 ounces) sugar
1 large egg
1 teaspoon vanilla extract
½ cup dried cranberries
½ cup white chocolate chips
½ cup sliced almonds

TOOLS:

Dry measuring cups
Measuring spoons
2 baking sheets
Small bowl
Medium bowl
Fork
Electric mixer
Flexible spatula
Small ice cream scoop or two teaspoons
Wire cooling racks
Wooden spoon

❶ Preheat the oven to 350°F. Line two baking sheets with parchment paper.

❷ In a small bowl, combine the flour, cornmeal, baking powder, and salt; stir with a fork to mix. In a medium bowl, using an electric mixer on medium-high speed, beat the butter and sugar until light and fluffy, about 3 minutes. Add the egg and vanilla and beat until well mixed. Scrape down the sides and bottom of bowl with a flexible spatula and beat again until incorporated. Add the flour mixture in three additions, beating well after each. Using a wooden spoon, stir the dried cranberries, white chocolate chips, and sliced almonds into the dough.

❸ Using two teaspoons or a small ice cream scoop, form the dough into clumps, and place them on the lined baking sheets, spacing them about 2 inches apart. Use your fingers to flatten the clumps into cookie-shaped discs.

❹ Bake for 13 to 15 minutes, until the edges are golden and set but the centers are still soft. Place the baking sheets on wire racks to cool for about 5 minutes, then use a spatula to remove the cookies from the baking sheets and place directly on the racks to cool completely. If you have dough left over, form it and bake it as above.

(See photo, page 153)

Good to know! You can swap in dried cherries or raisins for the cranberries, if you prefer.

If the cranberries or other fruit are hard, place them in a small saucepan with ½ cup orange juice or brandy over low heat until the mixture is warm, about 3 minutes. Remove from heat and let the mixture cool while you prepare the cookie dough. When it's time to add the fruit, drain well and pat the plumped-up fruit dry with paper towels. Discard the liquid. Stir in the fruit as instructed in the recipe.

CURRANT SCONES

Prep time: 15 minutes ⏱ Baking time: 15 to 18 minutes 🖐 Makes 10 to 12

Going to a brunch and don't know what to bring? These pretty little scones are perfect. Everyone will be so impressed—no need to tell them that it only took you about 30 minutes, and you mixed them in one bowl. These are best the day they're made.

INGREDIENTS:

2 cups (8.5 ounces) all-purpose flour
¼ cup (1.75 ounces) sugar, plus
    2 teaspoons
2 teaspoons baking powder
¼ teaspoon salt
5 tablespoons unsalted butter, cold
¾ cup heavy cream, plus 2 tablespoons
1 teaspoon vanilla extract
½ cup dried currants

TOOLS:

Dry measuring cups
Measuring spoons
Liquid measuring cup
Baking sheet
Large bowl
Whisk
Butter knife
Pastry blender
Flexible spatula or wooden spoon
2½–3-inch cookie cutter or chef's knife
Pastry brush
Wire cooling rack

❶ Preheat the oven to 375°F. Line a baking sheet with parchment paper.

❷ Place the flour, ¼ cup sugar, baking powder, and salt in a large bowl and stir with a whisk. Cut the butter into small pieces with a butter knife and add them to the dry ingredients. Press a pastry blender into the butter and dry ingredients repeatedly so that the butter gets cut into tiny pieces and incorporated into the dry ingredients; the mixture should resemble coarse sand (this is called "cutting in"; see page 185 for more information).

❸ Add ¾ cup plus 1 tablespoon cream and the vanilla to the flour mixture and stir with a flexible spatula or wooden spoon until nearly mixed, then add the currants and stir until completely mixed. Try to mix as little as possible—the more you mix, the tougher the scones will be.

❹ Sprinkle a little bit of flour on your countertop and dump the dough out on it. Using the heel of your hand, gently knead the dough three or four times to bring it together, then pat it into a circle about 7 inches wide. Use a 2½- to 3-inch round cookie cutter to cut the dough into scones, or use a chef's knife to cut it into 10 to 12 triangles. Place the scones on the baking sheet.

❺ Use a pastry brush to brush the scones with 1 tablespoon of cream, then sprinkle with 2 teaspoons sugar. Bake for 15 to 18 minutes, until the scones are lightly browned on top. Remove the scones to a wire rack to cool. Serve slightly warm or at room temperature.

(See photo, page 43)

"KITCHEN SINK" OATMEAL COOKIES

Prep time: 15 minutes ⏱ Baking time: 12 to 15 minutes (per batch) ✋ Makes 32

Oatmeal cookies are fun to make with kids because there's lots of measuring and stirring. I love oatmeal cookies that are chock-full of goodies like chocolate chips, raisins, and nuts—you could cut back and just do the classic raisins, or go crazy and add some coconut to these.

INGREDIENTS:

1¼ cups (5.4 ounces) all-purpose flour

1 teaspoon baking soda

½ teaspoon salt

12 tablespoons (1½ sticks) unsalted butter, softened

¼ cup (1.75 ounces) sugar

1 cup (8.4 ounces) packed dark brown sugar

2 large eggs, at room temperature

1 teaspoon vanilla extract

3 cups quick-cooking oats (do not use instant)

¾ cup chocolate chips

¾ cup raisins

¾ cup chopped walnuts

TOOLS:

Dry measuring cups

Measuring spoons

2 baking sheets

Small bowl

Large bowl

Fork

Electric mixer

Flexible spatula

Small ice cream scoop or two tablespoons

Wire cooling racks

❶ Preheat the oven to 350°F. Line two baking sheets with parchment paper. In a small bowl, combine the flour, baking soda, and salt, and stir with a fork to mix.

❷ In a large bowl, using an electric mixer on medium-high speed, beat the butter, sugar, and brown sugar until light and fluffy, about 3 minutes. Scrape down the sides and bottom of the bowl with a flexible spatula and beat again. Beat in the eggs and vanilla. Scrape down the sides and bottom of the bowl again, and beat until uniform. (Don't worry if the mixture looks curdled.)

❸ Using your flexible spatula or a wooden spoon, stir the flour mixture into the butter mixture until just combined—you want all of the dry ingredients incorporated, but don't beat it to death. Stir in the oats, chocolate chips, raisins, and walnuts. Make sure all of the ingredients are incorporated well.

❹ Using a small ice cream scoop or two tablespoons, portion the dough into clumps and place on baking sheets, spacing them 2 inches apart. (Don't try to use up all the dough—bake it in batches.) Bake for 12 to 15 minutes, until just set and light golden around the edges.

❺ Remove the baking sheets from oven, place them on wire racks to cool for 2 minutes, then remove the cookies from the sheets with a spatula and place them directly on wire racks to cool completely. Repeat with the remaining dough (you can reuse the same parchment).

(See photo, page 8)

Good to know! You can use old-fashioned oats instead of quick-cooking, if you like. They'll make the cookies, well, oatier—you'll see more oat flakes, and the cookies will be heartier. Don't use instant oats—they'll ruin the texture of your cookies.

Cakes

PERFECTLY SIMPLE POUND CAKE 31

PUMPKIN BREAD 32

SOUR CREAM COFFEE CAKE 35

RASPBERRY BUCKLE 36

CARROT CUPCAKES 37

DOUBLE APPLE STREUSEL COFFEE CAKE 38

WHITE CHOCOLATE–STRAWBERRY CUPCAKES 40

ORANGE CREAM CUPCAKES 42

CHEESECAKE CUPCAKES 44

CHOCOLATE–CHOCOLATE CHIP CUPCAKES 45

LIME-GLAZED CITRUS TEA CAKES 46

GERALDINE'S CHOCOLATE-DATE CAKE 48

GREAT BIG COCONUT CAKE 50

STRAWBERRY ICE CREAM CUPCAKES 52

PINEAPPLE UPSIDE-DOWN CAKE 54

CREAMY VANILLA CHEESECAKE 56

"ALMOND JOY" CHEESECAKE 58

TRES LECHES CAKE 62

TIRAMISU 64

MOLTEN DARK CHOCOLATE CAKES 66

BROWNIE ICE CREAM TORTE 68

FLOURLESS CHOCOLATE CAKE 70

ALMOND-RASPBERRY CAKE 74

CURRANT-CRANBERRY SPICE CAKE 76

BANANA SNACK CAKE 78

PEANUT BUTTER AND BANANA BREAD 80

SUSAN'S ZUCCHINI BREAD 81

PERFECTLY SIMPLE POUND CAKE

Prep time: 10 minutes ⏲ Baking time: 65 to 75 minutes ✋ Makes 1 9-inch loaf cake, serves 10

There are few things more versatile than a good pound cake. Have a slice on its own, top it
with ice cream and hot fudge, smother it in berries—you just can't go wrong.
This cake freezes well, so make an extra one and keep it in the freezer. It's also delicious
in the Black-and-White Trifles (see page 94).

INGREDIENTS:

2½ cups (10.6 ounces) all-purpose flour
    (plus 2 tablespoons for preparing
    pan)
1 teaspoon baking powder
¼ teaspoon salt
12 tablespoons (1½ sticks) unsalted
    butter, at room temperature (plus
    2 tablespoons for preparing pan)
1½ cups (10.5 ounces) sugar
3 large eggs, at room temperature
¾ cup sour cream, at room temperature
1 tablespoon vanilla extract

TOOLS:

5 x 9-inch loaf pan
Dry measuring cups
Measuring spoons
Medium bowl
Fork
Large bowl
Electric mixer
Flexible spatula
Toothpick
Wire cooling rack

❶ Preheat the oven to 350°F. Using your fingers or a piece of plastic wrap, apply a thin coat of butter to the inside of a 5 x 9-inch loaf pan, taking care to get it in all the corners. Spoon in 2 tablespoons flour and move the pan around until the inside of it is coated with a thin layer of flour. Tap out and discard the excess flour.

❷ In a medium bowl, combine the flour, baking powder, and salt; stir with a fork to mix. In a large bowl, using an electric mixer on medium-high speed, beat the butter and sugar until very light and fluffy, about 3 minutes. Add the eggs, one at a time, beating well after each. After the second egg has been beaten in, stop the mixer and use a flexible spatula to scrape down the sides and bottom of the bowl. Beat in the last egg, then the sour cream and vanilla.

❸ Stop the mixer and scrape down the beaters. Using a flexible spatula or a wooden spoon, stir in the dry ingredients all at once, mixing thoroughly, but try to mix the batter as little as possible. Pour the batter into the loaf pan and smooth the top with the same flexible spatula.

❹ Bake the cake for 65 to 75 minutes, until a toothpick inserted in the center comes out clean. Let the cake cool in the pan on a wire rack for 10 minutes, then turn it out of the pan and place right-side-up on a wire rack to cool completely.

(See photo, page 33)

PUMPKIN BREAD

Prep time: 15 minutes ⏱ Baking time: 1 hour, 10 minutes 🖐 Serves 10

This is one of my favorite things to bake on a chilly fall day. It's a great snack and a decadent treat for breakfast. For a different flavor, try swapping in raisins or dried cranberries for the chocolate, if you like.

INGREDIENTS:

Cooking spray
1½ cups (6.4 ounces) all-purpose flour
1 teaspoon baking soda
½ teaspoon baking powder
1 teaspoon salt
½ teaspoon cinnamon
¼ teaspoon nutmeg
¼ teaspoon ground cloves
8 tablespoons (1 stick) unsalted butter,
     at room temperature
1 cup (7 ounces) sugar
2 large eggs, at room temperature
1 15-ounce can solid-pack pure pumpkin
½ cup miniature chocolate chips
     (optional)
½ cup chopped walnuts (optional)

TOOLS:

5 x 9-inch loaf pan
Small bowl
Large bowl
Fork
Dry measuring cups
Measuring spoons
Electric mixer
Flexible spatula
Toothpick
Wire cooling rack

❶ Preheat the oven to 350°F. Mist a 5 x 9-inch loaf pan with cooking spray.

❷ In a small bowl, using a fork, mix together the flour, baking soda, baking powder, salt, cinnamon, nutmeg, and cloves.

❸ In a large bowl, using an electric mixer on medium speed, beat together the butter and sugar until light and fluffy, about 2 minutes. Beat in the eggs, one at a time, then beat in the pumpkin. Scrape down the sides and bottom of the bowl with a flexible spatula, then beat again just until the mixture is uniform.

❹ Pour the flour mixture into the pumpkin mixture and stir with a flexible spatula until the dry ingredients are just mixed in, taking care to scrape the bottom of the bowl but mixing as little as possible. Stir in the chocolate chips and/or walnuts, if using.

❺ Pour the batter into the loaf pan and spread evenly. Bake for 60 to 70 minutes, until a toothpick inserted into the center of the bread comes out clean. Let cool on a wire rack for 20 minutes before turning the bread out of the pan and letting it cool completely on the rack.

From top: Susan's Zucchini Bread, Perfectly Simple Pound Cake, and Pumpkin Bread

SOUR CREAM COFFEE CAKE

Prep time: 30 minutes ⏱ Baking time: 45 to 50 minutes ✋ Serves 12

While I was working on this book, I was often asked if I had a favorite recipe. I don't—but this would be on the short list. It has a ripple of cinnamon sugar and a cinnamon glaze—delicious with a cup of coffee. It keeps well for a few days and makes a perfect hostess gift.

INGREDIENTS:

Cooking spray

Cake:

2 cups (8.5 ounces) all-purpose flour

1 teaspoon baking powder

1 teaspoon baking soda

1 teaspoon salt

8 tablespoons (1 stick) unsalted butter,
    at room temperature

1 cup (7 ounces) sugar

3 large eggs, at room temperature

1 cup sour cream, at room temperature

2 teaspoons vanilla extract

½ cup (4.2 ounces) packed dark brown
    sugar

2 teaspoons cinnamon

Glaze:

½ cup (2 ounces) confectioners' sugar

1 teaspoon cinnamon

2½ teaspoons milk

TOOLS:

12-cup Bundt pan or 10-inch tube pan

Dry measuring cups

Measuring spoons

Small bowl

Large bowl

Fork

Electric mixer

Flexible spatula

Paring knife

Toothpick

Wire cooling rack

Sour Cream Coffee Cake, Double
Apple Streusel Coffee Cake,
and Raspberry Buckle

❶ Make the cake: Preheat the oven to 350°F. Generously mist a 10-inch tube pan or 12-cup Bundt pan with cooking spray. In a small bowl, combine the flour, baking powder, baking soda, and salt, stirring them together with a fork.

❷ In a large bowl, using an electric mixer, beat the butter and sugar until fluffy, about 2 minutes. Beat in the eggs, one at a time, beating until well mixed before adding the next one. Stop the mixer and scrape down the sides and bottom of the bowl with a flexible spatula after beating in the second and third eggs.

❸ Using a flexible spatula or wooden spoon, stir in half of the flour mixture until almost mixed in. Mix in the sour cream and vanilla all at once, then stir in the remaining flour mixture, taking care not to overmix. Using the flexible spatula, scrape the bottom of the bowl to make sure all the ingredients are incorporated. In a small bowl, stir the brown sugar and 2 teaspoons cinnamon together with a fork.

❹ Pour half of the batter into the pan, and use the flexible spatula to spread it evenly. Sprinkle the brown sugar–cinnamon mixture evenly over the batter (use your fingers). Spread the remaining batter over the brown sugar mixture. Bake the cake for 45 to 50 minutes, until a toothpick inserted in the center of the cake comes out clean.

❺ Let the cake cool in the pan on a wire rack for 10 minutes. Run a sharp paring knife along the outside of the cake, inside the pan, to separate the cake from the sides of the pan. Place the wire rack upside-down over the top of the cake pan and, holding on firmly to both the cake pan and the wire rack, quickly invert them so that the cake comes out of the pan and onto the rack. Gently lift the pan away, and let the cake cool for at least another 30 minutes.

❻ Just before serving, make the glaze: In a small bowl, using a fork, mix the confectioners' sugar, cinnamon, and milk. Use a fork to drizzle the glaze over the cake.

RASPBERRY BUCKLE

Prep time: 20 minutes ⏱ Baking time: 45 to 50 minutes ✋ Serves 8 to 10

"Buckle" is one of those funny fruit-dessert names, like brown betty or grunt or pandowdy. A buckle is basically a cake that sort of resembles a giant muffin with a streusel topping. This buckle, studded with fresh raspberries, is perfect for brunch, but could also work after dinner if served with ice cream.

INGREDIENTS:

Cooking spray

Topping:

¾ cup (5.25 ounces) sugar

¾ cup (3.2 ounces) all-purpose flour

2 teaspoons cinnamon

¼ teaspoon salt

5 tablespoons unsalted butter, cold,
   cut into 10 pieces

Cake:

2 cups (8.5 ounces) all-purpose flour

1 teaspoon baking powder

½ teaspoon salt

4 tablespoons (½ stick) unsalted butter,
   softened

¾ cup (5.25 ounces) sugar

2 large eggs, at room temperature

½ cup half-and-half, at room
   temperature

1 teaspoon vanilla extract

1½ cups fresh raspberries

TOOLS:

Dry measuring cups

Measuring spoons

Liquid measuring cup

9-inch round cake pan

Medium bowl

Fork

Pastry blender

Small bowl

Large bowl

Electric mixer

Flexible spatula

Toothpick

Wire cooling rack

❶ Preheat the oven to 350°F and mist a 9-inch round cake pan generously with cooking spray.

❷ Make the topping: In a medium bowl, combine the sugar, flour, cinnamon, and salt; mix well with a fork. Add the butter pieces and use your fingers or a pastry blender to "cut in" the butter (see page 185 for more information). To do this, press the pastry blender down onto the butter several times so that it gets cut into ever-smaller pieces and also becomes incorporated into the dry ingredients. What you want is for the whole mixture to look like coarse sand, with no large pieces of butter left, and no pockets of dry ingredients that don't have some butter in them. Place the bowl in the fridge.

❸ Make the cake: In a small bowl, mix the flour, baking powder, and salt; stir with a fork to combine. In a large bowl, using an electric mixer on medium speed, beat the butter and sugar until light and fluffy, about 2 minutes. Add 1 egg, beat well, then beat in the second egg. Stop the mixer and scrape down the sides and bottom of the bowl with a flexible spatula. Beat the mixture again until everything is well combined. Add the vanilla to the half-and-half.

❹ Using the flexible spatula, beat in half of the flour mixture until nearly combined, then stir in all of the half-and-half mixture. Mix in the remaining flour. Try to mix as little as possible—you want to make sure all the dry ingredients are incorporated, but don't mix the batter too much or your cake will be tough.

❺ Sprinkle the raspberries on top of the batter and gently mix them in with the flexible spatula. Pour the batter into the pan and spread it evenly with the flexible spatula. Get the topping out of the fridge and sprinkle it over the cake.

❻ Bake the cake for 45 to 50 minutes, until a toothpick inserted in the center comes out clean (with no clumps of batter clinging to the toothpick). Place the cake on a wire rack to cool for at least 10 minutes before serving.

(See photo, page 34)

CARROT CUPCAKES

Prep time: 25 minutes ⏱ Baking time: 22 to 25 minutes 🖐 Makes 12

These are classic carrot cupcakes, spicy and not overly sweet, studded with pineapple and walnuts. A bit of marmalade adds a subtle orange flavor and helps make the cupcakes really tender. You can shred the carrots on a box grater, or buy a bag of pre-shredded carrots from the supermarket.

INGREDIENTS:

1 cup (4.25 ounces) all-purpose flour

½ teaspoon baking powder

¼ teaspoon baking soda

¼ teaspoon salt

2 teaspoons cinnamon

1 teaspoon ground ginger

¼ teaspoon nutmeg

Pinch of ground cloves

⅔ cup (4.7 ounces) sugar

⅓ cup vegetable oil

2 tablespoons orange marmalade

1 teaspoon vanilla extract

2 large eggs, at room temperature, lightly beaten

1⅓ cups shredded carrots (from about 3 medium carrots)

8¼-ounce can crushed pineapple, drained well

½ cup chopped walnuts (optional)

TOOLS:

Standard 12-cup muffin tin

Paper or foil cupcake liners

Dry measuring cups

Small bowl

Medium bowl

Whisk

Flexible spatula

2 tablespoons or ice cream scoop

Wire cooling rack

❶ Preheat the oven to 350°F. Line all the cups of a standard 12-cup muffin tin with paper or foil cupcake liners.

❷ In a small bowl, combine the flour, baking powder, baking soda, salt, cinnamon, ginger, nutmeg, and cloves. Whisk to mix well.

❸ In a medium bowl, whisk together the sugar, vegetable oil, orange marmalade, vanilla, and beaten eggs until well mixed. Add the flour mixture and stir with a flexible spatula until all the ingredients are combined. Scrape down the bottom of the bowl and turn the spatula over to make sure all of the dry ingredients are incorporated. You want to stir everything together thoroughly, but try not to mix it too much—overmixing will result in tough cupcakes.

❹ Add the shredded carrots, drained pineapple, and chopped walnuts, if using, and stir with the flexible spatula just enough to mix them into the batter.

❺ Use two tablespoons or an ice cream scoop to evenly divide the batter among the lined muffin cups; the cups should be about three-quarters full. Bake the cupcakes for 22 to 25 minutes, until a toothpick inserted into the center of a cupcake comes out clean. Let the cupcakes cool in the pan on a wire rack for 10 minutes, then remove the cupcakes from the pan and let them cool completely on the wire rack.

(See photo, page 192)

Good to know! These are great with Cream Cheese Frosting (see page 168), or with a simple glaze (see page 40 for a lemon glaze, or page 35 for a cinnamon glaze). Or you can sift confectioners' sugar over them just before serving them. To do that, place 2 or 3 tablespoons confectioners' sugar in a fine-mesh sieve. Hold the sieve over the cupcakes and lightly tap the sides of the sieve with your fingers so that the sugar comes through as a light powder.

DOUBLE APPLE STREUSEL
COFFEE CAKE

Prep time: 25 minutes ⏱ Baking time: 50 to 55 minutes ✋ Serves 6 to 8

This moist, slightly spicy apple coffee cake, with its satisfying, crunchy topping, is great for brunch or in the afternoon. Kids and adults alike will love it! Don't use Red Delicious apples—they're too soft and mealy for baking.

INGREDIENTS:

Cooking spray

Streusel:

¼ cup (1.1 ounces) all-purpose flour

¼ cup (2.1 ounces) packed dark brown sugar

2 tablespoons sugar

½ teaspoon cinnamon

¼ teaspoon salt

3 tablespoons cold unsalted butter, cut into pieces

¼ cup chopped pecans

Cake:

1½ cups (6.4 ounces) all-purpose flour

1 cup (8.4 ounces) packed dark brown sugar

1 tablespoon cinnamon

1 teaspoon baking soda

½ teaspoon salt

¾ cup unsweetened applesauce, at room temperature

8 tablespoons (1 stick) unsalted butter, melted, cooled slightly

¼ cup plain yogurt, at room temperature (don't use nonfat; full fat is best, but low-fat is okay)

1 teaspoon vanilla extract

1 large egg, at room temperature

1 small sweet apple, such as Gala or Yellow Delicious

❶ Preheat the oven to 350°F. Mist an 8-inch square baking pan with cooking spray.

❷ Make the streusel: In a medium bowl, combine the flour, brown sugar, sugar, cinnamon, and salt; stir with a fork to mix well. Add the butter pieces. Use a pastry blender to crush the butter and combine it with the dry ingredients. (This is called "cutting in" the butter; see page 185 for more information.) It's done when all the lumps of butter are cut up and incorporated with the dry ingredients, and the whole thing looks like slightly lumpy coarse sand. Add the pecans and toss with your fingers to mix. Place the bowl with the streusel in the fridge.

❸ Make the cake: In a large bowl, combine the flour, brown sugar, cinnamon, baking soda, and salt; whisk well to combine, making sure to break up the brown sugar so there are no lumps. In a separate large bowl, combine the applesauce, melted butter, yogurt, vanilla extract, and egg; beat with a whisk to combine well.

❹ Peel the apple. On a cutting board, using a chef's knife, cut off the top and bottom to remove the stem and bottom bit. Cut the apple lengthwise into 4 pieces, cutting around the core to remove it; discard the core. Roughly chop the apple (you want pieces that are about ½ inch—but don't worry about the shape or about making the pieces exactly uniform).

5 Add the flour mixture to the applesauce mixture all at once, and use a flexible spatula to stir the two mixtures together. Add the chopped apple. Scrape the bottom of the bowl and flip the spatula over to be sure there are no pockets of flour mixture that don't get incorporated. You want to combine the two mixtures and the chopped apple thoroughly, but try not to stir it too much, because that will result in a tough cake.

6 Scrape the batter into the baking pan and spread it evenly. Sprinkle the streusel evenly over the top of the cake.

7 Bake the cake for 50 to 55 minutes, or until a toothpick inserted in the center of the cake comes out clean. Let the cake cool in the pan on a wire rack for at least 20 minutes. Cut into pieces and serve.

(See photo, page 34)

TOOLS:

Dry measuring cups
Measuring spoons
Liquid measuring cup
8-inch square baking pan
Medium bowl
Fork
Pastry blender
2 large bowls
Whisk
Peeler
Cutting board
Chef's knife
Flexible spatula
Toothpick
Wire cooling rack

WHITE CHOCOLATE–STRAWBERRY CUPCAKES

Prep time: 25 minutes ⏱ Baking time: 25 to 30 minutes ✋ Makes 12

I think these little cupcakes, with their pink and white hues and sweet lemony glaze,
would be perfect for a bridal or baby shower, or to take to a friend's house for a party.
Bake them in pink cupcake liners to go all-out cute.

INGREDIENTS:

Cupcakes:

$1/3$ cup white chocolate chips

12 small strawberries

$1^1/3$ cups (5.7 ounces) all-purpose flour

$3/4$ teaspoon baking powder

$1/8$ teaspoon salt

8 tablespoons (1 stick) unsalted butter,
      at room temperature

$3/4$ cup (5.25 ounces) sugar

2 teaspoons grated lemon zest

2 large eggs, at room temperature

$1/2$ cup half-and-half, at room
      temperature

1 teaspoon vanilla extract

Glaze:

1 cup (4 ounces) confectioners' sugar

3 tablespoons fresh lemon juice

12 small strawberries, for garnish
      (optional)

❶ On a cutting board, using a chef's knife, chop the chocolate chips into smaller pieces. Don't worry about making them tiny or uniform in size or shape—you just want the pieces smaller than regular chocolate chips. Transfer them to a small bowl.

❷ Rinse the strawberries well, pat dry with paper towels, and remove the stems. Place them on the same cutting board you used for the white chocolate and, using the same knife, chop them into $1/4$-inch pieces (don't worry about making them uniform, just chop them up).

❸ Preheat the oven to 350°F. Line the cups in a standard 12-cup muffin tin with paper or foil liners. In a small bowl, combine the flour, baking powder, and salt. Stir with a fork to mix well.

❹ Using an electric mixer on medium speed, beat the butter, sugar, and lemon zest in a large bowl until light and fluffy, about 2 minutes. Add the eggs, one at a time, beating well after each. Turn off the mixer and scrape down the sides and bottom of the bowl with a flexible spatula. Beat again with the mixer until the mixture is uniform.

❺ Add half of the flour mixture and stir with the flexible spatula until almost combined. Stir in the half-and-half and the vanilla. Add the rest of the dry ingredients and stir until almost combined, then add the white chocolate and strawberries and carefully stir everything together. Scrape down the bottom and sides of the bowl to make sure all the dry ingredients are incorporated, but try not to mix it all too much or you'll get tough cupcakes.

❻ Use a small ice cream scoop or two tablespoons to divide the batter among the paper or foil liners in the muffin pan, filling each about three-quarters full. Bake for 25 to 30 minutes, until a toothpick inserted into the center of a cupcake comes out clean. Remove the pan to a wire rack to cool for 5 minutes, then take the cupcakes out of the pan and place them on the rack to cool completely.

❼ Make the glaze: In a small bowl, stir together the sugar and juice with a fork until completely mixed and free of lumps. If the glaze is too runny, add more sugar, a few teaspoons at a time, and stir it in with the fork. If it's too thick, add more juice, 1 teaspoon at a time. Spoon the glaze over the cooled cupcakes. Top each with a strawberry, if desired.

(See photo, page 43)

TOOLS:

Dry measuring cups
Liquid measuring cup
Measuring spoons
Cutting board
Chef's knife
2 small bowls
Large bowl
Standard 12-cup muffin tin
Paper or foil cupcake liners
Fork
Rasp grater
Electric mixer
Flexible spatula
2 tablespoons or a small ice cream scoop
Toothpick
Wire cooling rack

Good to know! You can make these with blueberries or raspberries instead of the strawberries, if you prefer. Be careful when stirring in the berries so your cupcakes don't turn pink or blue.

You could make the glaze with orange juice instead of lemon, if you like. If you do, use orange zest in the batter instead of lemon.

ORANGE CREAM CUPCAKES

Prep time: 25 minutes ⏲ Baking time: 18 to 20 minutes ✋ Makes 12

These delicate cupcakes are very nice with just a dusting of powdered sugar on top, but spread with Cream Cheese Frosting (see recipe, page 168), they're like a Creamsicle. Chocolate frosting is also delicious on these (see recipe on page 167). The cupcakes taste best the day they're made.

INGREDIENTS:

1½ cups (6.4 ounces) all-purpose flour
¾ teaspoon baking powder
½ teaspoon baking soda
¼ teaspoon salt
2 medium-size navel oranges
2 teaspoons vanilla extract
½ cup half-and-half, at room
    temperature
2 tablespoons orange marmalade
8 tablespoons (1 stick) unsalted butter,
    at room temperature
¾ cup (5.25 ounces) sugar
2 large eggs, at room temperature

TOOLS:

Standard 12-cup muffin tin
Paper or foil cupcake liners
Fork
3 small bowls
Large bowl
Flexible spatula
Electric mixer (or wooden spoon)
Rasp grater
Dry measuring cups
Liquid measuring cup
Wire cooling rack
Measuring spoons

Opposite page: Currant Scones, Orange Cream Cupcakes, and White Chocolate–Strawberry Cupcakes

❶ Preheat the oven to 350°F and place a rack in the middle of the oven. Line the cups in a standard 12-cup muffin tin with paper or foil liners.

❷ In a small bowl, stir together the flour, baking powder, baking soda, and salt with a fork until combined.

❸ Wash the oranges and pat dry with paper towels. Remove the zest from both (see page 191) and place in a small bowl with the vanilla extract. You should have about 2 tablespoons of zest. Cut 1 orange in half and squeeze out the juice into a liquid measuring cup; you should have about ¼ cup. (If you don't have that much, squeeze enough juice from the other orange to equal ¼ cup.) Place the orange juice in another small bowl and stir in the vanilla, half-and-half, and marmalade.

❹ In a large bowl, using an electric mixer on medium speed, beat the butter, sugar, and zest mixture until light and fluffy, about 3 minutes. Scrape down the sides and bottom of the bowl with a flexible spatula. Add the eggs one at a time, beating for 15 seconds after each. Scrape down the bowl again.

❺ Add half of the flour mixture and stir with a flexible spatula until almost combined. Mix in all of the half-and-half–orange juice mixture. Add the rest of the flour mixture and stir until just combined. Scrape the sides and bottom of the bowl with the flexible spatula to be sure you've mixed in all of the flour, but try to keep the stirring to a minimum.

❻ Use a ¼-cup dry measure to scoop the batter into the lined muffin cups. Fill each cup about three-quarters full. Bake the cupcakes for 18 to 20 minutes, until the tops spring back when lightly touched with your finger.

❼ Remove the muffin tin to a wire rack and let cool 5 minutes, then remove the cupcakes from the pan and place them directly on the rack to cool completely.

You Made That Dessert?

CHEESECAKE CUPCAKES

Prep time: 10 minutes ⏱ Baking time: 25 minutes ⏱ Chilling time: 1 hour ✋ Makes 12 cupcakes

This is a fun take on both cupcakes and cheesecake. They're super-easy, but look really festive and fancy—perfect for a baby or bridal shower. A few fresh berries are all they really need, but you could also serve them with Raspberry Sauce or Brandied Cherries (see the recipes on pages 162 and 165). Swap Nilla wafers for the gingersnaps if you prefer.

INGREDIENTS:

16 gingersnaps (snack size, not jumbo)
2 8-ounce packages cream cheese, at room temperature
¾ cup (5.25 ounces) sugar
¼ cup sour cream, at room temperature
1 teaspoon vanilla extract
Grated zest of 1 small lemon
¼ teaspoon salt
2 large eggs, at room temperature
1½ cups strawberries, raspberries, or blueberries, for serving (optional)

TOOLS:

Standard 12-cup muffin tin
Paper or foil cupcake liners
Large bowl
Electric mixer
Rasp grater
Flexible spatula
¼ cup dry measure
Teaspoon
Wire rack

(See photo, page 192)

❶ Preheat the oven to 325°F. Line the cups of a standard 12-cup muffin tin with paper or foil liners and place a gingersnap in the bottom of each liner.

❷ Using an electric mixer on medium-high speed, beat the cream cheese and sugar in a large bowl until the mixture is light and smooth, and no lumps of cream cheese remain, about 3 minutes. Stop the mixer once or twice while beating and scrape down the sides and bottom of the bowl with a flexible spatula. Add the sour cream, vanilla, lemon zest, and salt to the cream cheese mixture and beat just to combine. Add 1 egg and beat until incorporated, then beat in the second egg. Stop the mixer, scrape down the sides and bottom of the bowl with the flexible spatula, and beat again until the mixture is fully incorporated (but try to beat as little as possible to achieve this—you want to avoid beating a lot of excess air into the mixture).

❸ Fill a ¼-cup dry measure to the brim with the cream cheese mixture and plop into one of the lined muffin cups, right on top of the gingersnap. Repeat with the remaining batter, filling the cups nearly all the way. Use the back of a teaspoon or your fingers to smooth the tops of the cupcakes.

❹ Bake for 25 minutes, until cheesecakes are just set (they will look puffed up and may crack a bit; that's okay). Transfer the pan to a wire rack for 15 minutes, then remove the cupcakes from the pan and place them directly on the rack to cool to room temperature. The cupcakes will sink slightly as they cool.

❺ Once the cheesecake cupcakes have cooled, place them in the refrigerator until cold and firm, at least 1 hour. Place a sliced strawberry or a few raspberries or blueberries on the top of each cupcake, if desired, and serve.

Good to know! You can freeze these cupcakes for up to 2 weeks. Place them in the freezer in the pan for about 30 minutes, until firm, then transfer them to a ziplock freezer bag. Seal the bag and place it in the freezer. To defrost, place the cupcakes in the fridge for about 4 hours.

CHOCOLATE–CHOCOLATE CHIP CUPCAKES

Prep time: 15 minutes ⏱ Baking time: 18 to 20 minutes ✋ Makes 12 cupcakes

Coffee adds a depth and richness to these yummy cupcakes, but you won't taste it.
These are best the day they're made. For a different take, swap in
white chocolate chips instead of semisweet.

INGREDIENTS:

½ cup (1.45 ounces) unsweetened cocoa
    powder
2/3 cup hot strongly brewed coffee
1 1/3 cups (5.7 ounces) all-purpose flour
¾ teaspoon baking soda
¼ teaspoon salt
8 tablespoons (1 stick) unsalted butter,
    at room temperature
½ cup (3.5 ounces) sugar
2 large eggs, at room temperature
1 teaspoon vanilla extract
1 cup semisweet chocolate chips

TOOLS:

Standard 12-cup muffin tin
Paper or foil cupcake liners
Liquid measuring cup
2 small bowls
Medium bowl
Whisk
Fork
Electric mixer
Flexible spatula
2 tablespoons or ice cream scoop
Wire cooling rack

❶ Preheat the oven to 350°F. Line all the cups of a standard 12-cup muffin tin with paper or foil liners.

❷ Place the cocoa powder in a small bowl. Whisk in the hot coffee until smooth and let cool until the mixture is lukewarm, about 5 minutes. In a separate small bowl, mix the flour, baking soda, and salt with a fork.

❸ In a medium bowl, using an electric mixer on medium speed, beat the butter and sugar until light and fluffy, about 3 to 4 minutes. Beat in the eggs, one at a time. After beating in the second egg, scrape down the sides and bottom of the bowl with a flexible spatula and beat the mixture again, until just combined. Beat in the vanilla and coffee mixture.

❹ Using the flexible spatula, stir in the flour mixture. Scrape the bottom of the bowl to make sure all the flour is incorporated, but try to mix as little as possible—the more you mix, the tougher your cupcakes will be. Stir in the chocolate chips.

❺ Use an ice cream scoop or two tablespoons to divide the batter evenly among the cupcake cups, filling each about three-quarters full. Bake 18 to 20 minutes, until a toothpick inserted in the center of a cupcake comes out clean. Do not overbake them, or they'll be dry. Transfer the muffin tin to a wire rack for 20 minutes to cool, then remove the cupcakes from the pan to a wire rack to cool completely.

(See photo, page 192)

Good to know! These cupcakes are great on their own with just a light dusting of confectioners' sugar—but they're really special when topped with Chocolate Frosting (see page 167 for a recipe) or, my favorite, Cream Cheese Frosting (page 168). My other favorite way to have these is with vanilla ice cream and Brandied Cherries (page 165).

LIME-GLAZED CITRUS TEA CAKES

Prep time: 15 minutes ⏱ Baking time: 40 minutes ✋ Makes 2 8-inch loaves, serves 12

These citrusy tea cakes are perfect to take to someone's house for a party, or as a hostess gift if you're visiting for a weekend. You can play around with the flavors a bit—try using the zest of a small orange and swapping in lemon juice for the orange juice, for example. The lime glaze would also be good on a regular pound cake (see page 31 for a recipe).

INGREDIENTS:

Cooking spray

Cakes:

2 cups (8.5 ounces) all-purpose flour

¾ teaspoon baking powder

½ teaspoon salt

¼ teaspoon baking soda

8 tablespoons (1 stick) unsalted butter, at room temperature

1¼ cups (8.75 ounces) sugar

Grated zest of 1 lemon

¾ cup sour cream, at room temperature

¼ cup fresh orange juice

1 teaspoon vanilla extract

3 large eggs, at room temperature

Glaze:

1 cup (4 ounces) confectioners' sugar

4–6 teaspoons lime juice

TOOLS:

2 4 x 8-inch loaf pans

2 medium bowls

Small bowl

Rasp grater

Dry measuring cups

Liquid measuring cup

Measuring spoons

Electric mixer

Flexible spatula

Toothpick

Paring knife

Wire cooling rack

Fork

❶ Preheat the oven to 350°F. Mist two 4 x 8-inch loaf pans with cooking spray.

❷ Make the cakes: In a medium bowl, combine the flour, baking powder, salt, and baking soda. Stir with a fork to combine.

❸ In a separate medium bowl, using an electric mixer on medium-high speed, beat together the butter, sugar, and lemon zest until light and fluffy, about 2 minutes. Beat in the sour cream, orange juice, and vanilla until well mixed, about 1 more minute, then beat in the eggs. Stop the mixer and use a flexible spatula to scrape down the sides and bottom of the bowl. Beat with the electric mixer again until the mixture is uniform.

❹ Stop the mixer again and use the flexible spatula to stir in the dry ingredients, using as few strokes as possible. Scrape down to the bottom of the bowl to make sure all of the dry ingredients are incorporated.

❺ Divide the batter between the two pans and smooth the tops with a flexible spatula. Bake for 40 minutes, or until a toothpick inserted into the center of each cake comes out clean (use one toothpick for each cake; don't "double-dip"). Let the cakes cool for 20 minutes in the pans on a wire rack, then run a sharp paring knife around the inside of the pans to loosen the cakes and turn them out of the pans. Turn the cakes right-side up on the rack and let them cool completely.

❻ Make the glaze: Just before serving the cakes, put the confectioners' sugar in a small bowl and add the lime juice. Stir with a fork until the sugar is completely moistened. Adjust the consistency by adding more confectioners' sugar if the glaze is too thin, or more lime juice (a few drops at a time) if it's too stiff. Spoon the glaze over the cakes, and let stand for about 10 minutes so the glaze can firm up. Slice the cakes and serve.

Lime-Glazed Citrus Tea Cakes

GERALDINE'S CHOCOLATE-DATE CAKE

Prep time: 20 minutes ⏱ Baking time: 55 to 60 minutes ✋ Makes 1 9-inch cake, serves 10

I love this recipe. I found it online and wrote to the author, a woman named Heather, whose grandmother Geraldine, created it. Heather graciously agreed to let me share it with you. Try it—you'll love this fabulous cake as much as I do.

INGREDIENTS:

Cooking spray

2 cups pitted dried dates, halved

1¼ cups hot strongly brewed coffee

11 tablespoons unsalted butter, at room temperature

½ cup (3.5 ounces) sugar

¼ cup (2.1 ounces) lightly packed dark brown sugar

2 large eggs, at room temperature

1 teaspoon vanilla extract

1 cup (4.25 ounces) all-purpose flour

½ cup (1.45 ounces) unsweetened cocoa powder

1 teaspoon baking soda

½ teaspoon salt

½ cup chocolate chips

TOOLS:

9-inch round cake pan

Liquid measuring cups

Dry measuring cups

Measuring spoons

Large bowl

Electric mixer

Flexible spatula

Fine-mesh sieve

Spoon

Blender or food processor

Wire cooling rack

Opposite page: Geraldine's Chocolate-Date Cake

❶ Preheat the oven to 350°F. Mist a 9-inch round cake pan with cooking spray. Place the pan on a sheet of parchment, trace the pan with a pencil, and cut out the parchment circle. Line the bottom of the pan with the parchment round and mist it with cooking spray. Loosely fill a 2-cup liquid measuring cup with the dates and cover with the hot coffee. Let it sit for 5 minutes while you prepare the other ingredients.

❷ In a large bowl, using an electric mixer on medium speed, beat together the butter, sugar, and brown sugar until fluffy, about 2 minutes. Beat in the eggs, one at a time, and the vanilla extract. Scrape down the sides and bottom of the bowl with a flexible spatula and then beat again until the mixture is uniform. Place a fine-mesh sieve over the bowl with the butter mixture and put the flour, cocoa powder, baking soda, and salt in the sieve. Sift the dry ingredients by holding the sieve over the bowl and lightly tapping the side with your fingers. If there are any lumps of dry ingredients left after you've finished sifting, rub the back of a spoon over the lumps to press them through the sieve. With a flexible spatula, mix the dry ingredients gently into the butter mixture until nearly combined.

❸ Pour the dates and coffee into a blender or food processor and blend to puree the mixture completely. Add the pureed dates to the batter and mix with the same flexible spatula until all the ingredients are combined.

❹ Pour the batter into the prepared pan and sprinkle the top evenly with the chocolate chips. Bake for 55 to 60 minutes or until the edges begin to pull away from the side of the pan and the cake springs back when you touch it lightly. Cool the cake in the pan on a wire rack until cool enough to handle, then gently turn the cake out onto the rack to cool further. Serve at room temperature. Cover leftover cake with plastic wrap and keep at room temperature for up to 4 days.

Good to know! If you cut a slice of cake, press some plastic wrap directly on the cut part of the cake to keep it from drying out, as well as covering the cake.

GREAT BIG COCONUT CAKE

Prep time: 20 minutes ⏱ Baking time: 1 hour 🖐 Serves 12

I know there are people out there who don't like coconut—but for those of you like me, who love it, this cake is for you. With plenty of fluffy coconut flakes and coconut milk, it's pretty much coconut heaven. It's a lovely addition to a dessert table for a party, and would be great for a shower.

INGREDIENTS:
Cooking spray
Cake:
2½ cups (10.6 ounces) all-purpose flour
    (plus 3 tablespoons for preparing
    the pan)
1 tablespoon baking powder
2 teaspoons baking soda
1 teaspoon salt
16 tablespoons (2 sticks) unsalted
    butter, at room temperature
1½ cups (10.5 ounces) sugar
3 large eggs, at room temperature
2 teaspoons vanilla extract
1 cup canned coconut milk (shake can
    well before opening)
1 cup sweetened flake coconut
Glaze:
1 cup (4 ounces) confectioners' sugar
3 tablespoons coconut milk
⅓ cup sweetened flake coconut

TOOLS:
12-cup Bundt pan or 10-inch tube pan
Small bowl
Large bowl
Dry measuring cups
Liquid measuring cup
Measuring spoons
Fork
Electric mixer
Toothpick
Flexible spatula
Paring knife
Wire cooling rack

❶ Make the cake: Preheat the oven to 350°F. Generously mist a 12-cup Bundt pan or a 10-inch tube pan with cooking spray. Spoon in 3 tablespoons flour and move the pan all around to coat it with a thin layer of flour. Tap out and discard any excess flour.

❷ In a small bowl, mix 2½ cups flour, the baking powder, baking soda, and salt, stirring with a fork to combine. In a large bowl, using an electric mixer at medium speed, beat the butter and sugar until light and fluffy, about 2 minutes. Add the eggs one at a time, beating well after each. Scrape down the sides and bottom of the bowl with a flexible spatula and beat again until the mixture is uniform. Beat in the vanilla.

❸ Add half of the flour mixture to the wet mixture and stir with your flexible spatula until nearly incorporated. Stir in the coconut milk. Add the remaining flour and stir until it's nearly mixed in, then stir in the flaked coconut. Try to mix as little as possible—the more you mix, the tougher your cake will be. Pour the batter into the prepared pan.

❹ Bake for 55 to 60 minutes, or until a toothpick inserted into the cake comes out clean. Set the pan on a wire cooling rack to cool. After about 15 minutes, run a thin, sharp paring knife around the small hole in the center of the cake, separating the inside edge of the cake from the pan. Place the wire rack upside down over the top of the pan, and, holding both the rack and the cake pan, quickly but carefully flip them over so that the cake comes out of the pan. Carefully lift the pan off the cake. Let the cake cool completely.

❺ Make the glaze: Put the confectioners' sugar in a bowl and add 2 tablespoons coconut milk. Stir briskly with a fork. Add more coconut milk if necessary to get the glaze fluid enough so that you can use the fork to drizzle it over the cake. After drizzling the cake with the glaze, sprinkle it with ⅓ cup coconut.

Great Big Coconut Cake

You Made That Dessert?

STRAWBERRY ICE CREAM CUPCAKES

Prep time: 20 minutes ⏲ Chilling time: 1 hour, 5 minutes ✋ Makes 12

These cute cupcakes couldn't be simpler, and they're perfect for a kid's birthday party (even if the "kid" is in her thirties . . .). You can vary the flavors as you like, using different cake and/or ice cream. I think the sprinkles make them extra-special.

INGREDIENTS:

2 pints strawberry ice cream
1 pound cake (store bought or
    homemade; see page 31 for a recipe)
6 teaspoons strawberry jam
2 cups heavy cream, chilled
2 tablespoons confectioners' sugar
Sprinkles, for decoration (optional)

TOOLS:

Standard 12-cup muffin tin
Paper or foil cupcake liners
Serrated knife
Round cookie cutter
Measuring spoons
2-inch ice cream scoop
Large bowl
Electric mixer
Ziplock bag
Scissors

❶ Line a standard 12-cup muffin tin with paper or foil cupcake liners. Take the ice cream out of the freezer for 10 minutes to soften enough to make it easy to scoop.

❷ Using a serrated knife, cut the pound cake into 6 slices, each about ¾-inch thick. Using a round cookie cutter, cut 12 rounds from the cake slices. Put a cake round in each muffin cup. (If you don't have a cookie cutter, find a glass that's the right size, and use it as a guide as you cut the rounds with a paring knife. You want the cake rounds to fit in the bottoms of the muffin cups.)

❸ Drop ½ teaspoon of strawberry jam onto each cake round. Using a 2-inch ice cream scoop, scoop 12 balls of ice cream, dropping them into the muffin cups as you scoop. The scoops should be large enough to peek out over the tops of the muffin cups. Put the muffin tin in the freezer to allow the ice cream to firm up again, at least 20 minutes or up to 2 hours.

❹ Place a metal mixing bowl and the beaters from your electric mixer in the refrigerator for 10 minutes. Pour the cream and confectioners' sugar into the chilled bowl. Using an electric mixer on medium speed, begin whipping the cream until it gets very foamy. Turn the mixer up to medium-high speed and beat the cream until it forms medium-firm peaks.

❺ Remove the muffin tin from the freezer. Gently spoon the whipped cream into a large ziplock bag, remove any excess air, seal the bag, and squeeze the cream over to one side. Snip a small corner off the side of the bag where the cream is, and gently squeeze the bag to pipe the whipped cream on top of each cupcake to resemble frosting. Start around the outer edges and swirl up in the middle. Decorate the tops with sprinkles, if desired, then place the muffin tin back in the freezer until the whipped cream firms up, about 45 minutes. Remove the cupcakes from the freezer about 5 minutes before serving.

Strawberry Ice Cream Cupcakes

PINEAPPLE UPSIDE-DOWN CAKE

Prep time: 20 minutes ⏱ Baking time: 40 to 45 minutes ✋ Serves 10

Upside-down cakes are pretty retro, but they've enjoyed a renaissance in recent years, and with good reason. I've had many kinds, but I still really love the classic pineapple. Use fresh pineapple, not canned, for the best flavor—you can usually find it precut in the supermarket. Try this cake with a scoop of coconut sorbet for a tropical treat.

INGREDIENTS:

1¾ cups (7.5 ounces) all-purpose flour

2 teaspoons baking powder

½ teaspoon salt

2 teaspoons ground ginger

10 tablespoons unsalted butter, at room temperature

¾ cup (5.75 ounces) packed light brown sugar

2 cups fresh pineapple pieces

¾ cup (5.25 ounces) sugar

2 teaspoons vanilla extract

1 tablespoon dark rum (optional)

2 large eggs, at room temperature

²/₃ cup sour cream, at room temperature

TOOLS:

Small bowl

Large bowl

Dry measuring cups

Measuring spoons

Fork

Saucepan

Flexible spatula

9-inch round cake pan

Electric mixer

Toothpick

Paring knife

Wire cooling rack

❶ Preheat the oven to 375°F. In a small bowl, mix the flour, baking powder, salt, and ginger and stir with a fork.

❷ In a saucepan, melt 4 tablespoons of the butter over medium heat. Add the brown sugar and stir with a flexible spatula to dissolve the sugar. Bring to a boil, stirring. When the mixture begins to boil, stop stirring and let it cook for 1 minute. Pour the caramel mixture into a 9-inch round cake pan and swirl the pan so that the caramel covers the bottom of the pan. Be careful not to touch the caramel—it is extremely hot. Arrange the pineapple decoratively in the caramel and carefully press it down. Rinse and dry the flexible spatula.

❸ In a large bowl, using an electric mixer, beat the remaining 6 tablespoons of the butter with the sugar until it's light and fluffy, about 2 minutes. Beat in the vanilla and rum, if using. Add the eggs, one at a time, beating after each until it's mixed in. After adding the second egg, stop the mixer and use the flexible spatula to scrape down the sides and bottom of the bowl, then beat again just until the mixture is uniform.

❹ Using the flexible spatula, stir in half of the flour mixture until it's almost mixed in. Add all of the sour cream and stir with the spatula until it's nearly mixed in. Add the remaining flour mixture and stir until the batter is uniform, scraping the bottom of the bowl to be sure the flour is completely incorporated. Try to do this with as few strokes as possible—the more you mix, the tougher your cake will be.

❺ Scrape the batter into the pan on top of the pineapple, and use the spatula to carefully spread the batter evenly, without moving the pineapple. Bake for 40 to 45 minutes, until a toothpick inserted in the center of the cake comes out clean. Remove the cake from the oven and place it on a wire cooling rack for 5 minutes.

Pineapple Upside-Down Cake

6 After 5 minutes, run a paring knife around the very outside of the pan to separate the sides of the cake from the pan. Then place a serving plate upside-down over the cake pan. Hold the cake pan and the plate together and carefully but swiftly flip them over, so that the cake falls out of the pan and onto the plate with the pineapple right-side up. Pull the pan away. If any pieces of pineapple have stuck to the pan, pull them out and place them back on the cake, and scrape any caramel still in the pan onto the cake with a flexible spatula. Wait 5 more minutes before cutting and serving.

CREAMY VANILLA CHEESECAKE

Prep time: 30 minutes ⏱ Baking time: 1 hour, 10 minutes ⏱ Chilling time: 7 hours ✋ Serves 10

This is a classic cheesecake, made extra creamy with the addition of a bit of heavy cream. It freezes well: Wrap it in foil (in the pan), put it in a heavy-duty ziplock freezer bag, and freeze for up to 2 months. To defrost, leave it in the fridge overnight. Try it with Raspberry Sauce, Brandied Cherries, or even Caramel Sauce (see recipes beginning on page 160).

INGREDIENTS:

Crust:

1½ cups graham cracker crumbs (from a box, or about 15 graham cracker sheets crushed in a food processor)

Pinch of salt

6 tablespoons unsalted butter, melted

Filling:

3 8-ounce packages cream cheese, at room temperature

1 cup (7 ounces) sugar

3 large eggs, at room temperature

½ cup sour cream, at room temperature

¼ cup heavy cream, at room temperature

2 tablespoons vanilla extract

¼ teaspoon salt

TOOLS:

8-inch springform pan

Medium bowl

Large bowl

Fork

Electric mixer

Flexible spatula

Roasting pan

Wire cooling rack

Measuring spoons

Dry measuring cups

Paring knife

❶ Preheat the oven to 350°F. Wrap the bottom and sides of an 8-inch springform pan tightly with two layers of foil.

❷ Make the crust: In a medium bowl, with a fork, stir together the graham cracker crumbs, salt, and melted butter until all of the crumbs are moistened. Transfer the mixture to the pan and use your fingers or the bottom of a glass to press it evenly into the bottom. Bake for 10 minutes, then remove to a wire rack to cool.

❸ Make the filling: In a large bowl, using an electric mixer at medium speed, beat the cream cheese and sugar until smooth and light, about 2 minutes. Scrape down the bowl with a flexible spatula and beat again to remove any remaining lumps. Beat in the eggs, one at a time. Scrape down the bowl again. Beat in the sour cream, heavy cream, vanilla, and salt.

❹ Pour the filling into the pan on top of the crust (it's okay if the crust is still warm). Pick up the springform pan about 1½ inches and drop it onto the counter. Repeat two or three times; this will force out any pockets of air in the cheesecake. Place the pan in a large roasting pan. Fill the roasting pan with hot water until it reaches about an inch up the sides of the springform pan. (This is called a "water bath"; see page 186 for more about this.)

❺ Bake the cake for 60 to 70 minutes, until the cake is just firm on the edges but still wiggles a little bit in the center when you gently shake it. It will firm up as it cools. Remove the pans from the oven and take the springform out of the roasting pan. Remove the foil, but leave the pan sides intact. Place the springform on a wire rack to cool for 1 hour, then cover with foil and refrigerate for at least 6 hours.

❻ To unmold, run a thin, sharp paring knife around the outside of the cake, pressing it against the inside of the pan so that you don't cut into the cake. Remove the sides of the pan.

Creamy Vanilla Cheesecake with Raspberry Sauce

"ALMOND JOY" CHEESECAKE

Prep time: 20 minutes ⏱ Baking time: 1 hour, 10 minutes ⏱ Chilling time: 7 hours ✋ Serves 10

I always loved Almond Joy candies (Mounds too), so the idea of mixing almonds, coconut, and chocolate into cheesecake form was a no-brainer. The toasted coconut and almond topping is optional, but it's quick to do and I think it adds a pretty, finished look. You'll have extra chocolate-coconut glaze left over—try it on ice cream.

INGREDIENTS:

Crust:

1¼ cups chocolate graham cracker crumbs (from a box, or about 12 graham cracker sheets crushed in a food processor)

½ cup sliced almonds

¼ teaspoon salt

4 tablespoons (½ stick) unsalted butter, melted

Filling:

2 8-ounce packages cream cheese, at room temperature

½ cup (3.5 ounces) sugar

3 large eggs, at room temperature

½ teaspoon vanilla extract

1 15-ounce can cream of coconut (shake well before opening can)

½ teaspoon salt

Topping (optional):

½ cup sweetened flaked coconut, for garnish

½ cup sliced almonds, for garnish

12 ounces semisweet chocolate

½ cup canned cream of coconut

½ cup heavy cream

❶ Preheat the oven to 350°F. Make the crust: In a medium bowl, mix the graham cracker crumbs, almonds, and salt with a flexible spatula. Stir in the melted butter until the dry ingredients are lightly moistened. Press the mixture into the bottom of a 9-inch springform pan. Wrap the outside of the pan tightly with two layers of foil. Bake for 10 minutes. Cool on a wire rack. Leave the foil on.

❷ Make the filling: Using an electric mixer on medium speed, beat the cream cheese and sugar until well combined and light, and no lumps remain, about 2 minutes. Scrape down the sides and bottom of the bowl with a flexible spatula and beat again until smooth. Beat in the eggs one at a time, beating well after each. Scrape down the sides and bottom of the bowl again. Beat in the vanilla, 1 cup cream of coconut, and the salt all at once. (Pour the remaining cream of coconut into a small bowl, cover it with plastic and refrigerate it. You'll use it for the topping.)

❸ Pour the filling into the crust. Gently transfer the springform pan into a roasting pan, and add enough hot tap water to the roasting pan to come about an inch up the sides of the springform pan. (This is called a "water bath," see page 186 for more about this.) Bake for 1 hour, until the filling is set but still a bit jiggly in the center when you gently shake the springform pan (it will firm up as it cools).

❹ Remove the springform pan from the roasting pan, remove the foil, and let the cake cool in the pan on a wire rack for 1 hour. Lightly cover the cheesecake with plastic wrap and refrigerate until it is cold and firm, at least 6 hours.

❺ Make the topping: If you're going to garnish the cake with the coconut and sliced almonds, place both on a rimmed baking sheet and bake in a preheated 350°F oven until light golden, about 5 to 8 minutes, stirring the coconut and almonds once or twice during baking for even toasting. Remove the sheet from oven, pour the nuts and coconut into a bowl, and let them cool completely.

❻ After the cheesecake has cooled, finish the topping: On a cutting board, using a chef's knife, finely chop the chocolate and place it in a large bowl (see page 187 for more on chopping chocolate). Pour the remaining ½ cup cream of coconut and heavy cream into a saucepan and warm it over medium-low heat until it's just simmering (hot, with tiny bubbles forming around the edges, but not boiling). Pour the cream mixture over the chocolate and whisk until the chocolate has melted and the mixture is smooth. Let it cool.

❼ Pour about ½ cup to 1 cup of the chocolate mixture on top of the cheesecake, spreading with an offset spatula or flexible spatula. Sprinkle with the toasted coconut and almond mixture, if using. Chill until the chocolate mixture has set, about 10 minutes.

❽ Run a sharp paring knife around the inside of the springform pan, then release the sides. To slice the cheesecake cleanly, run your chef's knife under hot water and wipe it clean and dry with a towel in between each cut.

(See photo, page 60)

TOOLS:

Medium bowl
Flexible spatula
9-inch springform pan
Wire cooling rack
Large bowl
Dry measuring cups
Electric mixer
Roasting pan
Rimmed baking sheet
Cutting board
Chef's knife
Paring knife
Liquid measuring cup
Measuring spoons
Saucepan
Whisk

Good to know! You will have about 1 cup of leftover chocolate topping. Pour it into a sealable container, cover, and refrigerate for up to 5 days. Rewarm it on low heat in a saucepan on the stove or in the microwave on low power to bring it back to a pourable consistency. Serve it spooned over ice cream or pound cake (see page 31 for a recipe).

"Almond Joy" Cheesecake

Tres Leches Cake

TRES LECHES CAKE

Prep time: 20 minutes ⏱ Baking time: 30 to 35 minutes ⏱ Chilling time: 2 hours, 30 minutes ✋ Serves 12

This rich cake is Latin American in origin—though no one knows exactly where. Some say it's Mexican, others claim it hails from Nicaragua or Cuba. To whoever did invent it, I say, *¡Gracias!* This is one of my favorites, and was our wedding cake (we got married near my in-laws' home in Mazatlan, Mexico).

INGREDIENTS:

Cake:

12 tablespoons (1½ sticks) unsalted butter, at room temperature (plus 2 tablespoons for preparing pan)

2 cups (8.5 ounces) all-purpose flour (plus 3 tablespoons for preparing pan)

2 teaspoons baking powder

½ teaspoon salt

1 cup (7 ounces) sugar

3 large eggs, at room temperature

2 teaspoons vanilla extract

1 cup milk, at room temperature

Glaze:

1 12-ounce can evaporated milk

1 14-ounce can sweetened condensed milk

1 cup half-and-half, or canned coconut milk (shake the can well before opening)

1 tablespoon dark rum

TOOLS:

Dry measuring cups

Liquid measuring cup

Measuring spoons

Medium bowl

Fork

Large bowl

Electric mixer

Flexible spatula

9 x 13-inch pan

Toothpick

Wire cooling rack

Whisk

❶ Preheat the oven to 350°F. Using your fingers or a piece of plastic wrap, spread 2 tablespoons butter in a thin layer over the inside of a 9 x 13-inch pan, taking care to get into all the corners. Spoon 3 tablespoons flour into the pan and move the pan all around until the inside is coated with a thin layer of flour. Tap out and discard the excess flour.

❷ Make the cake: Combine the flour, baking powder, and salt in a medium bowl; stir with a fork to mix well. Using an electric mixer on medium speed, beat the butter and sugar in a large bowl until light and fluffy, about 2 minutes. Add the eggs one at a time, beating well after each, then beat in the vanilla. Scrape down the sides of the bowl with a flexible spatula and beat again until mixture is uniform.

❸ Add half of the flour to the wet mixture and stir with the flexible spatula until the two are almost combined. Beat in the milk, then the remaining flour mixture, beating until just combined. Scrape down the bottom of the bowl to be sure all of the flour is mixed in, but try not to overmix.

❹ Pour the batter into the prepared pan. Bake for 30 to 35 minutes, or until a toothpick inserted into middle of the cake comes out clean and the cake springs back when touched lightly in the center. Remove the cake from the oven and let it cool on a wire rack for about 20 minutes.

❺ Meanwhile, make the glaze: In a large bowl, whisk together the evaporated milk, sweetened condensed milk, half-and-half (or coconut milk), and rum, just until combined.

❻ Using a fork or toothpick, carefully puncture the cake all over (being careful not to tear it). Pour the glaze over the cake, about ½ cup at a time, letting the glaze soak in before pouring in more. If the glaze stops seeping in, stop adding it. Let the cake stand at room temperature for 30 minutes, then cover the top with plastic wrap and refrigerate for at least 2 hours.

❼ To serve: You can serve this cake plain or with fresh fruit, toasted nuts, icing—you really can't go wrong. Personally, I like to spread it with a thin layer of sweetened whipped cream and serve it with a few sliced strawberries and/or mangoes.

(See photo, page 61)

Good to know! To make sweetened whipped cream, use an electric mixer to whip 1½ cups heavy cream until it starts to thicken. Add 2 to 3 tablespoons confectioners' sugar and continue to whip until the cream holds its shape. Don't overwhip the cream—you'll end up with a curdled, butter-like mess that can't be saved. Use a flexible spatula to gently spread the whipped cream in soft waves over the Tres Leches Cake just before serving.

TIRAMISU

Prep time: 25 minutes ⏱ Chilling time: 6 hours ✋ Serves 8

Tiramisu means "pick me up" in Italian, and between the coffee and the brandy in here, it does just that. There's no baking involved, so try this one out first if you're nervous about baking.

INGREDIENTS:

1 cup strongly brewed coffee, cooled
¼ cup brandy
24 ladyfingers
¾ cup heavy cream, chilled
8 ounces mascarpone, at room
    temperature (see "Good to Know")
2 teaspoons vanilla extract
½ cup sugar
Pinch of salt
¼ cup (0.73 ounce) unsweetened cocoa
    powder

TOOLS:

Liquid measuring cup
7 x 11-inch baking pan
Serrated knife
Cutting board
Large bowl
Electric mixer
Measuring spoons
Pastry brush
Flexible spatula
Fine-mesh sieve

Opposite page: Tiramisu

❶ In a 2-cup liquid measuring cup or small bowl, mix the cooled coffee and brandy. Place 12 ladyfingers in a single layer, lying flat, in a 7 x 11-inch baking pan. You may have to trim some of the ladyfingers to fit in the dish. (To trim a ladyfinger, place it on a cutting board, and saw it gently with a serrated knife.)

❷ In a large bowl, combine the cream, mascarpone, vanilla, sugar, and salt. Beat with an electric mixer on low speed at first, then increase to high speed, until the mixture forms stiff peaks (see page 190 to learn more about whipping cream). Remove the beaters (scrape any cream mixture clinging to them back into the bowl). Add 3 tablespoons of the coffee mixture to the cream mixture and carefully stir with the same flexible spatula.

❸ Using a pastry brush, brush the ladyfingers thoroughly with the coffee-brandy mixture, so that they're all well moistened but not soaked. Using the flexible spatula, scoop half of the mascarpone mixture into the dish and spread it carefully but evenly over the ladyfingers. Top the mascarpone layer with another layer of 12 ladyfingers, trimming to fit as necessary. Brush the ladyfingers with the coffee mixture (you may not use it all—that's okay). Top the ladyfingers with the remaining mascarpone mixture and spread it evenly. Cover the dish with foil and refrigerate for at least 6 hours, or as long as 24 hours.

❹ Just before serving, spoon the cocoa into a fine-mesh sieve. Uncover the tiramisu. Bring the sieve over the tiramisu and lightly tap the edge with your fingers to sift the cocoa evenly over the surface of the tiramisu. (You may not use all of the cocoa—that's okay.) Cut into pieces and serve.

Good to know!
Ladyfingers are traditional in tiramisu, but if you can't find them in your supermarket, buy a premade plain sponge cake. Slice the cake into ½-inch-thick slices, and use the cake slices instead of ladyfingers. Follow the recipe as written otherwise.

Mascarpone is a lusciously light, sweet Italian cream cheese, available in the dairy section of most higher-end supermarkets. If you can't find it, you can swap in regular cream cheese, but that will make your tiramisu a bit heavier.

MOLTEN DARK CHOCOLATE CAKES

Prep time: 25 minutes ⏱ Baking time: 10 minutes ✋ Makes 6

These decadent little cakes are basically dressed-up brownies, baked at a high temperature so the outsides get cooked while the insides remain soft and fluid. The best part about making molten chocolate cakes at home is that you can prepare the batter a day ahead—ideal for a date or a dinner party.

INGREDIENTS:

8 tablespoons (1 stick) unsalted butter (plus 1–2 tablespoons for preparing ramekins)
7 ounces bittersweet chocolate
½ cup (2.1 ounces) all-purpose flour
Pinch of salt
2 teaspoons instant espresso powder (optional)
2 large eggs
2 large egg yolks
¼ cup heavy cream
1 teaspoon vanilla extract
½ cup (2 ounces) confectioners' sugar, plus extra for dusting

TOOLS:

6 ¾-cup ramekins
Cutting board
Chef's knife
Dry measuring cups
Liquid measuring cup
Measuring spoons
Saucepan
Flexible spatula
Small bowl
Medium bowl
Large bowl
Fork
Whisk
Large spoon

Opposite page: Molten Dark Chocolate Cakes with Brandied Cherries

❶ Preheat the oven to 450°F. Using your fingers or a piece of plastic wrap, thoroughly coat six ¾-cup ramekins with 1 to 2 tablespoons butter (use as much as you need to coat them with a thin film).

❷ On a cutting board, using a sharp chef's knife, chop the chocolate into small pieces; see page 187 for more details on how to chop chocolate). Place the chocolate in a saucepan. Using the same knife and cutting board, cut the butter into 8 pieces and add them to the saucepan with the chocolate. Place the pan on the stove over the lowest possible heat setting and cook, stirring constantly with a flexible spatula, until the mixture is melted and smooth. Remove the pan from the stove, pour the mixture into a medium bowl, and let it cool slightly.

❸ In a small bowl, mix the flour and salt together with a fork. If using espresso powder, stir it into the flour mixture with the fork.

❹ In a large bowl, using a wire whisk, beat together the eggs, yolks, cream, and vanilla extract. Whisk in the confectioners' sugar, just until mixture is combined.

❺ Using the same flexible spatula, stir the chocolate mixture into the egg mixture, turning the mixtures over each other until they're combined (this is called "folding"; see page 185 for more information). Gently stir in the flour mixture (you shouldn't see any traces of flour, but try not to mix more than you have to).

❻ Use a large spoon to divide the chocolate mixture among the ramekins. (You can stop here, cover the ramekins tightly with foil, and refrigerate them for up to a day. Remove them from the fridge just before baking.)

❼ Place the ramekins in the oven and bake for 10 minutes. (If the cakes were refrigerated, bake 14 minutes.) Let them stand 1 minute. Place the hot ramekins on individual dessert plates to serve. Pass around ice cream or sorbet to go with the cakes, if desired.

You Made That Dessert?

BROWNIE ICE CREAM TORTE

Prep time: 10 minutes ⏱ Freezing time: 5 hours ✋ Serves 8 to 10

This is a fun, super-easy dessert that looks really impressive but is actually a breeze to put together. You can vary it however you like by simply swapping different flavors of ice cream. Or you could place a bit of of caramel sauce, chopped nuts, or sliced bananas between layers of ice cream. The possibilities are as open as your imagination.

INGREDIENTS:

Cooking spray

1 box brownie mix (see "Good to know!")

1 pint vanilla ice cream

1 pint sorbet, raspberry or strawberry

Hot Fudge Sauce (see page 159 for recipe) or chocolate syrup, for serving (optional)

Whipped cream, for serving (optional)

Raspberries, for serving (optional)

TOOLS:

Large bowl

Wooden spoon

Flexible spatula

9-inch springform pan

Wire cooling rack

Large spoon

Chef's knife

❶ Lightly mist a 9-inch springform pan with cooking spray. Prepare the brownie mix as package label directs. Pour the batter into the springform pan and spread it evenly with an offset spatula. Bake as the package label directs. Place the brownie on a wire rack to cool for 30 minutes.

❷ While the brownie is cooling, place the vanilla ice cream in the fridge. When the brownie has cooled, use a large spoon to scoop about two-thirds of the pint of ice cream into the center of the brownie. Spread the softened ice cream in an even layer over the brownie using the back of the spoon. Freeze for 30 minutes. While it's freezing, place the sorbet in the fridge.

❸ Use a large spoon to scoop about two-thirds of the pint of sorbet on top of the ice cream. Spread it out with the back of the spoon into an even layer. Place the pan in the freezer for 30 minutes, then cover the torte firmly with plastic wrap and freeze until it is completely firm, about 4 hours.

❹ Drizzle Hot Fudge Sauce or chocolate syrup over the top of the torte, if desired. Before serving, let the torte sit in the refrigerator for about 20 minutes. To slice, dip a chef's knife in a pitcher of very hot water and wipe dry with a clean kitchen towel between each cut. Top each slice with a dollop of whipped cream and fresh raspberries, if desired.

Good to know! When buying brownie mix, look for one that is baked in a 9-inch pan, not the 9 x 13-inch pan or "family size." If you can't find the smaller size, only use half of the batter in the springform pan.

Brownie Ice Cream Torte

FLOURLESS CHOCOLATE CAKE

Prep time: 20 minutes ⏱ Baking time: 20 to 25 minutes ⏱ Chilling time: 7 hours ✋ Serves 16

No doubt you've had some version of this cake at some point, likely in a restaurant.
It's one of those cakes that seems very difficult to make but is actually really easy. Try it
with fresh whipped cream and raspberries, or with Raspberry Sauce or Crème Anglaise
(see pages 162 and 166 for the recipes).

INGREDIENTS:

Cooking spray
8 ounces semisweet chocolate
8 ounces milk chocolate
16 tablespoons (2 sticks) unsalted
    butter, cut into pieces
1 teaspoon instant espresso powder
2 teaspoons vanilla extract
6 large eggs, at room temperature
¼ teaspoon salt

TOOLS:

9-inch springform pan
Cutting board
Chef's knife
Roasting pan
Saucepan
Flexible spatula
2 large bowls
Measuring spoons
Cup
Electric mixer
Wire cooling rack
Paring knife

❶ Preheat the oven to 325°F. Mist a 9-inch springform pan with cooking spray. Trace the bottom of the pan onto a piece of parchment paper, then cut out the paper round. Lock the springform pan together, then place the paper round on the bottom, pressing it down. Mist the parchment with cooking spray. Wrap the bottom of the springform pan tightly with two layers of foil, then place the pan into a large roasting pan.

❷ On a cutting board, using a sharp chef's knife, chop both chocolates (see page 187 for more on how to do this). Combine the butter and chopped chocolates in a saucepan. Place the pan on the stove over the very lowest heat setting. Cook, stirring constantly with a flexible spatula, until the mixture is melted and smooth. Remove it from the heat and pour it into a large bowl. In a cup, dissolve the instant espresso in the vanilla extract. Scrape the vanilla mixture into the chocolate mixture and stir to combine.

❸ In a large bowl, using an electric mixer, beat the eggs and salt until pale and nearly double in volume, about 5 to 8 minutes. Pour about one-third of the egg mixture into the chocolate mixture and use your flexible spatula to turn the two mixtures over each other, scraping down the bottom of the bowl and turning it over the top (this is called "folding," see page 185 for more on this). The idea is to mix the two items together, but gently, so they get thoroughly incorporated but you don't deflate all the air that you've beaten into the eggs. Pour another one-third of the egg mixture into the chocolate mixture and fold it in, then do the same with the final third.

❹ Pour the batter into the springform pan and smooth the top with the flexible spatula. Place the roasting pan in the oven, then pour enough hot tap water into the roasting pan, around the outside of the springform pan, to reach about one-third of the way up the outside of the springform pan (this is called a "water bath"; see page 186). Bake until the edges of the cake are beginning to look dry and set, 20 to 25 minutes (if you gently wiggle the springform pan, the center of the cake will still jiggle a bit—that's okay, the cake will firm up as it cools).

❺ Take the roasting pan out of the oven, remove the springform pan from the water bath, remove the foil, and place the springform pan on a wire rack to cool to room temperature, about 1 hour. Cover the springform pan with foil or plastic wrap and refrigerate the cake for 6 hours or overnight.

❻ Remember to take the cake out of the fridge about 30 minutes before serving. To remove it from the pan, run a sharp paring knife along the inside edge of the pan, then unlock the sides and remove them. Turn a plate upside down over the top of the cake and flip over both the cake and the pan bottom. Remove the pan bottom and peel off the parchment, then place a serving plate upside down over the cake. Flip both over. Cut the cake into very thin slices and serve.

(See photo, page 73)

Currant-Cranberry Spice Cake

Flourless Chocolate Cake with
Crème Anglaise

ALMOND-RASPBERRY CAKE

Prep time: 20 minutes ⏱ Baking time: 35 minutes ✋ Serves 8

This sophisticated single-layer cake is perfect to serve in the afternoon with coffee or tea, and it also makes a nice dessert after dinner or brunch. Sift a tablespoon of confectioners' sugar over the top just before serving, if you like. Be sure to use almond paste and not marzipan—the latter is much sweeter than almond paste and has a different texture.

INGREDIENTS:

4 tablespoons (½ stick) unsalted butter, at room temperature (plus 1–2 tablespoons for preparing pan)
¼ cup (1.75 ounces) sugar
1 7-ounce tube almond paste, broken up into pieces
3 large eggs, at room temperature
1 teaspoon vanilla or almond extract
¾ cup (3.2 ounces) all-purpose flour (plus 2 tablespoons for preparing pan)
½ teaspoon baking powder
½ teaspoon salt
1 6-ounce box fresh raspberries
¼ cup sliced almonds

TOOLS:

9-inch round baking pan
Measuring spoons
Dry measuring cups
Large bowl
Small bowl
Electric mixer
Flexible spatula
Fork
Wire cooling rack
Toothpick

Opposite page: Almond-Raspberry Cake

❶ Preheat the oven to 350°F. Using your fingers or a piece of plastic wrap, coat a 9-inch round baking pan with a thin layer of butter. Place the pan over a sheet of parchment paper, trace the pan with a pencil, then cut the circle out of the parchment. Place the parchment circle in the bottom of the pan, then coat the parchment with a thin layer of butter. Spoon 2 tablespoons flour into the pan and move the pan all around to coat the parchment and the pan sides with a thin layer of flour. Tap the excess flour out and discard it.

❷ Place the sugar and almond paste in a large bowl and beat with an electric mixer on low speed until thoroughly mixed, about 1 to 2 minutes. Add the butter, then raise the mixer speed to medium and beat well. When the mixture forms a cohesive paste, raise the speed to medium-high and beat until it gets fluffy, about 2 to 3 minutes. Add the eggs, one at a time, beating until each egg is incorporated before adding the next one. Beat in the vanilla. Stop the mixer and use a flexible spatula to scrape down the sides and bottom of the bowl, then beat again until everything is thoroughly mixed.

❸ In a small bowl, stir together the flour, baking powder, and salt with a fork. Add the flour mixture to the almond paste mixture and stir them together with the flexible spatula. Stir well and scrape the bottom of the bowl to make sure all the flour is mixed in, but try not to overmix, or your cake will be tough.

❹ Carefully mix the raspberries into the batter with the flexible spatula; try to avoid breaking them up. Pour the batter into the prepared pan, using the flexible spatula to gently spread it out evenly. Sprinkle the sliced almonds over the top.

❺ Bake the cake until a toothpick inserted in the center comes out clean or with just a few crumbs attached, about 35 minutes. Cool on a wire rack for 10 minutes, then turn the cake out onto a wire rack. Carefully flip it over again, so it's right-side up on the rack as it cools. Serve the cake warm; or let it cool completely, wrap it tightly in plastic, and keep it at room temperature for up to 3 days.

CURRANT-CRANBERRY SPICE CAKE

Prep time: 20 minutes ⏱ Baking time: 50 to 55 minutes ✋ Serves 12

If you need something to bring to a holiday party, look no further. This festive, spicy cake is easy, pretty, keeps well for a few days (wrapped and kept at room temperature), and is a crowd-pleaser. Dress it up by sifting some confectioners' sugar over it, or spoon on a simple glaze.

INGREDIENTS:

Cooking spray
2 cups (8.5 ounces) all-purpose flour
   (plus 3 tablespoons for preparing
   the pan)
1 teaspoon baking soda
1 teaspoon cinnamon
½ teaspoon ground ginger
¼ teaspoon nutmeg
Pinch of ground cloves
¾ teaspoon salt
8 tablespoons (1 stick) unsalted butter,
   at room temperature
¾ cup (6.3 ounces) packed dark brown
   sugar
2 large eggs, at room temperature
1 cup canned cranberry sauce
1 teaspoon vanilla extract
½ cup sour cream, at room temperature
¼ cup milk, at room temperature
1 cup dried currants
1 cup chopped walnuts (optional)

TOOLS:

12-cup Bundt pan or 10-inch tube pan
Dry measuring cups
Liquid measuring cup
Measuring spoons
2 large bowls
Fork
Electric mixer
Flexible spatula
Toothpick
Paring knife
Wire cooling rack

❶ Preheat the oven to 350°F. Generously mist a 12-cup Bundt pan or a 10-inch tube pan with cooking spray, taking care to get every corner and crevice. Spoon in 3 tablespoons flour and move the pan all around to coat it with a thin layer of flour. Tap out and discard any excess flour.

❷ Combine 2 cups flour, the baking soda, cinnamon, ginger, nutmeg, cloves, and salt in a large bowl and stir with a fork to mix well. In a large bowl, using an electric mixer on medium speed, beat the butter and brown sugar until light and fluffy. Add the eggs, one at a time, beating well after each. Stop the mixer and scrape down the sides and bottom of the bowl with a flexible spatula, then beat again until the mixture is uniform. Beat in the cranberry sauce and vanilla. (Don't worry if the mixture looks curdled or separated—it will come back together when the other ingredients are added.)

❸ Stop the mixer, and scrape down the beaters and the sides and bottom of the bowl with the flexible spatula. Add half of the flour mixture to the butter mixture and stir it in gently with the spatula or a wooden spoon. Stir in the sour cream and milk and mix it in until it's almost fully incorporated, then add the rest of the flour mixture, the currants, and the walnuts (if using). Stir until the flour mixture is completely incorporated. Be sure to scrape down the bottom of the bowl to mix in any pockets of flour, but try to mix the batter as little as possible; overmixing will give you a tough cake.

You Made That Dessert?

❹ Pour the batter into the prepared pan and gently smooth the top of the cake with the spatula. Bake for 50 to 55 minutes, until a toothpick inserted near the center of the cake comes out clean. Place the pan on a wire rack to cool for 15 minutes.

❺ Slide a paring knife around the inner and outer edges of the cake, then set the wire rack upside down on top of the cake pan and, holding the rack and pan together, quickly flip them over so that the cake comes out of the pan onto the rack. Let the cake cool completely.

(See photo, page 72)

Good to know! A simple glaze dresses this cake up for a party. Place 1¼ cups confectioners' sugar in a small bowl. Pour in 2 to 3 tablespoons milk and stir well with a fork until the glaze is smooth and free of lumps. Add ½ teaspoon vanilla extract if you like. If the glaze is too thin, add more confectioners' sugar, 1 teaspoon at a time; if it's too thick, add more milk, 1 teaspoon at a time, until you reach the right consistency. You want to be able to drizzle the glaze over the cake, but you don't want it so thin that it runs off the cake too much.

BANANA SNACK CAKE

Prep time: 15 minutes ⏱ Baking time: 45 to 50 minutes 🖐 Serves 12

This is one of those old-fashioned single-layer cakes you probably had at birthday parties as a kid. I love this cake—especially with the whole-wheat flour, it has a comforting wholesomeness that's just great on a cold fall day. I like it with caramel or chocolate frosting, but a dusting of confectioners' sugar is really all it needs. Kids and adults alike will ask for seconds.

INGREDIENTS:

8 tablespoons (1 stick) unsalted butter, at room temperature (plus 2 tablespoons for preparing baking pan)

1½ cups (6.4 ounces) all-purpose flour (plus 3 tablespoons for preparing baking pan)

1 cup (4.5 ounces) whole-wheat flour (or all-purpose)

1 teaspoon baking powder

1 teaspoon baking soda

½ teaspoon salt

4 large ripe bananas

1 cup sour cream, at room temperature

2 teaspoons vanilla extract

1 cup (8.4 ounces) packed dark brown sugar

2 large eggs, at room temperature

½ cup finely chopped walnuts or pecans (optional)

TOOLS:

9 x 13-inch baking pan

Small bowl

2 large bowls

Fork

Electric mixer

Flexible spatula

Toothpick

Wire cooling rack

❶ Preheat the oven to 350°F. Coat a 9 x 13-inch baking pan with a thin layer of butter. Spoon 3 tablespoons flour into the pan and move the pan all around to coat the bottom and sides with a thin layer of flour. Tap out and discard the excess flour.

❷ In a small bowl, mix together the all-purpose and whole-wheat flour (if using), baking powder, baking soda, and salt, and stir with a fork. In a large bowl, mash the bananas with a fork, leaving some chunks, then stir in the sour cream and vanilla.

❸ In a separate large bowl, with an electric mixer on medium speed, beat the butter and brown sugar until fluffy, about 2 minutes. Scrape down the sides of the bowl with a flexible spatula and beat again for 30 seconds. Add 1 egg, beat until incorporated, then beat in the next one. After adding the second egg, scrape the sides and bottom of the bowl with the spatula and beat again until uniform.

❹ Using your flexible spatula, stir half of the dry ingredients into the butter mixture, mixing until the two are nearly combined. Stir in the mashed banana mixture, then add the remaining flour and walnuts (if using) and stir until completely combined, taking care to scrape the bottom of the bowl to incorporate all of the flour. Try to mix the batter as little as possible.

❺ Pour the batter into the pan, smooth the top with your flexible spatula, and bake for 45 to 50 minutes, until a toothpick inserted in the center of the cake comes out clean and the cake springs back when lightly pressed. Let it cool completely in the pan on a wire rack. Dust the top with powdered sugar, or frost the cake with Rich Caramel Frosting (see page 169 for recipe) or Chocolate Frosting (recipe on page 167).

Banana Snack Cake with Rich Caramel Frosting

Good to know! Make sure you use very ripe bananas for this cake—they should have at least a few brown spots on the peel and be very soft and smell banana-y. If your bananas are not very ripe, don't bother making this cake. Seriously! It's just not the same with hard bananas.

PEANUT BUTTER AND BANANA BREAD

Prep time: 10 minutes ⏲ Baking time: 55 to 60 minutes ✋ Makes 1 9-inch loaf, serves 8

This is one of those happy-accident recipes. While I was baking at a bed-and-breakfast in Venice Beach, California, a guest requested banana bread. I didn't have enough butter, so I swapped in peanut butter—and I've been making banana bread this way ever since.

INGREDIENTS:

Cooking spray

1¼ cups (5.35 ounces) all-purpose flour

1 teaspoon baking soda

½ teaspoon salt

½ cup creamy peanut butter (do not use "natural")

⅔ cup sugar

3 large ripe bananas, mashed with a fork

2 large eggs, at room temperature, lightly beaten

½ cup chopped walnuts or chopped pecans (optional)

½ cup miniature chocolate chips (optional)

TOOLS:

5 x 9-inch loaf pan

Small bowl

Large bowl

Dry measuring cups

Measuring spoons

Fork

Electric mixer

Flexible spatula (or wooden spoon)

Toothpick

Paring knife

Wire cooling rack

❶ Preheat the oven to 350°F. Mist a 5 x 9-inch loaf pan with cooking spray.

❷ In a small bowl, mix the flour, baking soda, and salt with a fork. In a large bowl, using an electric mixer on medium-low speed, beat the peanut butter and sugar together until well blended, about 2 minutes. Beat in the mashed banana and eggs; mix well.

❸ Using a wooden spoon or flexible spatula, stir the flour mixture into the peanut butter–banana mixture, mixing until just combined, scraping down the sides of the bowl with a flexible spatula if needed. Stir in the chopped nuts and/or chocolate chips, if using.

❹ Pour the batter into the pan and gently smooth the top with the flexible spatula. Bake 45 minutes. Cover the pan loosely with foil and bake 10 to 15 minutes longer, until a toothpick inserted in the center comes out clean. Let the bread cool on a wire rack for 10 minutes in the pan.

❺ Remove the bread by running a paring knife around the inside of the pan to loosen it, then inverting the pan to release the bread onto a wire rack. Carefully turn the bread right-side up and cool completely. Slice and serve. Wrap any leftovers tightly in plastic wrap and foil; keep at room temperature for up to 3 days, or freeze for up to 1 month.

(See photo, page 23)

SUSAN'S ZUCCHINI BREAD

Prep time: 15 minutes ⏱ Baking time: 65 to 75 minutes ✋ Makes 1 8-inch loaf, serves 8

When my pal Jen McDonald told me her mom was famous for her zucchini bread, I had to try her recipe for myself. I did, and she deserves to be famous! This is the best zucchini bread I've ever had, and I'm grateful to Jen's mom, Susan Balderama, for sharing her fabulous recipe.

INGREDIENTS:

Cooking spray
1½ cups (6.4 ounces) all-purpose flour
½ teaspoon baking soda
1/8 teaspoon baking powder
½ teaspoon salt
2 teaspoons cinnamon
2 large eggs, at room temperature
¾ cup (5.25 ounces) sugar
½ cup (4.2 ounces) packed dark brown sugar
½ cup vegetable oil
1½ teaspoons vanilla extract
1 cup grated zucchini (from 1–1½ small zucchini)
¼ cup chopped walnuts (optional)

TOOLS:

4 x 8-inch loaf pan
Dry measuring cups
Measuring spoons
Liquid measuring cup
Small bowl
Large bowl
Whisk
Grater
Flexible spatula
Toothpick
Paring knife
Wire cooling rack

❶ Preheat the oven to 325°F. Mist a 4 x 8-inch loaf pan generously with cooking spray.

❷ In a small bowl, combine the flour, baking soda, baking powder, salt, and cinnamon; stir together with a fork to mix well.

❸ In a large bowl, using a whisk, beat the eggs. Add the sugar, brown sugar, oil, and vanilla, and beat well for about 2 minutes, until the ingredients are well blended.

❹ Add the flour mixture to the egg mixture and mix gently, but thoroughly, with a flexible spatula until the flour is fully incorporated. Scrape down the bottom of the bowl and turn the spatula over to be sure all of the dry ingredients are mixed in. Stir in the zucchini and walnuts (if using).

❺ Pour the batter into the loaf pan and bake for 65 to 75 minutes, or until a toothpick placed in the center of the loaf comes out clean. Transfer the pan to a wire rack to cool for 10 minutes.

❻ Remove the bread by running a sharp paring knife around the inside of the loaf pan to loosen it, then invert the pan. Turn the bread right-side up and place it on the wire rack to cool completely. Wrap in plastic wrap and keep at room temperature for up to 3 days.

(See photo, page 33)

Good to know! This bread freezes well. Once it has cooled completely, wrap it tightly in plastic wrap and then in foil; freeze for up to 1 month.

CUSTARDS AND PUDDINGS

DARK CHOCOLATE PUDDING 83

BUTTERSCOTCH PUDDING 84

CLASSIC RICE PUDDING 86

COCONUT RICE PUDDING 87

YOGURT PANNA COTTA 89

DOUBLE CHOCOLATE CROISSANT
    BREAD PUDDING 90

CARAMELIZED BANANA BREAD
    PUDDING 92

BLACK-AND-WHITE TRIFLES 94

WARM GINGERBREAD PUDDING CAKE 96

SILKY CHOCOLATE NUTELLA MOUSSE 98

DOTTIE'S DELUXE NOODLE PUDDING 99

PUMPKIN MOUSSE 100

CHAI POTS DE CRÈME 102

DARK CHOCOLATE PUDDING

Prep time: 20 minutes ⏱ Chilling time: 4 hours ✋ Serves 4

Many of us grew up on instant pudding, but after making it from scratch, I promise you'll never go back. This pudding, with both semisweet chocolate and cocoa powder, is so rich and velvety— nothing out of a box could compare. And the best part? It's easy to make and very quick.

INGREDIENTS:

1½ ounces semisweet chocolate

½ cup (4.2 ounces) packed dark brown sugar

¼ cup (0.73 ounce) unsweetened cocoa powder

3 tablespoons cornstarch

⅛ teaspoon salt

1 cup half-and-half

1 cup whole milk

2 tablespoons unsalted butter, cut into pieces

1 teaspoon vanilla extract

TOOLS:

Cutting board

Chef's knife

Dry measuring cups

Measuring spoons

Liquid measuring cup

Saucepan

Whisk

Flexible spatula

Large bowl

❶ On a cutting board, using a sharp chef's knife, chop the chocolate (see page 187 for more on how to do this); set it aside. In a saucepan, whisk together the brown sugar, cocoa, cornstarch, and salt. Get out as many lumps as you can. Place the pan on the stove over medium heat and gradually add the half-and-half, whisking until the mixture is smooth. Whisk in the milk.

❷ Cook the mixture, whisking constantly, until the pudding thickens and begins to boil, about 5 to 7 minutes. Be sure to get your whisk (or a flexible spatula) into the corners and all around the bottom of the saucepan while the pudding is cooking to get any bits sticking to the pan and incorporate them into the pudding.

❸ Remove the pan from the heat and whisk in the butter, chopped chocolate, and vanilla, whisking until the butter and chocolate have melted and all the ingredients are thoroughly mixed together. Pour the pudding into a large bowl and cover with plastic wrap, gently pressing the plastic directly onto the surface of the pudding (this will keep a skin from forming).

❹ Let the pudding cool slightly to serve warm; or let it cool to lukewarm, then refrigerate until cold (at least 4 hours). The pudding will keep in the refrigerator for up to 3 days.

(See photo, page 85)

BUTTERSCOTCH PUDDING

Prep time: 30 minutes ⏱ Chilling time: 2 to 5 hours ✋ Serves 6

Technically, butterscotch doesn't really have scotch in it—some say the "scotch" refers to Scotland, while others say "scotch" is a derivation of "scorch," which is what happens to the sugar to give butterscotch its distinctive flavor. I added a bit of scotch to this pudding anyway, to give it a kick—but you can certainly leave it out if you prefer.

INGREDIENTS:

1 cup (8.4 ounces) packed dark brown sugar
3 tablespoons cornstarch
½ teaspoon salt
3 large egg yolks
2 tablespoons scotch
2 tablespoons vanilla extract
1½ cups half-and-half
1½ cups heavy cream
3 tablespoons unsalted butter, cut into small pieces

TOOLS:

Dry measuring cups
Measuring spoons
Liquid measuring cup
Saucepan
Medium bowl
Whisk
Flexible spatula
Large bowl or 6 ramekins
Kitchen towel

❶ In a saucepan, whisk together the brown sugar, cornstarch, and salt. In a medium bowl, with the same whisk, beat together the yolks, scotch, and vanilla. Place the saucepan with the cornstarch mixture on the stove and turn the heat on to low. Whisk in 1 cup half-and-half, beating well to get rid of any lumps. Raise the heat to medium and whisk in the remaining ½ cup half-and-half and all of the heavy cream.

❷ Cook the mixture, stirring well with a flexible spatula and carefully scraping the mixture on the bottom and in the corners of the pan, until the mixture thickens and starts to bubble, 5 to 7 minutes. Remove the pan from the heat.

❸ Place a slightly damp kitchen towel under the bowl with the yolk mixture and re-whisk the mixture. Whisking constantly, slowly pour about one-third of the hot cream mixture from the saucepan into the yolk mixture. It's important that you whisk vigorously while you're pouring the cream mixture—this will keep the yolks from getting scrambled (and the towel under the bowl will help keep it in place).

❹ Whisk the mixture in the bowl back into the saucepan. Turn the heat back on to medium-low, add the butter, and cook, stirring constantly with the flexible spatula, taking care to scrape the bottom and corners of the pan, for 2 to 4 minutes, until the mixture is hot (don't let it boil).

❺ Pour the pudding into six ramekins, or into a clean, large bowl. Cover the pudding with plastic wrap, gently pressing the plastic directly onto the surface to keep a skin from forming. Let it cool to room temperature, then chill in the refrigerator until cold, about 2 hours for ramekins or 5 hours for a bowl.

Clockwise from top: Dark Chocolate Pudding, Butterscotch Pudding, Classic Rice Pudding, and Yogurt Panna Cotta

CLASSIC RICE PUDDING

Prep time: 40 minutes (if using uncooked rice), or 20 minutes (if starting with cooked rice) 🖐 Serves 6

Talk about comfort food—it's hard to get more comforting than a nice bowl of good, old-fashioned rice pudding. I like it very creamy and cinnamon-y, with raisins, but you can leave out the raisins if you like, and add more or less cinnamon—or try it with another kind of fruit, like dried apples.

INGREDIENTS:

½ teaspoon salt
¾ cup uncooked rice (or 1½ cups cooked)
1½ cups whole milk
⅓ cup (2.3 ounces) sugar
2 large eggs
½ cup half-and-half
1 tablespoon honey
1 teaspoon vanilla extract
⅔ cup golden raisins (optional)
1 tablespoon unsalted butter
1 teaspoon cinnamon

TOOLS:

Dry measuring cups
Liquid measuring cup
Measuring spoons
Saucepan
Fork
Flexible spatula
Whisk
Large bowl

❶ If you're starting with uncooked rice, bring 1½ cups of water to a boil in a medium saucepan. Add the salt and ¾ cup uncooked rice, and stir. Reduce the heat to low, cover the pan, and cook for 15 to 20 minutes, until the water is absorbed and the rice is cooked. (If you're starting with cooked rice, you can skip this step.)

❷ Once the rice is cooked, fluff it up with a fork, then add the milk and sugar (if you started with cooked rice, add the salt now). Turn the heat to medium-low and cook, stirring often with a flexible spatula, for 15 minutes, until the pudding begins to thicken.

❸ Whisk the eggs just until the yolks and whites are combined, then whisk in the half-and-half, honey, and vanilla. Turn the heat under the saucepan to low and whisk the rice mixture; while doing so, slowly pour in the egg mixture. It's very important that you keep whisking so that the egg mixture gets combined into the pudding and not scrambled.

❹ Once the egg mixture is thoroughly incorporated, switch back to your spatula or wooden spoon, add the raisins (if using), and cook the pudding for 2 minutes more, stirring constantly. Remove it from the heat, add the butter, and stir until the butter is melted and well incorporated. Pour the pudding into a bowl.

❺ Serve the pudding warm, or cover with plastic wrap (pressing the plastic directly onto the surface) and refrigerate to serve cold. Sprinkle the cinnamon on top just before serving. The pudding will keep in the fridge for up to 4 days.

(See photo, page 85)

COCONUT RICE PUDDING

Prep time: 5 minutes ⏱ Cooking time: 30 to 35 minutes ✋ Serves 6

Coconut milk lends a festive, tropical taste to comforting rice pudding. For even more of an island flavor, top it with chopped fresh pineapple.

INGREDIENTS:

1 cup sweetened flake coconut

2 tablespoons unsalted butter

½ cup uncooked jasmine rice

1/3 cup (2.3 ounces) sugar

Zest of 1 small lemon

2 14-ounce cans unsweetened coconut milk (shake cans before opening them)

½ teaspoon salt

2 tablespoons dark rum or 1 tablespoon vanilla extract

TOOLS:

Dry measuring cups

Rasp grater

Measuring spoons

Food processor

Large saucepan

Wooden spoon or flexible spatula

Large bowl

Small bowl

Baking sheet

❶ Put ½ cup coconut in a food processor and pulse until finely chopped (or spread it on a cutting board and chop it as finely as you can with a chef's knife). In a large saucepan, melt the butter over medium heat. Add the rice and cook, stirring with a wooden spoon or flexible spatula, for 1 minute. Stir in the chopped coconut, sugar, lemon zest, coconut milk, and salt and bring to a simmer, about 5 minutes (tiny bubbles will form along the edges and the mixture may steam a little bit, but don't let it boil).

❷ Turn the heat down to low and cook, stirring often, until the pudding has thickened (it will be about the same consistency as runny oatmeal; it will firm up as it cools), about 25 minutes. Remove the saucepan from the heat, pour the pudding into a large bowl, and stir in the rum or vanilla. Cover the pudding with plastic wrap, pressing down carefully so that the plastic lightly touches the whole surface of the pudding. Let the pudding cool for 15 minutes to serve it warm, or let it cool to room temperature and then refrigerate it to serve cold.

❸ While the pudding is cooling, toast the remaining coconut: Preheat the oven to 350°F. Spread the remaining ½ cup coconut in a single layer on a rimmed baking sheet (no need to grease the baking sheet or line it). Bake it for 5 to 8 minutes, stirring every 2 minutes, until the coconut is golden brown (be careful—the coconut can get too dark very quickly if you don't stir it often and keep an eye on it). Pour the toasted coconut into a small bowl to cool.

❹ Spoon the pudding into individual dessert bowls, top with toasted coconut, and serve.

(See photo, page 88)

YOGURT PANNA COTTA

Prep time: 10 minutes ⏱ Chilling time: 6 hours 🖐 Serves 6

Panna cotta—literally "cooked cream" in Italian—is a silky custard traditionally made with cream and plain gelatin. It's deceptively easy to make, and it's a perfectly elegant finish to a dinner party. This tangy panna cotta is especially good with fresh berries, or you could serve it with Brandied Cherries (see page 165 for the recipe).

INGREDIENTS:

1 tablespoon cold water
1 teaspoon plain gelatin
1 cup half-and-half
¾ cup (5.25 ounces) sugar
Pinch of salt
1 17.6-ounce container plain Greek
    yogurt (do not use fat-free yogurt)
1 tablespoon vanilla extract

TOOLS:

Liquid measuring cup
Measuring spoons
Small bowl
Saucepan
Whisk
Flexible spatula
Large bowl
6 wineglasses or small bowls

❶ Pour water into a small bowl and sprinkle the gelatin on top. Let it stand at room temperature for 5 minutes (it will firm up).

❷ In a saucepan, whisk together the half-and-half, sugar, and salt. Place the pan on the stove over medium-high heat and cook, stirring often with a whisk or flexible spatula, until the sugar dissolves and the mixture is just simmering, about 3 minutes (it will be hot and you'll see a bit of steam, but it shouldn't boil).

❸ Remove the pan from the heat and scrape in the gelatin mixture with a flexible spatula, then whisk until the gelatin has dissolved. In a large bowl, combine the yogurt and vanilla. Stir in the half-and-half mixture with the same whisk until all the ingredients are well combined.

❹ Divide the mixture among six wineglasses or small bowls. Cover each with plastic wrap and refrigerate for at least 6 hours, or overnight. To serve, uncover the glasses. Serve the panna cotta with fresh berries, Raspberry Sauce (see page 162), Brandied Cherries (page 165), or Wine-Poached Peaches (page 148).

(See photo, page 85)

Good to know! Be sure to use Greek yogurt for this—it's been strained, so it's far richer and creamier than standard yogurt.

Black-and-White Trifles, Coconut Rice Pudding, and "New Wave" Lemon Meringue Pie

DOUBLE CHOCOLATE CROISSANT BREAD PUDDING

Prep time: 25 minutes ⏱ Resting time: 30 minutes ⏱ Baking time: 50 to 55 minutes ✋ Serves 10

This is a super-rich dessert, not for the faint of heart or the non–chocolate lover.
Serve it with the best vanilla ice cream or fresh whipped cream.

INGREDIENTS:

7 chocolate croissants
8 ounces semisweet chocolate
4 ounces milk chocolate
4 cups half-and-half
5 large eggs
1 tablespoon vanilla extract
2 tablespoons bourbon or dark rum
    (optional)
1 teaspoon salt
Vanilla ice cream or whipped cream, for
    serving (optional)

TOOLS:

Liquid measuring cup
Measuring spoons
9 x 13-inch baking pan
Cutting board
Chef's knife
Saucepan
Whisk
Large bowl
Wire cooling rack

❶ Chop or tear the croissants into 1-inch pieces (don't worry about making the pieces perfectly uniform in size or shape, just generally chop or tear them up) and place in a 9 x 13-inch baking pan.

❷ On a cutting board with a sharp chef's knife, chop both chocolates (see page 187 for more on how to do this). Warm the half-and-half in a saucepan over medium-low heat until it just begins to form small bubbles around the edges, not quite to a boil. Add the chocolate to the half-and-half and turn off the heat. Stir with a whisk until the chocolate has melted and the mixture is smooth.

❸ Whisk the eggs in a large bowl just to mix them. Whisking constantly, slowly pour the warm chocolate mixture into the eggs. Whisk until well combined. Whisk in the vanilla, bourbon (if using), and salt. Pour the chocolate mixture over the croissants, and press down on the croissants to make sure they're all moistened.

❹ Let the mixture sit on the counter for 30 minutes. After 15 minutes, preheat the oven to 350°F. Bake for 50 to 55 minutes, until the pudding is puffed up and the center is set.

❺ Let the pudding cool for at least 10 minutes on a wire rack before serving (it will fall—don't worry, it's supposed to). Serve it with ice cream or whipped cream, if desired.

Good to know! You can prepare this dish up to 24 hours before you need it, through step 3. Don't bake it—cover it with foil and refrigerate it. Let it come to room temperature (by letting it stand on a countertop for about 30 minutes) before baking as directed.

You can make this recipe even if you can't find chocolate croissants. Use regular ones, and stir in 1 cup of chocolate chips just before baking.

Double Chocolate Croissant Bread Pudding and Carmelized Banana Bread Pudding

CARAMELIZED BANANA
BREAD PUDDING

Prep time: 35 minutes ⏱ Resting time: 30 minutes ⏱ Baking time: 60 to 65 minutes ✋ Serves 8

Bread pudding is one of my favorite desserts for three reasons: it's so simple to make but really impressive, it's inexpensive but doesn't seem so, and it can be prepared in advance and then simply baked just in time to serve it.

INGREDIENTS:

Cooking spray

4 tablespoons (½ stick) unsalted butter

1 cup (8.4 ounces) packed dark brown
   sugar

4 large ripe bananas, peeled

1 small loaf (12 ounces) challah, or other
   egg bread

6 large eggs

4 cups half-and-half

½ cup (3.5 ounces) sugar

2 tablespoons vanilla extract

2 tablespoons bourbon or dark rum
   (optional)

1 teaspoon salt

TOOLS:

9 x 13-inch baking dish

Dry measuring cups

Liquid measuring cup

Measuring spoons

Flexible spatula

Skillet

Paring knife

Cutting board

Serrated knife

Large bowl

Whisk

Wire cooling rack

❶ Lightly mist a 9 x 13-inch baking dish with cooking spray; set aside. Place a large skillet over medium heat. Cut the butter into slices, adding to the skillet as you go. When all the butter is in the skillet, add the brown sugar, stirring quickly with a flexible spatula to moisten the sugar with the butter. This is your caramel. Cook the caramel, stirring with the spatula, until the sugar has melted and is beginning to bubble, about 5 minutes.

❷ Slice the bananas into the skillet with a paring knife—you want them about twice as thick as slices you would put on a bowl of cereal (about ¾ inch), and try to cut them on the diagonal. Use the flexible spatula to stir the bananas around in the brown sugar mixture until the caramel is bubbling and the bananas are coated with caramel and beginning to soften, about 2 minutes. Remove the skillet from the heat.

❸ On a cutting board, using a serrated knife, cut the bread into cubes, about ½ inch (don't worry about making them exactly that size or perfectly even). Place the bread cubes in the baking dish. Using the same flexible spatula you used to stir the bananas, scrape the banana mixture into the baking dish with the bread cubes, spreading them all around. When all the bananas are in, stir the mixture by placing the spatula under the bread and turning it over the bananas. Do this repeatedly until the bananas and bread cubes are well combined.

❹ In a large bowl, using a whisk, beat the eggs until they're fully blended. Whisk in 1 cup of the half-and-half until the mixture is well combined. Whisk in the sugar until it has dissolved. Whisk in the remaining 3 cups half-and-half, vanilla, bourbon (if using), and salt. Pour this mixture into the baking dish with the bananas and bread cubes, making sure to distribute it evenly. Press the bread down into the half-and-half mixture with your fingers to make sure all of it is well coated. Let the baking dish stand at room temperature for 30 minutes.

❺ Preheat the oven to 350°F. Tear a sheet of foil that is about 2 inches wider than your baking dish and place it on the center rack in the oven. Place the baking dish on top of the foil, so that there's about an inch of foil showing on both sides. Bake the pudding for 60 to 65 minutes, until puffed and golden brown on top, and just set in the center. Let cool on a wire rack for about 10 minutes before serving.

(See photo, page 91)

Good to know! You can make this dish up to 24 hours before you need it. Just make the pudding through step 4; don't bake it. Cover the baking dish with foil and put it in the refrigerator. Let it come to room temperature (by letting it stand on a countertop for about 30 minutes) before baking as directed.

BLACK-AND-WHITE TRIFLES

Prep time: 35 minutes ⏲ Chilling time: 4 hours total ✋ Makes 6

Trifle is a traditional British dessert, in which cake or ladyfingers are layered with jam and custard in a large glass bowl. This is a modern version, with vanilla and chocolate pudding, pound cake, and berries. Individual servings mean you don't need a huge serving bowl.

INGREDIENTS:
Puddings:

3 ounces semisweet chocolate
¼ cup cornstarch
¾ cup milk
3 cups half-and-half
1 cup (7 ounces) sugar
¼ teaspoon salt
3 tablespoons unsalted butter, at room temperature
1 tablespoon vanilla extract

Trifles:

1 pound-cake loaf, store-bought or homemade (see page 31 for a recipe)
12 strawberries
¼ cup Grand Marnier, or other orange liqueur (or orange juice)
½ cup heavy cream, cold
2 teaspoons confectioners' sugar

TOOLS:

Dry measuring cups
Measuring spoons
Liquid measuring cup
Cutting board
Chef's knife
Serrated knife
Paring knife
Small bowl
Fork or small whisk
Spoon
Saucepan
Whisk
Flexible spatula
3 medium bowls
Electric mixer

❶ Make the puddings: On a cutting board, using a sharp chef's knife, chop the chocolate (see page 187 for more on how to do this); set it aside. In a small bowl, mix the cornstarch and milk, beating with a fork or small whisk to get out all the lumps.

❷ In a saucepan, combine the half-and-half, sugar, and salt; mix with a whisk. Place the pan over medium heat and cook, stirring often with the whisk, until it just starts to bubble a tiny bit on the edges (don't let it boil). Use a flexible spatula to scrape the cornstarch mixture into the pan with the half-and-half. Bring to a boil, whisking constantly, until the pudding thickens, about 15 to 17 minutes (be sure to scrape the bottom and corners of the pan with a flexible spatula while cooking; use the whisk to beat out any lumps). Remove the pan from the heat and stir in the butter and vanilla, stirring until the butter is melted and incorporated.

❸ Divide the pudding into two medium bowls. Cover one with plastic wrap, gently pressing the plastic directly against the surface of the pudding. Add the chopped chocolate to the other bowl and whisk until the chocolate is melted and fully incorporated into the pudding. Cover with plastic wrap, gently pressing the plastic directly onto the surface of the pudding. Let both cool at room temperature until lukewarm, then refrigerate until cold, at least 3 hours. (The puddings can be made up to 2 days ahead; keep them covered and refrigerated.)

❹ On a cutting board, using a serrated knife, trim the top, bottom, and sides off the pound cake to remove the crust. Cut the remaining cake into ½-inch cubes. Pull the green leaves off the strawberries and use a paring knife to cut out the hulls (see "Good to Know!" for more detailed instructions). On a cutting board, using the paring knife, slice the strawberries.

⑤ Assemble the trifles: Place six wineglasses or dessert bowls on a counter. Put a few cake cubes in each glass, enough to just cover the bottom of the glass. Using a spoon, sprinkle some Grand Marnier over the cake cubes, using about half. Put some sliced strawberries on top of the cake in the glasses, using about half (don't worry about being precise here). Divide the vanilla pudding between the glasses (it will be about ¼ cup per glass), spreading it out with the back of a spoon. Cover the pudding with another layer of cake cubes (you may not use up all of the cake). Sprinkle the cake cubes with the remaining Grand Marnier and top them with the remaining sliced strawberries. Cover the berries with the chocolate pudding, dividing it among the glasses (again, you'll have about ¼ cup per glass). Spread the pudding with the back of a spoon. Cover the glasses and refrigerate the trifles for at least 1 hour, or up to overnight.

⑥ When you're about ready to serve the trifles, place a medium bowl and beaters in the fridge for 5 minutes. Pour the heavy cream into the chilled bowl and beat with the chilled beaters (in an electric mixer) until the cream is foamy. Add the confectioners' sugar and continue beating the cream until medium-firm peaks form. Uncover the trifles, top each with a dollop of whipped cream, and serve.

(See photo, page 88)

Good to Know! The hull is the green leafy stem and soft white core of a strawberry. To remove it, gently ease a sharp paring knife into the flesh next to the stem, slightly angled inward. Carefully turn the strawberry around so that the knife moves through the berry, separating the hull. When you've gone all the way around, gently pull out the cone-shaped hull and discard.

WARM GINGERBREAD PUDDING CAKE

Prep time: 20 minutes ⏱ Baking time: 30 to 35 minutes ✋ Makes 1 8-inch cake, serves 6

Pudding cakes are amazing—pull one out of the oven, and you have a fluffy cake with a warm, gooey sauce underneath it, all in the same pan. Instead of the traditional lemon or chocolate pudding cake, I decided to give gingerbread a spin. The recipe may look weird, but try it, especially at the holidays—you'll get lots of ooohs and ahhhs.

INGREDIENTS:

Cooking spray
1¼ cups (5.4 ounces) all-purpose flour
1½ teaspoons baking soda
¼ teaspoon salt
1 tablespoon ground ginger
1½ teaspoons cinnamon
¼ teaspoon ground cloves
1/8 teaspoon nutmeg
Pinch of black pepper
3 tablespoons finely chopped crystallized ginger
½ cup molasses (do not use extra strong or blackstrap)
1¼ cups boiling water
4 tablespoons (½ stick) unsalted butter, at room temperature
¼ cup (2.1 ounces) packed plus 1/3 cup (2.8 ounces) packed dark brown sugar
1 large egg, at room temperature
2 tablespoons unsalted butter, melted
Whipped cream, for serving (optional)

TOOLS:

Dry measuring cups
Measuring spoons
Fork
Liquid measuring cup
Whisk
Two small bowls
Medium bowl
Electric mixer
Flexible spatula
8-inch square baking pan
Wire cooling rack

❶ Preheat the oven to 350°F. Lightly mist an 8-inch square baking pan with cooking spray.

❷ In a small bowl, mix together the flour, baking soda, salt, ground ginger, cinnamon, cloves, nutmeg, and pepper; stir with a fork to combine well. Stir in the chopped crystallized ginger. In a separate small bowl, whisk together the molasses and ½ cup boiling water; set aside.

❸ In a medium bowl, using an electric mixer on medium-low speed, beat together 4 tablespoons butter and ¼ cup brown sugar until fluffy, about 2 minutes. Beat in the egg. Scrape down the sides and bottom of the bowl with a flexible spatula, and beat again with the electric mixer until the mixture is uniform.

❹ Add half of the flour mixture to the butter mixture and stir with the flexible spatula just to combine. Stir in the molasses mixture. Stir in the remaining flour mixture and mix until all the ingredients are just combined. Scrape down the sides and bottom of the bowl to make sure all the dry ingredients are incorporated. Scrape the batter into the baking pan and spread it evenly. Sprinkle 1/3 cup brown sugar evenly over the top.

❺ In a bowl, whisk together the remaining ¾ cup of boiling water and the 2 tablespoons melted butter. Now, here's where it gets a little weird: Pour the water-butter mixture over the brown sugar and batter in the pan, but *do not stir*. This layer of water on top of the batter will look strange and wrong, but it's okay—resist the urge to mix the layers together. Carefully place the pan in the oven and bake for 30 to 35 minutes, until the cake is cracked on top, set, and spongy when you lightly press the surface with your fingers. Remove the cake to a wire rack to cool for 5 minutes. Serve hot, with whipped cream, if desired.

Warm Gingerbread Pudding Cake

SILKY CHOCOLATE NUTELLA MOUSSE

Prep time: 20 minutes ⏱ Chilling time: 4 hours ✋ Serves 8 to 10

Chocolate mousse—what could be more rich, decadent, and satisfying? A touch of the chocolate-hazelnut spread Nutella adds silkiness; you won't taste the hazelnut flavor. And this mousse has no raw egg whites, as many traditional chocolate mousses do, so you can feed it to kids and pregnant women without worry.

INGREDIENTS:

10 ounces semisweet chocolate

1 teaspoon vanilla extract

Pinch of salt

3 cups heavy cream, chilled

½ cup Nutella chocolate-hazelnut spread

TOOLS:

Cutting board

Chef's knife

2 large bowls

Measuring spoons

Liquid measuring cup

Saucepan

Whisk

Dry measuring cups

Electric mixer

Flexible spatula

❶ On a cutting board, using a sharp chef's knife, chop the chocolate into small pieces (see page 187 for more on how to do this). Place the chopped chocolate in a large bowl, and add the vanilla and salt.

❷ Bring 1 cup cream to boil in a saucepan. Pour the hot cream onto the chocolate mixture and whisk until the chocolate is melted and the mixture is smooth. Whisk in the Nutella. Let the mixture stand on counter until it comes to room temperature, stirring occasionally with a flexible spatula, about 10 minutes.

❸ Using an electric mixer on high speed, beat the 2 remaining cups of cream in a large bowl until it forms firm peaks (see page 190 for more about whipping cream). Using a flexible spatula, plop about one-third of the whipped cream into the bowl with the cooled chocolate mixture. Stir the two together by scraping the bottom of the bowl and turning the two mixtures over each other (this is called "folding," see page 185 for more on this) until they're mostly combined (you may have a few streaks of cream left; that's okay). Fold another third of the cream into the chocolate mixture, then the last third. When you fold in the last bit of cream, make sure there are no visible streaks of cream left—the mixture should be uniform in color.

❹ Pour the mousse into a serving bowl or eight individual glasses, cover loosely with plastic wrap, and chill until set, about 4 hours for a bowl or 2 hours for glasses.

(See photo, page 101)

Good to know! You can make this up to a day ahead of serving. If you like a darker, richer mousse, use half bittersweet and half semisweet chocolate.

DOTTIE'S DELUXE NOODLE PUDDING

Prep time: 30 minutes ⏱ Baking time: 50 to 55 minutes ✋ Serves 12

This recipe is very special to me. I first had this amazingly delicious noodle pudding at my dear friend Jen Chernaik's baby shower. I asked her close friend Laura Salamone for the recipe, and it turns out it was her late mother's. Sadly, I never got to meet Dottie Salamone, but by all accounts she was a lovely and exceptional person, and I'm honored that Laura shared her recipe.

INGREDIENTS:

Cooking spray

Topping:

3 cups cornflakes

¼ cup (1.75 ounces) sugar

1 tablespoon cinnamon

¼ teaspoon salt

5 tablespoons unsalted butter, melted

Pudding:

8 ounces large egg noodles

6 tablespoons unsalted butter, at room temperature, cut into 8 pieces

8 ounces cream cheese, at room temperature

¾ cup (5.25 ounces) sugar

¼ teaspoon salt

4 large eggs, at room temperature

1¼ cups milk, at room temperature

1¼ cups apricot nectar

TOOLS:

9 x 13-inch baking dish

Dry measuring cups

Food processor

Measuring spoons

Liquid measuring cup

Saucepan

Medium bowl

Pot

Colander

Fork

Flexible spatula

2 large bowls

Electric mixer

Wire cooling rack

❶ Preheat the oven to 350°F. Lightly mist a 9 x 13-inch baking dish with cooking spray.

❷ Make the topping: Crush the cornflakes in a food processor; or put them in a large ziplock bag, seal the bag, and beat them with a rolling pin or skillet until they're crushed. In a medium bowl, combine the crushed cornflakes, sugar, cinnamon, and salt, and stir with a fork to mix. Pour in the melted butter and stir until all the cornflakes are moistened and all the ingredients are thoroughly mixed together.

❸ Make the pudding: Cook the egg noodles in a pot of boiling water for as long as the package label directs. Drain the noodles and place them in a large bowl. Add the 8 pieces of butter and stir with a flexible spatula until the butter is melted and the noodles are coated.

❹ In a large bowl, with an electric mixer on medium speed, beat the cream cheese, sugar, and salt until well mixed and smooth, about 2 minutes. Add the eggs one at a time, beating well after each. Stop the mixer and scrape down the sides and bottom of the bowl with a flexible spatula. Beat again with the electric mixer to make sure everything is combined well. Turn the mixer speed down to low and slowly pour in the milk and apricot nectar. Beat until thoroughly mixed.

❺ Pour the cream cheese mixture into the bowl with the noodles and stir well with the flexible spatula to completely coat the noodles. Pour the mixture into the prepared baking dish and spread evenly. Sprinkle the topping evenly over the top.

❻ Bake the pudding for 50 to 55 minutes, until the center is set (it shouldn't jiggle when you gently shake the pan). Let it cool on a wire rack. Serve it warm or at room temperature, or cover and chill to serve it later.

(See photo, page 194)

PUMPKIN MOUSSE

Prep time: 15 minutes ⏱ Chilling time: 4 hours, 40 minutes ✋ Serves 6

Love pumpkin, but tired of traditional pumpkin pie? This mousse is a great departure, with the same warm spices and creamy texture. Dress it up by sprinkling chopped crystallized ginger on top, or serve it with gingersnaps on the side (see page 7 for a recipe).

INGREDIENTS:

1 15-ounce can solid-pack pumpkin
2 cups heavy cream, chilled
¾ cup (5.75 ounces) packed light brown sugar
1 tablespoon plus 1½ teaspoons pumpkin pie spice
¼ teaspoon salt
1 tablespoon vanilla extract

TOOLS:

Liquid measuring cup
Dry measuring cups
Measuring spoons
Saucepan
Flexible spatula
2 large bowls
Electric mixer

❶ In a saucepan, mix the pumpkin, ½ cup cream, sugar, pumpkin pie spice, and salt with a flexible spatula until well combined. Place it on the stove, turn the heat to medium, and cook for 5 minutes, stirring about every 30 seconds. Remove the pan from the heat, pour the mixture into a large bowl, and let it cool on a countertop until it reaches room temperature, about 30 to 40 minutes, stirring every 10 minutes with a flexible spatula.

❷ In a large bowl, with an electric mixer on high speed, beat the remaining 1½ cups of cream and vanilla until medium peaks form (see page 190 to read more about whipping cream). Using the same flexible spatula from step 1, plop about one-third of the cream into the bowl with the pumpkin mixture. Stir the two together by scraping the bottom of the bowl and turning the two mixtures over each other (this is called "folding," see page 185 for more on this) until they're mostly combined (you may have a few streaks of cream left; that's okay). Fold another third of the cream into the pumpkin mixture, then the last third. When folding in the last bit of cream, make sure there are no streaks of cream left; the mixture should be uniform in color.

❸ Pour the mousse into a large serving bowl or divide into six glasses, cover loosely with plastic wrap, and refrigerate until firm, 4 hours for the large bowl and 2 hours for individual glasses.

Good to know! Be sure to use 100 percent pure pumpkin in this recipe, not canned pumpkin pie filling. The pie filling is already sweetened, so it would make the mousse far too sweet.

Pumpkin Mousse, Chai Pots de Crème, and Silky Chocolate Nutella Mousse

CHAI POTS DE CRÈME

Prep time: 25 minutes ⏱ Baking time: 25 to 30 minutes ⏱ Chilling time: 2 hours ✋ Makes 6

Here's a dessert with a fancy French name that's really just baked individual custards.
I like pots de crème (pronounced "poe de crem") because they're so elemental—the
simplest ingredients easily combined to make something truly elegant and satisfying.
You can make them up to a day ahead.

INGREDIENTS:

2 cups half-and-half
1 chai tea bag
6 large egg yolks
½ cup (3.5 ounces) sugar
Pinch of salt
Whipped cream, for garnish (optional)

TOOLS:

Liquid measuring cup
Saucepan
Large bowl
Dry measuring cups
Whisk
Dish towel
Fine-mesh sieve
6 ¾-cup ramekins
Roasting pan
Wire cooling rack

❶ Preheat the oven to 325°F. Place six ¾-cup ramekins in a large roasting pan.

❷ Pour the half-and-half into a saucepan and add the tea bag (if there is a string attached to the tea bag, snip it off with scissors before adding the bag to the pan). Cook it over low heat until the half-and-half is hot but not quite boiling.

❸ Meanwhile, place the egg yolks in a large bowl and add the sugar and salt. Use a whisk to combine them well. Lightly dampen a kitchen towel and place it under the bowl with the yolk mixture.

❹ Remove the tea bag from the hot half-and-half, squeezing it lightly. Discard the tea bag. Pour the half-and-half in a slow stream into the egg yolk mixture, whisking constantly; this is important, to keep the eggs from cooking. (Don't worry—the damp towel will keep the bowl in place as you whisk and pour.)

❺ Pour the mixture through a sieve into a liquid measuring cup. Spoon off any foam (don't worry if you don't get it all). Pour the custard mixture into the ramekins, dividing it evenly among them.

❻ Place the roasting pan with the ramekins on a rack in the center of the oven. Rinse the measuring cup, then use it to pour hot tap water into the roasting pan around the ramekins (not in them), so that the water comes about one-third of the way up the sides of the ramekins (this is called a "water bath," see page 186 for more information). Lay a piece of aluminum foil loosely over the top of the roasting pan and close the oven door.

❼ Bake the pots de crème for 25 to 30 minutes, until the custards are just set; if you lightly shake one, it should be mostly firm but still a little jiggly in the center. (The custards will firm up more as they cool in the fridge.) Remove the roasting pan from the oven and take off the foil. Remove the ramekins from the water bath and place them on a wire rack to cool. (You won't need the roasting pan or water anymore.)

❽ Once the custards have cooled, cover each one with plastic wrap and refrigerate them for at least 2 hours, or up to overnight. Spoon a little whipped cream over each one before serving, if desired.

(See photo, page 101)

Good to know! You can make these with another kind of tea (jasmine is a good choice), or by dissolving 1 to 2 tablespoons instant coffee or instant espresso powder in the half-and-half. Follow the directions the same way.

Pies and Fruit Desserts

TIPSY KEY LIME PIE 105

BUTTERMILK PIE 107

CHOCOLATE–PEANUT BUTTER PIE 108

FRESH BERRY SHORTCAKES 112

NECTARINE-BLUEBERRY CRISP 114

RUSTIC PLUM GALETTE 116

BAKED APPLES 117

GRAPEFRUIT GRANITA 118

MOCHA CREAM PIE 120

LEMON-BERRY SEMIFREDDO 124

COOL BLUEBERRY SOUP 126

APPLE CRUMBLE 128

ELEGANT APPLE TARTLETS 130

PEAR–TART CHERRY CRISP 132

MAPLE WALNUT PIE 133

BLACKBERRY COBBLER 136

SWEET POTATO PIE WITH STREUSEL TOPPING 137

BANANA-NUTELLA WONTONS 138

CHERRY CLAFOUTI 140

CHERRY-BERRY STOVETOP COBBLER 142

"NEW WAVE" LEMON MERINGUE PIE 144

DRUNKEN PEARS STUFFED WITH COOKIE CRUMBLE 146

WINE-POACHED PEACHES 148

TIPSY KEY LIME PIE

Prep time: 20 minutes ⏱ Baking time: 27 to 29 minutes ⏱ Chilling time: 3 hours ✋ Serves 8

Key limes are different from the regular "Persian" limes you get in the supermarket. They're much smaller with a very thin peel, bright aroma, and distinctly sour taste. I recommend buying bottled Key lime juice instead of juicing all those tiny limes—or you can juice regular limes. The rum gives this pie a little extra bite.

INGREDIENTS:

Crust:

1½ cups graham cracker crumbs (from a box, or crush about 15 graham crackers in a food processor)

3 tablespoons sugar

¼ teaspoon salt

4 tablespoons (½ stick) unsalted butter, melted

Filling:

4 large egg yolks

1 14-ounce can sweetened condensed milk

⅔ cup bottled Key lime juice (Nellie & Joe's brand is sold in most supermarkets)

¼ cup light rum

1 pinch salt

Whipped cream, for serving (optional)

TOOLS:

Measuring spoons

Liquid measuring cup

Dry measuring cups

Baking sheet

Large bowl

Fork

9-inch pie plate

Wire cooling rack

Medium bowl

Whisk

❶ Preheat the oven to 375°F. Line a rimmed baking sheet with aluminum foil.

❷ Make the crust: In a large bowl, combine the graham cracker crumbs, sugar, and salt; stir with a fork to mix. Add the melted butter and stir again with the fork until all ingredients are moistened. Transfer the mixture to a 9-inch pie plate. Press with your fingers to cover the bottom and sides of the pie plate. Use the back of a spoon or the bottom of a dry measuring cup to gently press the crust into an even layer. Bake for 10 minutes. Remove to a wire rack to cool.

❸ Make the filling: In a medium bowl, whisk together the yolks, condensed milk, lime juice, rum, and salt until well combined. Place the crust on a foil-lined baking sheet. Pour the Key lime mixture into the crust.

❹ Bake for 17 to 19 minutes, until just set and the filling looks slightly jiggly when you gently shake the pie plate (it will firm up as it cools). Transfer the pie to the wire rack and let it cool to room temperature, about 30 to 40 minutes; then refrigerate it until cold, about 3 hours. Serve with whipped cream, if desired.

(See photo, page 106)

BUTTERMILK PIE

Prep time: 30 minutes ⏱ Baking time: 65 to 70 minutes ✋ Serves 8

This simple, old-fashioned pie is a Southern classic. Don't be scared off by the idea
of buttermilk—its tangy flavor mixes beautifully with the sugar and lemon zest,
and the result is a creamy custard pie that melts on the tongue.

INGREDIENTS:

Crust:

1 frozen, prepackaged 9-inch piecrust

1½ cups rice, uncooked

Filling:

4 tablespoons (½ stick) unsalted butter,
at room temperature

1 cup (7 ounces) sugar

Grated zest of 1 lemon

3 tablespoons all-purpose flour

3 large eggs, at room temperature,
lightly beaten

1 cup buttermilk, at room temperature

2 teaspoons vanilla extract

¼ teaspoon ground nutmeg

¼ teaspoon salt

TOOLS:

Measuring spoons

Dry measuring cups

Liquid measuring cup

Rasp grater

Fork

Baking sheet

Saucepan

Large bowl

Whisk

Flexible spatula

Wire cooling rack

Buttermilk Pie and Tipsy Key Lime Pie

❶ You need to partially pre-bake the piecrust before pouring
in the custard, to keep it from getting soggy. Here's how (this is
called "blind-baking"): Preheat the oven to 425°F. Cut out a 12-
inch sheet of parchment (don't worry about measuring exactly)
and place it inside the frozen piecrust. Fill the parchment with the
raw rice, spreading it out with your fingers so that it fills in all the
corners. Bake the piecrust this way for 20 minutes, then remove
it from the oven. Carefully pull off the parchment, taking care not
to spill any of the rice into the pie. (Discard the parchment and
rice.) Poke the crust along the bottom and around the sides with a
fork. Bake the piecrust for another 5 minutes, or until it turns light
golden, then remove it and place it on a wire rack.

❷ Reduce the oven temperature to 325°F and line a baking sheet
with foil.

❸ Make the filling (you can do this while the piecrust is baking):
In a saucepan, melt the butter over the lowest heat setting on your
stove. Pour the melted butter into a large bowl and let it cool for
5 minutes. Whisk in the sugar, lemon zest, and flour, beating until
there are no lumps. Whisk in the eggs, buttermilk, vanilla, nutmeg,
and salt, and mix until all the ingredients are well combined and
the mixture is smooth.

❹ Place the pie shell on the lined baking sheet. Pour the buttermilk
mixture into the crust. Bake for 40 to 45 minutes (check after 40),
until the filling is light golden and set (it should jiggle slightly
when you gently shake it—it will firm up as it cools).

❺ Take the pie off the baking sheet, place it on a wire rack, and let
it cool completely. Cover lightly with plastic wrap and refrigerate
until chilled, at least 2 hours.

Good to know! Turn the oven light on after 20 minutes—if the rim of the crust is turning dark brown, tear a piece of
foil, cut it in half, and fold both pieces into strips that will cover the rim of the crust. Take the pie out of the oven (on the baking sheet) and quickly but gently cover the rim with the foil strips. Place the pie back in the oven and continue to bake.

CHOCOLATE–PEANUT BUTTER PIE

Prep time: 40 minutes ⓘ Baking time: 10 minutes ⓘ Chilling time: 4 hours ✋ Serves 10 to 12

Chocolate, peanut butter, graham crackers, a few salty pretzels—this pie has it all if you're trying to satisfy a craving for something rich and decadent. A small slice is all you need. If you want to go peanut-butter crazy, garnish the pie with peanut butter–filled pretzels.

INGREDIENTS:

Crust:

1½ cups graham cracker crumbs (from a box, or crush 15 graham crackers in a food processor)

3 tablespoons sugar

¼ teaspoon salt

4 tablespoons unsalted butter, melted

Filling:

4 ounces cream cheese, at room temperature

3 tablespoons sugar

¾ cup creamy peanut butter (don't use "natural")

½ teaspoon vanilla extract

Pinch of salt

1/3 cup heavy cream, chilled

Topping:

6 ounces semisweet chocolate

½ cup heavy cream

1 tablespoon unsalted butter

Mini pretzel twists or nuggets, for garnish (optional)

❶ Preheat the oven to 375°F. Line a rimmed baking sheet with aluminum foil.

❷ Make the crust: In a large bowl, combine the graham cracker crumbs, sugar, and salt; stir with a fork to mix. Add the melted butter and stir again with the fork until all the ingredients are moistened. Transfer the mixture to a 9-inch pie plate.

❸ Press the crust mixture with your fingers to cover the bottom and sides of the pie plate. Use the back of a spoon or the bottom of a dry measuring cup to gently press the crust into an even layer. Bake the crust for 10 minutes, then set the pie plate on a wire rack to cool completely. (Wash and dry the large bowl.)

❹ Make the filling: Using an electric mixer at medium-high speed, beat the cream cheese and sugar in a large bowl until light and fluffy, about 1 to 2 minutes. Beat in the peanut butter, vanilla, and salt. Scrape down the sides and bottom of the bowl with a flexible spatula and beat again until all of the ingredients are well combined. (Wash and dry the beaters from the mixer.)

❺ In a separate large bowl, with an electric mixer at medium-high speed or a whisk, beat the cream until firm peaks form (see page 190 for more about whipping cream). Plop about one-third of the whipped cream into the bowl with the peanut butter mixture and use a flexible spatula to turn the mixtures over each other (this is called "folding," see page 185 for more on this) until the cream is mixed into the peanut butter filling. Try to mix as little as possible so that you don't deflate the cream too much. Add the rest of the cream to the bowl and fold it in the same way.

You Made That Dessert?

⑥ Spoon the filling into the cooled crust, smooth the top with the same flexible spatula, cover with plastic wrap, and refrigerate the pie until the filling is firm, about 3 hours.

⑦ Make the topping: On a cutting board, using a sharp chef's knife, chop the chocolate (see page 187 for more on how to do this). Place the chocolate in a medium bowl. Heat the ½ cup cream and butter in a saucepan until the butter has melted and the cream is simmering. Pour the cream mixture over the chocolate and whisk it until the chocolate has melted and the mixture is smooth.

⑧ Let the chocolate topping cool until it's lukewarm but still pourable, about 10 minutes. Pour the topping over the peanut butter filling, spreading it with a flexible or offset spatula to cover the filling. Garnish the top with pretzels, if desired. Refrigerate the pie until the topping is firm, about 1 hour.

(See photo, page 110)

TOOLS:

Baking sheet

2 large bowls

Fork

Dry measuring cups

Measuring spoons

Liquid measuring cup

9-inch pie plate

Wire cooling rack

Electric mixer

Flexible spatula

2 medium bowls

Cutting board

Chef's knife

Saucepan

Whisk

Chocolate–Peanut Butter Pie

Fresh Berry Shortcakes

FRESH BERRY SHORTCAKES

Prep time: 20 minutes ⏱ Baking time: 12 to 14 minutes ✋ Serves 8

There are many versions of strawberry shortcake, but I've always been partial to the kind made with biscuits. I love the contrast of the buttery biscuits with the sweet berries and rich whipped cream. Using a variety of berries gives these a little something extra.

INGREDIENTS:

Biscuits:

2 cups (8.5 ounces) all-purpose flour

2 teaspoons baking powder

½ teaspoon salt

¼ cup (1.75 ounces) plus 1 tablespoon sugar

6 tablespoons (¾ stick) unsalted butter, chilled, cut into pieces

¾ cup half-and-half

2 tablespoons heavy cream

Topping:

4 cups mixed berries, such as strawberries, blueberries, and raspberries

3 tablespoons sugar

1 cup heavy cream, chilled

2 tablespoons confectioners' sugar

1 teaspoon vanilla extract

❶ Make the biscuits: Preheat the oven to 450°F and line a baking sheet with parchment paper. In a large bowl, mix the flour, baking powder, salt, and ¼ cup sugar; stir them together with a fork. Toss in the pieces of butter and use a pastry blender to mix it into the dry ingredients by pushing down on the butter so that it gets cut up into ever-smaller pieces (this is called "cutting in"; see page 185 for more information). Keep blending the butter into the dry ingredients with the pastry blender until the butter is all cut in and the mixture is crumbly.

❷ Pour the half-and-half into the crumbly mixture and stir with a fork just until a dough forms. Sprinkle your countertop lightly with flour and dump the dough out onto it. Rub a little bit of flour onto your hands. Press the heel of one of your hands into the dough firmly to press it together, then turn the dough about a quarter of the way around and do it again (this is "kneading"). Sprinkle a little more flour onto the countertop or rub a little more onto your hands if the dough gets sticky. Knead the dough with the heel of your hand about 6 or 7 times, just until it's smooth and holds together.

❸ Pat the dough down into a ½-inch thick disc and cut it into 8 roughly even pieces with a chef's knife. (If you have a 3-inch round biscuit or cookie cutter, feel free to use it, but cutting the dough with a knife works just fine.) Wash and dry the bowl.

❹ Place the biscuits about 1 inch apart on the baking sheet. Brush them with the remaining heavy cream and sprinkle them with 1 tablespoon sugar. Bake the biscuits until golden brown, about 12 to 14 minutes. Remove the biscuits to a wire rack to cool.

⑤ Place a medium bowl and the beaters from your electric mixer in the freezer. If you're using strawberries, remove the hulls (see page 95 for more information) and slice the berries into a separate large bowl. Add the other berries. Add 3 tablespoons sugar and toss with the berries. Cover the bowl with plastic wrap and set aside.

⑥ Pour the chilled cream into your chilled bowl and add 2 tablespoons confectioners' sugar and the vanilla. Beat the cream with an electric mixer on medium-high speed until it forms medium-firm peaks.

⑦ To serve, split each biscuit in half (like an English muffin, so there's a top and a bottom) and place each one, open-faced, on a plate. Divide the berries among the biscuits, and finish by spooning a dollop of the whipped cream over each. Serve immediately.

(See photo, page 111)

TOOLS:
Dry measuring cups
Measuring spoons
Liquid measuring cup
Baking sheet
Large bowl
Pastry blender
Fork
Chef's knife (or 3-inch biscuit cutter)
Wire cooling rack
Medium bowl
Electric mixer
Paring knife
Tablespoon
Pastry brush

Good to know! You may want to add more sugar to your berries, depending on how sweet they are. Taste a few and add more sugar, if you like.

NECTARINE-BLUEBERRY CRISP

Prep time: 35 minutes ⏱ Baking time: 50 to 60 minutes ✋ Serves 6 to 8

This is my husband Mark's favorite dessert in this book. Juicy nectarines and blueberries are a perfect summer-fruit combo, and they're made even more luscious with a crunchy cinnamon-sugar topping. Whipped cream or ice cream is a must.

INGREDIENTS:

Filling:

2 pounds nectarines

2 cups blueberries

1/3 cup (2.3 ounces) sugar

3 tablespoons instant tapioca

Pinch of salt

Topping:

3/4 cup (3.2 ounces) all-purpose flour

3/4 cup (5.25 ounces) sugar

1/4 teaspoon salt

1 teaspoon cinnamon

6 tablespoons (3/4 stick) unsalted butter, cold, cut into 12 pieces

Whipped cream or vanilla ice cream, for serving (optional)

TOOLS:

Dry measuring cups

Measuring spoons

Baking sheet

Paring knife

Cutting board

Large bowl

Flexible spatula

Food processor

8-inch baking dish

Wire cooling rack

❶ Preheat the oven to 375°F. Line a rimmed baking sheet with parchment or foil.

❷ Make the filling: Using a sharp paring knife, cut the nectarines in half lengthwise (cutting from the stem end to the bottom). Pull the two halves of each nectarine apart and pull or cut out the pits (use the knife to cut around the pit to help it along if it doesn't pop right out). On a cutting board, using the same paring knife, cut each nectarine half into 5 or 6 slices. Place the nectarine slices in a large bowl and add the blueberries, sugar, tapioca, and salt. Mix gently with a flexible spatula until all the ingredients are combined. Let the fruit mixture stand for 15 minutes at room temperature.

❸ Make the topping: Place the flour, sugar, salt, and cinnamon in a food processor and use a few quick on-and-off turns to mix (this is called "pulsing"). Add the cold butter pieces and pulse several times, until the mixture resembles coarse sand and there are no more large pieces of butter.

❹ Spoon the fruit mixture into an ungreased 8-inch baking dish, scraping any juices from the bowl into the dish with a flexible spatula. Use the spatula to spread the fruit out into an even layer. Pour the topping over the fruit, spreading it out with your fingers into an even layer. Place the baking dish on the lined baking sheet and bake the crisp for 50 to 60 minutes, until the topping is golden brown and the fruit is bubbling.

❺ Remove the baking sheet from the oven and transfer the baking dish to a wire rack to cool. Let the crisp cool for at least 20 minutes. Serve warm, with whipped cream or ice cream.

Nectarine-Blueberry Crisp and
Rustic Plum Galette

You Made That Dessert?

RUSTIC PLUM GALETTE

Prep time: 25 minutes ⏱ Baking time: 35 to 40 minutes ✋ Serves 6

"Galette" is a fancy name for a free-form tart, no tart pan required—and they're great for new bakers because they're meant to be rustic, so you don't have to worry about making them look perfect. Wait until plums are at their sweetest, usually late summer and early fall, to make this simple tart, which is only lightly sweetened to allow the fruit's flavor to shine.

INGREDIENTS:

1 sheet frozen puff pastry, thawed
1½ pounds firm, ripe plums (about 10 to 12 medium)
3 tablespoons all-purpose flour
5 tablespoons sugar
Pinch of salt
1 tablespoon unsalted butter, melted

TOOLS:

Measuring spoons
Baking sheet
Rolling pin (or wine bottle)
Paring knife
Small bowl
Large bowl
Flexible spatula
Fork
Pastry brush
Wire cooling rack

(See photo, page 115)

❶ Preheat the oven to 400°F. Place the puff pastry on a large sheet of parchment on your countertop or table. Lay another sheet of parchment on top. Using a rolling pin (or a full wine bottle), roll out the dough to about a 12-inch circle (don't worry about making it a precise circle—circle-ish is fine). Pull off the top sheet of parchment and slide the bottom piece of parchment with the dough onto the baking sheet (some of the dough may hang over the sides; that's okay). Put the baking sheet in the fridge.

❷ Using a sharp paring knife, cut the plums in half and remove the pits. Cut each plum half into 5 or 6 slices.

❸ In a large bowl, mix the flour with 3 tablespoons sugar and the salt; stir with a fork to combine. Add the plum slices and gently mix with a flexible spatula until the plums are coated with the flour mixture.

❹ Take the baking sheet out of the fridge and set it on the counter. Place the plums on the dough, either in concentric circles or just piled on, whichever you prefer—but be sure to leave a 2-inch border around all the edges.

❺ Gently fold the dough edges over the fruit, just covering the sides (the middle of the galette will remain uncovered). Fold the dough over itself in pleats—again, don't worry about being precise, this is meant to be a rustic-looking tart. Just be sure there are no openings or cracks in the sides of the dough. When you have all the sides folded up, lightly brush the edges of the dough with the melted butter (use a pastry brush or your fingers), then sprinkle the edges of the dough and the exposed plums with the remaining 2 tablespoons of sugar.

❻ Bake the tart for 35 to 40 minutes, until the dough is lightly browned, puffed and crisp, and the fruit is juicy and bubbling. Place the baking sheet on a wire rack. Gently dip a pastry brush into the pockets of bubbling juices and brush the juice over the drier-looking plums to glaze them. Cool the tart on a wire rack for at least 15 minutes before slicing and serving.

BAKED APPLES

Prep time: 15 minutes ⏱ Baking time: 40 minutes 🖐 Makes 4

The first time I made these for my husband, Mark, he said, "Mmmm, it's like having a little apple crisp, all for me!" If you tend to like the fruit with just a little bit of the topping (or if you're watching your calories), this is for you. It's very comforting on a cold autumn evening, and easy enough for a weeknight dinner.

INGREDIENTS:

4 firm apples (Granny Smith, Rome, or Gala are all good choices)
1 tablespoon lemon juice
¼ cup raisins (or dried cranberries or dried cherries)
¼ cup quick-cooking oats (do not use instant)
¼ cup (2.1 ounces) packed dark brown sugar
1 teaspoon cinnamon
Pinch of salt
4 tablespoons (½ stick) unsalted butter, at room temperature
¾ cup apple cider
1 tablespoon whiskey or bourbon (optional)
Vanilla ice cream or whipped cream, for serving (optional)

TOOLS:

Vegetable peeler
Dry measuring cups
Measuring spoons
Liquid measuring cup
Melon baller
9-inch pie or baking dish
Pastry brush
Medium bowl
Tablespoon
Wire cooling rack

❶ Preheat the oven to 425°F. Using a vegetable peeler, peel off the skin from the top third of the apples (this will keep the skin from cracking). Use a melon baller to scoop out the seeds and cores, taking care not to puncture a hole in the bottom of the apples (leave about an inch of flesh in the bottom). Stand the apples up in a 9-inch pie dish or baking dish. Brush the insides and peeled parts of the apples with the lemon juice.

❷ In a medium bowl, mix together the raisins, oats, brown sugar, cinnamon, and salt; toss together with your fingers. Add the butter and mush it around with your fingers to mix it in with the oat mixture. When you're done, it should look like a big soft clump.

❸ Use your fingers to stuff each of the apples with one-fourth of the oat mixture, pressing it in and piling it at the top of each apple. If there are any raisins peeking out the top, push them under with your finger or a toothpick—raisins sticking out can burn during baking.

❹ Pour the cider and whiskey (if using) into the baking dish around the apples. Bake them for 10 minutes. Remove the dish from the oven (leave it on, but shut the door) and baste the apples with the cider mixture by spooning it over the tops of the apples, especially on the peeled parts. Return the dish to the oven for 15 minutes, then baste again. Place the dish back in the oven and bake 15 minutes longer.

❺ Remove the dish to a wire rack to let the apples cool for 5 to 10 minutes (now you can turn the oven off). Spoon each apple onto a plate or into a bowl and serve with ice cream or whipped cream.

(See photo, page 147)

Good to know! You can prep these up to a day ahead—get them ready, but don't pour the cider or whiskey into the pan. Cover the apples and refrigerate for up to a day. When you're ready to bake, uncover the apples, pour in the cider and whiskey, and bake as directed. You may need about 5 to 10 extra minutes of baking time.

GRAPEFRUIT GRANITA

Prep time: 20 minutes ⏱ Chilling time: 3 to 4 hours 🖐 Serves 8

This incredibly refreshing treat is also one of the easiest things you'll ever make.
It's the perfect ending for dinner on a hot summer night.

INGREDIENTS:

1 cup (7 ounces) sugar
¾ cup water
Pinch of salt
3 cups fresh grapefruit juice, from 4–5
    large grapefruits (preferably pink)
⅓ cup vodka

TOOLS:

Saucepan
Whisk or flexible spatula
Large bowl
9 x 13-inch baking pan
Liquid measuring cup
Dry measuring cups
Fork

❶ Mix the sugar with the water in a small saucepan and place over medium-low heat. Cook, stirring with a whisk or flexible spatula until the sugar has dissolved (do not boil). Remove from the heat and pour the syrup into a large bowl to cool, about 10 minutes.

❷ When the syrup is cool, add the salt, grapefruit juice, and vodka and mix well. Pour the mixture into a 9 x 13-inch baking pan and freeze for 3 to 4 hours, until firm. Every 45 minutes, stir with a fork to break up lumps.

❸ To serve, spoon granita into eight chilled wine glasses.

Grapefruit Granita

MOCHA CREAM PIE

Prep time: 20 minutes ⏲ Baking time: 15 minutes ⏲ Chilling time: 4 hours, 30 minutes ✋ Serves 12

This rich, chocolaty pie is creamy and delicious, and the hint of mocha gives it a distinctly grown-up flavor. If you prefer chocolate to mocha, simply leave out the espresso powder. Don't be intimidated by the number of steps—the pie is a bit time consuming, but all of the steps are easy and it's worth the effort!

INGREDIENTS:
Crust:
14 Oreo cookies
Pinch of salt
2 tablespoons unsalted butter, melted
Filling:
1 tablespoon vanilla extract
1 tablespoon instant espresso powder
3 ounces semisweet chocolate
1 ounce unsweetened chocolate
2 cups half-and-half
½ cup (3.5 ounces) plus 1 tablespoon sugar
¼ cup cornstarch
¼ teaspoon salt
4 large egg yolks
4 tablespoons (½ stick) unsalted butter, at room temperature
Topping:
1 cup heavy cream, chilled
1 tablespoon confectioners' sugar

❶ Make the crust: Preheat the oven to 350°F. Place the cookies and salt in a food processor and blend until the cookies are completely ground. Transfer the crumbs to a medium bowl. Pour in the melted butter and mix with a flexible spatula until all the crumbs are moistened.

❷ Transfer the mixture into a 9-inch pie plate and use your hands or the bottom of a glass to press the crumbs evenly over the bottom and up the sides of the pie dish to form a crust. Bake 15 minutes, until firm. Let the crust cool on a wire rack. (Turn the oven off.)

❸ Make the filling: In a small cup, combine the vanilla and instant espresso powder; stir with a spoon until the espresso powder has dissolved. On a cutting board, using a sharp chef's knife, chop both chocolates (see page 187 for more on how to do this).

❹ Mix 1 cup of the half-and-half with both chocolates in a saucepan and place on the stove over low heat. Cook, whisking often, until the chocolates have melted and the mixture is hot, about 5 minutes (it may look grainy—don't worry about that). Meanwhile, in a large bowl, whisk together the sugar, cornstarch, and salt. Pour the remaining cup of half-and-half into the sugar mixture and whisk until no lumps remain. Whisk in the egg yolks until everything is thoroughly mixed.

❺ When the chocolate mixture is hot, pour it very slowly into the cornstarch mixture—be sure that when you do this, you are whisking the cornstarch mixture vigorously at the same time. (Place a damp kitchen towel under the bowl; that will help keep it from sliding.) Doing this will keep the egg yolks from scrambling as you hit them with the hot chocolate mixture. When both mixtures are combined, pour them back into the saucepan and place it back on the stove over medium-low heat. Cook, stirring constantly with the whisk, until the mixture is thickened and beginning to boil, about 5 to 7 minutes. (It will look like pudding, because that's what it is!)

6 Pour the hot pudding into a clean medium bowl, and stir in the butter and the reserved vanilla-coffee mixture with a flexible spatula. Cover with plastic wrap, pressing the plastic directly onto the surface of the pudding (this keeps it from forming a skin). Let the pudding cool at room temperature for 1 hour.

7 Pour the pudding into the pie shell, cover with a fresh piece of plastic wrap (press it directly on the surface of the pudding again), and refrigerate for at least 3 hours; overnight is best.

8 A half hour before you're ready to serve the pie, pour the heavy cream and confectioners' sugar into a chilled bowl and beat with an electric mixer at medium-high speed (or beat vigorously with a whisk) until firm peaks form. (See page 190 to learn more about whipping cream.) Remove the plastic from the pie and spoon the whipped cream on top, spreading it with a flexible spatula. Refrigerate for 30 minutes, then slice and serve.

(See photo, page 122)

TOOLS:
Food processor
2 medium bowls
Flexible spatula
9-inch pie plate
Wire cooling rack
Measuring spoons
Spoon
Liquid measuring cup
Dry measuring cups
Cutting board
Chef's knife
Small cup
Saucepan
Whisk
2 large bowls
Electric mixer
Kitchen towel

Good to know! You can garnish this pie with chocolate curls or shavings. Use a vegetable peeler to peel the edge of a chocolate bar. Peel it right over the pie, so the shavings fall directly onto the whipped cream. Or sprinkle on a small handful of miniature chocolate chips.

Mocha Cream Pie

Lemon-Berry Semifreddo

LEMON-BERRY SEMIFREDDO

Prep time: 50 minutes ⏱ Freezing time: 3 hours 🖐 Makes 8

Semifreddo means "half cold" in Italian, and it refers to any dessert that is cold or partly frozen, especially semi-frozen custards like this one. This is one of the more ambitious recipes in this book. It isn't difficult at all, but it has a lot of steps and you'll dirty a lot of dishes. But it's delicious, refreshing, and very sophisticated—like a homemade ice cream that you can make without an ice cream maker.

INGREDIENTS:

4 cups mixed berries (such as raspberries, blueberries, and blackberries)

¼ cup lemon juice

1¼ cups (8.75 ounces) sugar

1½ cups chilled heavy cream

6 large egg yolks

1 tablespoon finely grated lemon zest

¼ teaspoon salt

Whipped cream and extra berries for serving (optional)

❶ Have ready 8 7-ounce waxed paper cups (such as Dixie cups). Place a large bowl and the beaters from an electric mixer in the freezer.

❷ In a food processor or blender, combine the berries, lemon juice, and ¼ cup sugar. Blend until smooth. Place a fine-mesh sieve over a medium bowl and pour the berry puree into the sieve. Stir the puree with a whisk or flexible spatula to force as much puree through as possible while removing the seeds. You should end up with about 1½ cups of berry puree. Place the strained puree in the fridge (no need to cover it) and discard the seeds.

❸ Pour the heavy cream into the bowl you had chilling in the freezer. Using the chilled beaters in your electric mixer, beat the cream until soft peaks form. Place the bowl with the whipped cream in the fridge (no need to cover it). Clean and dry the beaters.

❹ Place a saucepan with about 2 inches of water in it on the stove over medium heat. Heat the water until it simmers—that is, it should be hot and beginning to steam, with small bubbles beginning to form, but not quite boiling. When the water is simmering, turn the heat down to low. In a large bowl, whisk together 1 cup sugar, the egg yolks, lemon zest, and salt until just blended.

❺ Set the bowl with the yolk mixture over the saucepan of simmering water and whisk the egg yolk mixture vigorously until the mixture thickens, lightens to a pale yellow, and feels hot to the touch, about 10 minutes. The sugar should also dissolve. Remove the bowl from over the saucepan. Using an electric mixer on medium-high speed, beat the yolk mixture until it's cool, even thicker than before, and about doubled in volume, about 8 minutes.

❻ Take the whipped cream and the berry puree out of the fridge. Using a flexible spatula, plop the whipped cream into the bowl with the yolk mixture. Scrape in the berry puree. Mix the three together by scraping the bottom of the bowl with the flexible spatula and turning the mixtures over and over each other (this is called "folding," see page 185 for more information). Keep folding until the mixtures are completely combined.

❼ Transfer the mixture to a large liquid measuring cup, and divide it among the eight paper cups. Tap the cups lightly on the countertop to pop any air bubbles. Cover each cup tightly with plastic wrap and freeze (if you have space in the freezer, put all the cups in a 9 x 13-inch pan and set the pan in the freezer) until the semifreddos are firm, at least 3 hours.

❽ To serve, remove the plastic wrap from the cups. Place each semifreddo on a small plate upside-down, and peel off the paper cup. Serve with a small dollop of whipped cream and additional berries on the side, if desired.

(See photo, page 123)

TOOLS:
8 7-ounce waxed paper cups
Food processor or blender
Fine-mesh sieve
Medium bowl
Dry measuring cups
Liquid measuring cup
Rasp grater
Measuring spoons
Whisk
2 large bowls
Electric mixer
Saucepan
Flexible spatula
9 x 13-inch pan

Good to know! A few delicate little store-bought butter or lemon cookies would also go well with these.
You can use frozen berries for this, just thaw them before you begin.
If you can't find 7-ounce cups, use 9-ounce cups and don't fill them all the way.

COOL BLUEBERRY SOUP

Prep time: 30 minutes ⏱ Chilling time: 3 hours 🖐 Serves 4 to 6

Talk about a light, refreshing, sophisticated finish to a summer meal! Plus, there's no baking, so your kitchen stays cool. You could also serve this pretty soup as an appetizer. I grew up enjoying my mom's delicious blueberry soup—and she inspired this one.

INGREDIENTS:

1-pound bag frozen blueberries
(or 4 cups fresh)
1 cup dry white wine (such as Sauvignon
Blanc or Pinot Grigio)
3 tablespoons lemon juice (from 1 or
2 medium lemons)
1/3 cup (2.3 ounces) sugar
1 cinnamon stick (optional)
1 cup plain yogurt (preferably Greek),
or crème fraîche or sour cream (see
"The Skinny on Yogurt")
Additional yogurt and/or fresh
blueberries, for garnish (optional)

TOOLS:

Saucepan
Liquid measuring cup
Measuring spoons
Dry measuring cups
Large spoon
Large bowl
Blender or food processor (optional)
Wire whisk or fork

❶ Place the blueberries, wine, lemon juice, sugar, and cinnamon stick (if using) in a saucepan (don't cover it). Bring the mixture to a boil over medium heat, stirring a few times with a large spoon to dissolve the sugar and defrost berries. Once it has come to a boil, turn the heat down to low and let the mixture simmer for 10 minutes. Take the pan off the heat and let cool for 10 minutes, stirring once or twice during cooling time. Remove cinnamon stick.

❷ Pour the blueberry mixture into a blender or food processor—be careful, it will splatter!—and puree (or, if you don't have a blender or food processor, mash up the mixture as best you can with a fork). Don't worry if it isn't perfectly smooth—a rougher texture with some of the berries left intact will be equally delicious. Pour the blueberry soup into a large bowl and refrigerate it uncovered until cold, at least 3 hours.

❸ If any foam has formed on the top of the soup, skim it off with a spoon and discard it (don't worry if you don't get it all). Just before serving, gently stir the yogurt into the soup with a whisk or fork until blended (you shouldn't see any white streaks). Ladle or spoon the soup into cups or small bowls, top with a small dollop of yogurt and a few berries, and serve.

Cool Blueberry Soup and Wine-Poached Peaches

Good to know!
This fruit soup is best made a day ahead, to let the flavors develop, but it's very good the same day, too—just be sure to leave enough time for it to cool.

Use plain frozen blueberries—avoid any that are in syrup or have sugar or other sweeteners added.

If you want to include the cinnamon stick, most likely you'll have to buy a small container of them (unless your supermarket or natural food store sells bulk spices, in which case you can probably just buy one). Keep the extras in your pantry—use them as stirrers for hot apple cider, tea, or hot chocolate in cooler weather.

The Skinny on Yogurt
Greek yogurt is strained, so the excess water is removed, leaving behind a much richer and creamier yogurt than American brands. Crème fraîche is a slightly tangy, nutty, thick cultured cream, similar to sour cream but with a fluffier texture. Either of these or regular sour cream will work well in the soup. It comes down to personal taste (and budget—crème fraîche can be expensive).

APPLE CRUMBLE

Prep time: 20 minutes ⏱ Baking time: 50 to 55 minutes ✋ Serves 6

This dessert is like a really good date—you can bring it anywhere, dress it up
(by baking it in a pretty dish and serving it with the best vanilla ice cream you can find) or not,
and feel confident that it will hold its own. And I hope that like a great date,
you'll want to come back to it again and again.

INGREDIENTS:

Cooking spray

Filling:

5 Granny Smith apples

3 tablespoons lemon juice

¼ cup (1.75 ounces) sugar

Topping:

²/₃ cup (2.8 ounces) flour

½ cup quick-cooking oats (do not use
   instant)

½ cup (4.2 ounces) packed dark brown
   sugar

2 teaspoons cinnamon

¼ teaspoon salt

8 tablespoons (1 stick) unsalted butter,
   cold

Ice cream or whipped cream, for serving
   (optional)

TOOLS:

Dry measuring cups

Measuring spoons

Vegetable peeler

Chef's knife

Cutting board

Wooden spoon

2 large bowls

9-inch baking dish

Pastry blender or food processor

Wire cooling rack

❶ Make the filling: Peel the apples. Core them by cutting each apple into 4 pieces with a chef's knife, cutting around the core. Cut each piece of apple into slices (don't worry about making the apple slices exactly uniform, but you want them to be about ¼-inch thick). Place the apple slices in a large bowl, add the lemon juice and sugar, and toss with a wooden spoon or your hands to coat the apple slices with both the juice and sugar.

❷ Preheat the oven to 350°F. Mist a 9-inch baking dish with cooking spray. Spoon the apples into the pan, spreading them out evenly and pouring in any juice that's left in the bowl.

❸ Make the topping: In a large bowl stir together the flour, oats, brown sugar, cinnamon, and salt. Cut the butter into about 10 slices and add it to the dry ingredients. Press a pastry blender into the butter and dry ingredients repeatedly to cut up the butter and incorporate it into the dry ingredients (this is called "cutting in"; see page 185 for more information) until the mixture is similar to coarse sand. (Alternatively, place the dry ingredients in a food processor, turn on and off quickly a few times to mix, then add the pieces of butter and turn on and off quickly a few times again until the mixture resembles coarse sand.)

❹ Sprinkle the topping over the filling, covering it evenly. Bake 50 to 55 minutes, until the apple filling is bubbling and the topping is crisp. Let the crumble cool on a wire rack for at least 15 minutes before serving. Spoon it into dishes and top with ice cream or whipped cream, if desired.

From top left: Apple Crumble, Elegant Apple
Tartlets, and Pear–Tart Cherry Crisp

You Made That Dessert?

ELEGANT APPLE TARTLETS

Prep time: 30 minutes ⏱ Baking time: 20 to 23 minutes ✋ Makes 6 4-inch tartlets

Frozen puff pastry is one of my favorite "dirty little secrets." It makes any dessert look super-fancy, and it requires almost no work on your part. Don't feel ashamed to use it—chefs often do. Make sure the pastry has thawed before you try to unroll it.

INGREDIENTS:

2 Golden Delicious apples

3 tablespoons sugar

1 teaspoon cinnamon

Pinch of salt

1 sheet frozen puff pastry, thawed (half of a 17.3-ounce package)

2 tablespoons unsalted butter, melted

2 tablespoons turbinado sugar (such as Sugar in the Raw)

Ice cream or whipped cream, for serving (optional)

TOOLS:

Baking sheet

Vegetable peeler

Cutting board

Chef's knife

Fork

Small bowl

Measuring spoons

Rolling pin (or wine bottle)

4-inch plate or wide mug

Paring knife

Pastry brush

Wire cooling rack

❶ Preheat the oven to 400°F. Line a large rimmed baking sheet with parchment paper.

❷ Peel the apples. On a cutting board, using a chef's knife, cut each apple into 4 pieces, cutting around the core. Discard the core. Cut each apple quarter into thin slices, about ⅛ to ¼ inch. (Don't drive yourself crazy trying to get all the slices paper-thin or making them all the exact same width—just do your best to slice carefully and get them as thin as you can.)

❸ In a small bowl, combine the 3 tablespoons regular sugar, the cinnamon, and the salt, and stir with a fork to mix. Place two large sheets of plastic wrap on your counter (each about 12 inches wide), so that they overlap just slightly. Carefully uncurl the thawed puff pastry sheet (they're usually folded into thirds to fit in the box) and lay it in the center of the plastic wrap (you should have some extra plastic wrap around all sides of the pastry). Lay two more sheets of plastic wrap on top, the same way as the ones below the pastry. Using a rolling pin (or a full wine bottle), roll the pastry so that it's very thin, about half as thick as when you started, into an approximately 6 x 15-inch rectangle. Be sure to roll in all directions, and roll to the ends, so the pastry is fairly even all over. Remove the top sheets of plastic wrap.

❹ Using a 4-inch plate or wide mug as a guide, very lightly trace the outline of six circles by pressing the guide into the puff pastry (do not press too hard; all you are looking for is an outline of each circle). This will help to ensure that you've rolled the puff pastry thin enough. If you can't trace six circles, roll the pastry thinner until you can. Cut out the six 4-inch circles from the pastry with a sharp paring knife, following the lines you traced.

❺ Place the dough circles on the lined baking sheet; discard any leftover pastry. Place 8 to 10 slices of apple on each pastry round, in a row, overlapping the slices somewhat and leaving about ¼ to ½ inch around the edges. (You may not use up all of your apple slices—that's okay.) Brush the apples with the melted butter, and sprinkle with the cinnamon-sugar mixture. Sprinkle the turbinado sugar over each tartlet.

❻ Bake for 20 to 23 minutes, until the pastry is golden brown and slightly puffed on the edges and the apples are soft. Transfer the baking sheet to a wire rack and let the tartlets cool for 5 minutes. Serve warm, with ice cream or whipped cream.

(See photo, page 129)

Good to know! These are lovely with a drizzle of Caramel Sauce (see page 160 for a recipe).

PEAR–TART CHERRY CRISP

Prep time: 20 minutes ⏱ Baking time: 1 hour ✋ Serves 8

The best part about fruit crisps and crumbles is that they're so easy to make. Slice up some fruit and toss it with a bit of sugar and flour, top it with crumbly bits made from the simplest ingredients, and an hour later you have amazing smells coming from the kitchen and a dessert that's sure to please. What could be better?

INGREDIENTS:

Cooking spray

Topping:

1 cup (4.25 ounces) all-purpose flour

½ cup (4.2 ounces) packed dark brown sugar

2 tablespoons sugar

1 tablespoon ground ginger

2 teaspoons cinnamon

¼ teaspoon salt

8 tablespoons (1 stick) cold unsalted butter, cut into about 10 pieces

Filling:

3 15-ounce cans pear halves, packed in juice

1 cup dried cherries

3 tablespoons all-purpose flour

3 tablespoons sugar

2 tablespoons lemon juice

¼ teaspoon salt

Whipped cream or vanilla ice cream, for serving (optional)

TOOLS:

Baking sheet

Dry measuring cups

Measuring spoons

9-inch deep-dish pie plate

Food processor

Cutting board

Paring knife

Large bowl

Flexible spatula

Wire cooling rack

❶ Preheat the oven to 375°F; line a baking sheet with foil or parchment paper. Mist a 9-inch deep-dish pie plate with cooking spray.

❷ Make the topping: Place the flour, brown sugar, sugar, ginger, cinnamon, and salt in a food processor and mix using quick on-off turns (this is called "pulsing," see page 186 for more). Toss the butter pieces into the food processor all at once. Pulse seven or eight times, or until the butter is completely chopped up and the flour-butter mixture looks like coarse sand.

❸ Make the filling: Drain the canned pears. On a cutting board, using a sharp paring knife, cut each pear half lengthwise into 6 pieces. Place the slices in a large bowl, add the cherries, flour, sugar, lemon juice, and salt, and stir using a flexible spatula until all the ingredients are well mixed. Spoon the filling into the pie plate, scraping out any juices that have collected in the bowl and evenly spreading the fruit. Spread the topping evenly over the fruit in the pie plate. Gently press it down with your fingers to lightly pack it on.

❹ Place the pie plate on the lined baking sheet and bake for 1 hour, or until the topping is golden brown and the fruit is bubbling. Remove the dish from the baking sheet and place it on a wire rack to cool for at least 15 minutes before serving. Serve with whipped cream or ice cream, if desired.

(See photo, page 129)

MAPLE WALNUT PIE

Prep time: 20 minutes ⏱ Baking time: 40 minutes ✋ Serves 10

If you like pecan pie, give this one a shot. It has walnuts instead and is sweetened with maple syrup. Try to find grade B maple syrup if you can—it's richer and more flavorful than grade A (though that works well in this pie, too).

INGREDIENTS:

1½ cups chopped walnuts

1 unbaked frozen store-bought 9-inch piecrust in foil pan (not deep-dish)

2 large eggs, lightly beaten

¼ cup (2.1 ounces) packed dark brown sugar

¼ cup heavy cream

¾ cup pure maple syrup

2 tablespoons unsalted butter, melted and slightly cooled

1 tablespoon bourbon

2 tablespoons all-purpose flour

½ teaspoon salt

Vanilla ice cream or whipped cream, for serving (optional)

TOOLS:

Dry measuring cups

Baking sheet

Medium bowl

Measuring spoons

Liquid measuring cup

Large bowl

Whisk

Wire cooling rack

❶ Place a rack on the bottom third of the oven and preheat to 375°F. Spread the walnuts out on a baking sheet and bake for 7 to 10 minutes, shaking the pan every 2 minutes to let the walnuts toast evenly. Transfer the walnuts to a medium bowl; let them cool for 10 minutes. Wipe down the baking sheet.

❷ Line the same baking sheet with aluminum foil. Spread the walnuts evenly in the pie crust, and place the crust on the lined baking sheet. In a large bowl, whisk together the eggs, brown sugar, cream, maple syrup, butter, bourbon, flour, and salt. Be sure to break up all the lumps of brown sugar and get all the ingredients well incorporated. Pour this mixture over the nuts in the pie shell (it will be very full).

❸ Bake until the crust is golden and the filling is just firm in the center and puffed up, about 40 minutes. (Check the pie every 10 minutes during baking—if the crust is getting too dark, cut a piece of foil and fold it to about the width of the crust edge. Carefully place the foil over the crust.)

❹ Let the pie cool completely on a wire rack before serving. The filling will sink—that's okay. Serve with vanilla ice cream or whipped cream, if desired.

(See photos, pages 134 and 149)

From top left: Maple Walnut Pie and Sweet Potato Pie with Streusel Topping

Blackberry Cobbler

BLACKBERRY COBBLER

Prep time: 20 minutes ⏱ Baking time: 45 to 50 minutes 🖐 Serves 6

All year I look forward to the summer months—for the warm weather, sure, but mostly for the fruit! I love the sweet peaches, juicy nectarines, and, of course, all the beautiful berries. When you see boxes and boxes of fresh blackberries on store shelves or at a farmers' market, grab them and whip up this easy cobbler. Don't forget the vanilla ice cream.

INGREDIENTS:

Filling:
5 cups blackberries
½ cup (3.5 ounces) sugar
⅛ teaspoon salt
2 tablespoons instant tapioca

Biscuits:
1½ cups (6.4 ounces) all-purpose flour
1½ teaspoons baking powder
¼ teaspoon salt
3 tablespoons sugar, plus 1 teaspoon for sprinkling on top
4½ tablespoons unsalted butter, cold, cut into pieces (2¼ ounces)
½ cup half-and-half, plus 1 tablespoon

TOOLS:
Dry measuring cups
Measuring spoons
Liquid measuring cup
2 large bowls
Flexible spatula
Fork
Pastry blender
9-inch pie plate
2 tablespoons
Wire cooling rack

❶ Make the filling: In a large bowl, combine the berries, sugar, salt, and tapioca, and stir well with a flexible spatula. Set aside for 10 to 15 minutes.

❷ Meanwhile, make the biscuits: Preheat the oven to 375°F; place a sheet of aluminum foil on the center oven rack that is wider than your 9-inch pie plate. In a large bowl, combine the flour, baking powder, salt, and sugar; stir with a fork to mix well. Add the pieces of butter and use a pastry blender to push down on the butter, cutting it up into ever-smaller pieces and mixing into the dry ingredients at the same time (this is called "cutting in" the butter; see page 185 for more information). Keep cutting in the butter until the whole mixture is crumbly and looks like coarse sand, with no more big lumps of butter.

❸ Pour the half-and-half into the flour mixture and stir with the fork just until the dry ingredients are moistened and a rough dough forms. You'll still see tiny pieces of butter in the dough; that's okay.

❹ Give the berry filling a stir with a flexible spatula, then scrape the berries and any juices that have accumulated in the bowl into a 9-inch pie plate.

❺ Gather up a chunk of biscuit dough in a tablespoon and use another tablespoon to scrape it off and drop it onto the fruit. Repeat this with the remaining dough until you've used it all— you'll have around 6 to 8 lumps of dough. Sprinkle the tops of the biscuits with the remaining 1 teaspoon of sugar. Place the pie plate in the oven on top of the foil and bake the cobbler for 45 to 50 minutes, until the fruit is bubbling and the biscuits are golden brown. Let the cobbler cool for at least 10 minutes on a wire rack before serving.

(See photo, page 135)

You Made That Dessert?

SWEET POTATO PIE
WITH STREUSEL TOPPING

Prep time: 20 minutes ⓘ Baking time: 45 to 50 minutes ✋ Serves 10 to 12

This home-style dessert is lovely to bring to a Thanksgiving dinner. It's a nice break from pumpkin, but with the same satisfying spices and richness.

INGREDIENTS:

Pie:

1 15- to 17-ounce can mashed sweet potatoes

1 can (14 ounces) sweetened condensed milk

2 large eggs

1 tablespoon pumpkin pie spice

1/8 teaspoon salt

1 unbaked frozen store-bought 9-inch piecrust in foil pan (not deep-dish)

Topping:

1/2 cup (2.1 ounces) all-purpose flour

1/3 cup (2.8 ounces) packed dark brown sugar

1/4 cup (1.75 ounces) sugar

1/4 cup quick-cooking oats

1/8 teaspoon salt

4 tablespoons (1/2 stick) unsalted butter, melted

1/3 cup chopped pecans or walnuts (optional)

Whipped cream, for serving (optional)

TOOLS:

Fork

Paring knife

Spoon

Whisk

Large bowl

Small bowl

Medium bowl

Baking sheet

Dry measuring cups

Measuring spoons

Wire cooling rack

❶ Preheat the oven to 375°F; place an oven rack in the bottom third of the oven.

❷ In a large bowl, using a wire whisk, mix the mashed sweet potatoes and condensed milk until just combined. In a separate small bowl, whisk the eggs until lightly beaten, then whisk the eggs into the sweet potato mixture. Whisk in pumpkin pie spice and salt. Pour the mixture into the piecrust; smooth the top with the back of the spoon.

❸ Make the topping: Whisk together the flour, both sugars, oats, and salt in a medium bowl. Pour in the melted butter and stir with a fork until all dry ingredients are incorporated and the mixture is crumbly (if it appears wet, add more flour, a tablespoon at a time, until it looks crumbly and just slightly moist). Stir in the nuts with the fork (if using). Sprinkle the topping evenly on top of the sweet potato mixture.

❹ Line a baking sheet with foil, and place the pie on top. Bake the pie 25 minutes. Carefully rotate the baking sheet so that the side of the pie that was facing you is now facing the back of the oven, then bake another 20 to 25 minutes, until a paring knife inserted in the center comes out clean. Let the pie cool on a wire rack and serve at room temperature, or cover and refrigerate it to serve cold. Serve with whipped cream, if desired.

(See photos, pages 134 and 149)

Good to know!
Buy pure mashed sweet potatoes, not candied yams, which will be too sweet. If you can't find plain canned mashed sweet potatoes, it's easy to make them. Preheat the oven to 450°F. Prick 4 medium-sized sweet potatoes all over with a fork. When the oven is hot, place the potatoes directly on the middle oven rack and bake until soft, about 1 hour. Remove the potatoes from the oven and let them sit on the countertop until they're cool enough to handle. Then, slice them in half lengthwise and scoop out the flesh with a spoon into a large bowl. Mash the flesh with a fork until smooth. (You should have about 1 1/2 cups.)

BANANA-NUTELLA WONTONS

Prep time: 20 minutes ⏱ Baking time: 8 to 10 minutes ✋ Makes 16 wontons

This is a really fun dessert and would be great to make with kids. They can help fill the wonton wrappers, seal them, brush them, and sprinkle them. You'll find pre-made wonton wrappers in the refrigerator or freezer section of most supermarkets.

INGREDIENTS:

2 tablespoons sugar

2 teaspoons cinnamon

16 wonton wrappers, defrosted if frozen

5 tablespoons Nutella chocolate-
    hazelnut spread

1 medium ripe banana

2 tablespoons unsalted butter, melted

TOOLS:

Measuring spoons

Fork

Baking sheet

Small bowl

Paring knife

Pastry brush

Teaspoon

❶ Preheat the oven to 350°F. Line a baking sheet with parchment. Have a small glass of water ready. In a small bowl, mix the sugar and cinnamon with a fork until combined well.

❷ Lay 4 wonton wrappers out on a clean countertop. Place 1 teaspoon Nutella in the center of each wrapper. Cut the banana into very thin slices with a paring knife and place 2 slices on top of the Nutella on each wrapper. Dip your finger into the glass of water and run it along the edges of a wonton wrapper. Fold the wrapper in half diagonally, forming a triangle. Press on the edges well with your fingers to seal. Repeat with the remaining 3 wontons. Place the 4 on the baking sheet (you can place them close together; they won't spread).

❸ Repeat with the remaining wonton wrappers, Nutella, and bananas, working in batches of 4 wontons at a time. When all the wontons have been made, lightly brush the sides facing up with the melted butter and sprinkle with the cinnamon-sugar. Place the baking sheet in the oven and bake the wontons for 8 to 10 minutes, until crisp and lightly browned. Let cool for 1 minute before serving.

Good to know! These are best served hot. To reheat them after they've cooled, place them in a 350°F oven on a parchment-lined baking sheet for 5 minutes.

Banana-Nutella Wontons

CHERRY CLAFOUTI

Prep time: 10 minutes ⏱ Baking time: 45 to 50 minutes ✋ Serves 4 to 6

Don't let the French name intimidate you—this simple, rustic dessert (pronounced clah-foo-TEE), somewhere between a custard and a pancake, couldn't be easier to make. Plus, it looks beautiful and is sure to please. It's lovely after dinner, but because it isn't very sweet, it would also work well for brunch.

INGREDIENTS:

1 tablespoon unsalted butter (for preparing pie plate)

1½ cups frozen dark sweet cherries, not thawed

4 large eggs

½ cup (2 ounces) confectioners' sugar, plus 1 to 2 tablespoons for serving

½ cup (2.1 ounces) all-purpose flour

Pinch of salt

1½ cups half-and-half

½ teaspoon vanilla extract or pure almond extract

TOOLS:

Large bowl

Whisk

Dry measuring cups

Liquid measuring cup

Measuring spoons

9-inch pie plate

Fine-mesh sieve

Wire cooling rack

❶ Preheat the oven to 325°F. Using your fingers or a piece of plastic wrap, lightly coat a 9-inch pie plate with a thin film of butter. Spread the cherries evenly in the pie dish.

❷ Separate 3 of the eggs, placing the yolks in a large bowl (put the whites in a small bowl, cover, and refrigerate for another use—scramble them for breakfast tomorrow). Break the fourth egg and put the whole thing (not the shells, of course) in the bowl with the yolks. Add ½ cup confectioners' sugar, flour, and salt and whisk to combine. Pour in the half-and-half and vanilla, and whisk until well mixed (there should be no lumps).

❸ Carefully pour the egg mixture over the cherries in the pie plate. The cherries will float and move around a bit—this is fine, but redistribute them if they gather too much on one side.

❹ Carefully set the pie plate on the middle rack of the oven and bake for 45 to 50 minutes, until the clafouti is lightly puffed and set and no longer looks wet. (Check it after 45 minutes. If the clafouti is still liquid in the center when you gently wobble the pie plate, give it another 5 minutes.) Remove the clafouti to a wire rack to cool for at least 10 to 15 minutes (or let it sit longer and serve it at room temperature, if you like).

❺ Using a fine-mesh sieve, sift 1 to 2 tablespoons confectioners' sugar evenly over the clafouti. Slice and serve.

Good to know! Cherries are traditional in clafouti, and they look particularly pretty surrounded by the creamy custard. But you can use just about any fruit—raisins, plums, raspberries, blueberries, peaches. Frozen fruit is especially convenient—no peeling, pitting, or other prep work.

Vanilla or almond extract is easy, but if you have a sweet liqueur around—kirsch or cassis, for example—by all means, use that instead (add a tablespoon or two and bake as the recipe directs).

A glass pie plate is ideal for this dessert. It allows for the most even baking, and it makes a pretty presentation.

Cherry Clafouti

CHERRY-BERRY STOVETOP COBBLER

Prep time: 25 minutes ⏱ Cooking time: 32 minutes ✋ Serves 4 to 6

Fruit desserts have some seriously funny names—aside from the well-known cobblers, crisps, and crumbles, there are grunts, slumps, and pandowdies. Technically this dessert is a slump, because it's a cobbler cooked on the stove instead of in the oven, but I'm sure you'll understand why I declined to call it that.

INGREDIENTS:

Dumplings:

1½ cups (6.4 ounces) all-purpose flour

⅓ cup (2.3 ounces), plus 1 tablespoon sugar

1½ teaspoons baking powder

¼ teaspoon salt

¾ cup half-and-half

3 tablespoons unsalted butter, melted and cooled slightly

½ teaspoon cinnamon

Filling:

¼ cup (1.75 ounces) sugar

1 tablespoon, plus 1½ teaspoons cornstarch

Pinch of salt

½ cup juice (such as orange, berry, or pomegranate)

4 cups sweet cherries, pitted (if frozen, thaw and drain before measuring)

5 cups mixed berries, such as raspberries, blueberries, and blackberries

Ice cream or whipped cream (optional)

TOOLS:

Dry measuring cups

Measuring spoons

Liquid measuring cup

2 medium bowls

Whisk

Fork

Flexible spatula

Small bowl

Large skillet

Teaspoon

2 tablespoons

❶ Make the dumpling batter: In a medium bowl, combine the flour, ⅓ cup sugar, the baking powder, and salt; whisk to mix well. In another medium bowl, whisk together the half-and-half and melted butter.

❷ Pour the half-and-half mixture into the flour mixture and stir them together with a flexible spatula just until all the ingredients are incorporated. Scrape down the bottom of the bowl and turn the spatula over to make sure all of the dry ingredients are incorporated. In a small bowl, mix the remaining 1 tablespoon sugar with cinnamon; stir with a fork to combine.

❸ Make the filling: Combine ¼ cup sugar, the cornstarch, and the salt in a large skillet; whisk until no lumps remain. Add the juice and whisk to mix everything together. Add the cherries and berries and stir with a clean flexible spatula. Place on the stove over medium heat and cook, stirring often, for about 7 minutes, until the mixture begins to bubble and thicken.

❹ Using two tablespoons, drop heaping spoonfuls of dumpling batter over the fruit (it's okay if they touch or overlap a bit). Using a teaspoon, sprinkle the dumplings with the cinnamon-sugar. Reduce the heat on the stove to low, cover the skillet (use foil if your skillet doesn't have a lid), and let the cobbler simmer until the dumplings are cooked through and the liquid around the fruit has thickened, about 20 minutes (the dumplings may be a bit sticky, but they should feel firm to the touch). Uncover the cobbler and cook 5 minutes longer, until the dumplings spring back lightly when pressed gently with your fingers. Remove the cobbler from the heat and let cool for 5 to 10 minutes.

❺ Serve warm, with ice cream or whipped cream.

Cherry-Berry Stovetop Cobbler

"NEW WAVE" LEMON MERINGUE PIE

Prep time: 1 hour 20 minutes ⏱ Baking time: 15 to 18 minutes (shortbread), 1 hour, 45 minutes (meringues)

⏱ Chilling time: 2 hours ✋ Serves 6

My husband and I created this dessert one Thanksgiving in honor of my father-in-law, Steve, who loves lemon meringue pie. You don't have to make all the elements—you can make just one or two, and buy the others. If you end up with extra meringues and shortbread, serve them on the side.

INGREDIENTS:

Shortbread:

8 tablespoons (1 stick) unsalted butter, at room temperature

1/3 cup (2.3 ounces) sugar

1 teaspoon vanilla extract

1 cup (4.25 ounces) all-purpose flour

1/4 teaspoon salt

Lemon curd:

6 large egg yolks (place 2 of the whites in a separate bowl, cover and refrigerate—you'll need them for the meringues)

2/3 cup (4.7 ounces) sugar

1 tablespoon grated lemon zest (from 2 lemons)

1/2 cup fresh lemon juice (from about 3 to 4 lemons)

4 tablespoons (1/2 stick) unsalted butter, at room temperature, cut into 8 pieces

1/8 teaspoon salt

Meringues:

2 large egg whites

1/2 cup (3.5 ounces) sugar

❶ Make the shortbread: Preheat the oven to 375°F. Using a wooden spoon or flexible spatula, mix together the butter, sugar, and vanilla. Add the flour and salt, and mix until a soft dough forms. Using your fingers, press the dough into a 9-inch square baking pan.

❷ Prick the dough all over with a fork. Using a sharp paring knife, cut the dough into 8 pieces, but take care not to cut all the way through the dough (this is called "scoring").

❸ Bake the shortbread 15 to 18 minutes, until the edges are light golden. Remove the pan to a wire rack to cool for 10 minutes, then cut along the lines you scored before baking. Use a small offset spatula to lift out the shortbread and place them on the wire rack to cool completely. (You can make this up to 1 day ahead; store in an airtight container at room temperature.)

❹ Make the lemon curd: Fill a saucepan with about 1 inch of hot tap water, place it on the stove over medium-low heat, and let it come to a simmer (steaming but not quite boiling), then reduce the heat to low. In a metal bowl that will fit on top of the saucepan, whisk together the yolks, sugar, and zest, then whisk in the lemon juice.

❺ Place the bowl over the pan and whisk well. Add the butter a few pieces at a time and the salt, whisking well. Cook, whisking constantly, until the mixture thickens, about 12 to 15 minutes—don't let it boil. Pour the mixture through a fine-mesh sieve into a medium bowl. Cover with plastic wrap, pressing the plastic directly onto the curd, and refrigerate until cold, at least 2 hours. (You can make this up to 2 days ahead; keep covered and refrigerated.)

❻ Make the meringues: Preheat the oven to 200°F. Line a baking sheet with parchment paper.

❼ In a large bowl, using an electric mixer, beat the egg whites until they get very foamy. With the beaters going, add the sugar, 1 tablespoon at a time, until the meringue looks glossy and holds stiff peaks. Use a teaspoon to spoon out globs of meringue and plop them on the baking sheet about ½ to 1 inch apart (they won't spread).

❽ Bake for 45 minutes, then turn the oven off and leave the meringues inside for another 60 minutes. Remove them from the oven. Carefully remove the meringues from the parchment and place them on a wire rack to cool completely. (These are best eaten the day they're made.)

❾ Assemble the dessert: Spoon the lemon curd into six small bowls. Top each with a meringue or two and stick a shortbread into one side of each bowl. Serve with spoons.

(See photo, page 88)

TOOLS:
(for the shortbread)
Wooden spoon or flexible spatula
Medium bowl
9-inch square baking pan
Fork
Paring knife
Small offset spatula
Wire cooling rack
(for the lemon curd)
Saucepan
2 metal bowls (1 must be metal)
Whisk
Fine-mesh sieve
Liquid measuring cup
Measuring spoons
Rasp grater
Dry measuring cups
(for the meringues)
Baking sheet
Large bowl
Electric mixer
Measuring spoons
Teaspoon
Wire cooling rack

DRUNKEN PEARS STUFFED WITH COOKIE CRUMBLE

Prep time: 30 minutes 🕐 Baking time: 25 to 30 minutes 🖐 Serves 4

If you like poached pears, you'll love this dessert, in which the pears are basically poached in the oven. The cookie crumb mixture in the core of each pear half is reminiscent of the topping on a fruit crisp. These are perfect for an autumn dinner party.

INGREDIENTS:

4 Bosc pears, ripe but not mushy
1 cup red wine
3 tablespoons sugar
4 to 6 homemade or store-bought
   gingersnaps, crushed
2 tablespoons finely chopped walnuts
2 tablespoons unsalted butter, melted
2 teaspoons honey
Vanilla ice cream or whipped cream
   (optional)

TOOLS:

Measuring spoons
Liquid measuring cup
Vegetable peeler
Chef's knife
Melon baller or spoon
Paring knife
Whisk
Medium bowl
Fork
Spoon
9 x 13-inch baking dish
Wire cooling rack

Opposite page: Baked Apple and Drunken Pears Stuffed with Cookie Crumble

❶ Preheat the oven to 400°F. Using a vegetable peeler, peel the pears. Slice them in half lengthwise using a sharp chef's knife. Using a melon baller or spoon, scoop out the cores. Using a sharp paring knife, trim off the base of each pear half and gently cut out the stem. Cut a very thin slice off the rounded edge of each pear half, so they lie flat when placed round-side down.

❷ Pour the wine into a 9 x 13-inch baking dish. Whisk in the sugar until dissolved. Place the pears in the pan with the wine mixture (for now, set them so that the flat sides are face-down). Bake 15 minutes. Halfway through the baking time, baste the pears by spooning the wine mixture over them.

❸ Meanwhile, in a medium bowl, mix the crushed cookies and nuts together with a fork. Pour in the melted butter and honey, and stir with a fork until the nuts and cookie crumbs are completely moistened (add another ½ teaspoon honey if it seems dry).

❹ Pull the baking dish out of the oven and close the oven door (but leave it on). Using a spoon, carefully turn over the pears so that the cores are facing up. Using the melon baller, fill each pear core with the cookie mixture, mounding it slightly. Baste the pears with the wine (which should now have a more syrupy consistency than it did when you started).

❺ Bake the pears for another 10 to 15 minutes, until the filling is golden brown. Remove the pan from the oven and let cool on a wire rack for about 10 minutes. Place 2 pear halves on each plate and spoon some wine syrup over. Serve warm with vanilla ice cream or whipped cream, if desired.

Good to know! You can swap in another type of cookie for the gingersnaps. Pepperidge Farm Bordeaux cookies work well, or crisp oatmeal cookies (the kind without raisins).

Try chopped hazelnuts instead of walnuts.

If you find yourself with extra cookie crumbs, throw them into a zip-top plastic bag and freeze them. You can sprinkle them on top of ice cream for a treat.

You Made That Dessert?

WINE-POACHED PEACHES

Prep time: 10 minutes ⏲ Cooking time: 35 to 40 minutes ⏲ Cooling time: 20 minutes ✋ Serves 4

I'm all for rich, decadent desserts—but sometimes, especially in the summer, what you want is something light and not too sweet. This recipe is just right for those moments. It's simple, sophisticated, and you can make it ahead, so it's truly no fuss.

INGREDIENTS:

4 peaches, firm but ripe
1 bottle (750ml) rosé wine
¾ cup water
¾ cup (5.25 ounces) sugar
2 teaspoons lemon juice
Pinch of salt

TOOLS:

Paring knife
Dry measuring cups
Liquid measuring cup
Measuring spoons
Melon baller
Large pot
Whisk or flexible spatula
Spoon
Large bowl

❶ Using a sharp paring knife, cut the peaches in half. Use a melon baller to scoop out the pits.

❷ In a large pot, combine the wine, water, sugar, lemon juice, and salt. Warm over medium heat until just beginning to boil, stirring with a whisk or flexible spatula until the sugar dissolves. Reduce the heat to medium-low. Add the peaches and cook over low heat until tender, about 10 to 15 minutes (how long it takes will depend on how ripe the peaches are). Every 3 or 4 minutes, turn the peaches over with a spoon. Test the peaches by gently poking them with the tip of your paring knife—the knife should pierce the peaches easily. Remove the peaches with a spoon and place them in a large bowl or on a plate.

❸ Increase the heat to high and boil the wine mixture until it's thickened into a syrup consistency and reduced by half, about 20 to 25 minutes.

❹ Meanwhile, when the peaches are cool enough to handle, slip off the skins (they should come off easily in your fingers). Discard the skins.

❺ When the wine mixture has reduced, take the pot off the stove and pour the syrup into a large bowl. Let it cool to room temperature, stirring occasionally with a spoon or flexible spatula. Serve the peach halves with the syrup spooned on top. Or you can add the cooled syrup to the bowl with the peaches, cover, and refrigerate to serve chilled later.

(See photo, page 127)

Good to know! You can serve these peaches in their syrup on their own, or with a dollop of crème fraîche. A few small store-bought butter cookies would go nicely, too.

From top: Sweet Potato Pie with Streusel Topping and Maple Walnut Pie

You Made That Dessert?

CANDIES

HONEYED FUDGE 151

PEANUT-BUTTERSCOTCH BITES 152

CHOCOLATE RUM BALLS 154

MINT CHOCOLATE TRUFFLES 156

PUMPKIN-CHOCOLATE TRUFFLES 157

HONEYED FUDGE

Prep time: 5 minutes ⏲ Cooking time: 10 minutes ⏲ Chill: 6 hours ✋ Makes 30 pieces

There are two kinds of fudge recipes—those that "cheat" by using condensed milk or marshmallows, and the more traditional ones in which you have to use a candy thermometer. This one is a "cheat." But I've used both methods, and I think this way yields a result every bit as good as the trickier way, so why make it harder than it has to be?

INGREDIENTS:

Cooking spray
8 ounces semisweet chocolate
8 ounces bittersweet chocolate
¼ cup honey
1 can (14 ounces) sweetened condensed milk
1 teaspoon vanilla extract
¼ teaspoon salt
¾ cup chopped walnuts

TOOLS:

8-inch square baking pan
Cutting board
Chef's knife
Liquid measuring cup
Measuring spoons
Flexible spatula
Saucepan
Whisk
Wire cooling rack

❶ Line an 8-inch square pan with foil, leaving a 2-inch overhang on two sides. Mist it lightly with cooking spray.

❷ On a cutting board, using a sharp chef's knife, chop both chocolates into very small pieces. It's okay to mix them. (See page 187 to learn more about chopping chocolate.) Set the chocolate aside.

❸ In a saucepan, mix the honey, condensed milk, vanilla, and salt. Cook over medium-low heat, stirring constantly with a whisk, until mixture boils. Be very careful, as the honey and condensed milk can scorch if you don't keep stirring. Reduce the heat to the lowest it will go and simmer for 2 minutes, stirring often.

❹ Remove the pan from the heat and add the chopped chocolate. Let it sit for 1 minute, then stir with a whisk or flexible spatula until the chocolate has melted and the mixture is smooth (if all the chocolate doesn't melt, place the pan back over the lowest heat setting your stove has and cook, stirring constantly, until the mixture is completely smooth). Add the walnuts, stirring well. Pour the mixture into the prepared pan, using your spatula to spread it evenly. Let the fudge cool to room temperature on a wire rack, then cover it with foil and refrigerate until cold and firm, about 6 hours.

❺ To cut, use the foil overhang to lift the fudge out of the pan. Place it on a cutting board. Use a sharp chef's knife to cut, running the blade under hot water and wiping it dry between each cut.

(See photo, page 153)

Good to know! You can vary this recipe depending on your tastes, changing the nuts or playing with the ratio of semisweet to bittersweet chocolate.

For a pretty holiday gift, omit the nuts and stir in ½ cup crushed candy canes (crush them coarsely in a blender or food processor). Sprinkle some extra crushed peppermint candy on top for a festive look.

PEANUT-BUTTERSCOTCH BITES

Prep time: 15 minutes ⏱ Chilling time: 1 hour 🖐 Makes 35

Someone gave me these as a secret Santa gift when I was in college. Once I tried one, I couldn't stop eating them! I asked my Santa for the recipe, and I've been making these ever since, with lots of different variations. I've changed the type of chips, the cereal—the choices are endless. But this version is close to the original one I had all those years ago, and it's still my favorite.

INGREDIENTS:

3 cups cornflakes
1 11-ounce bag butterscotch chips
¾ cup peanut butter, crunchy or creamy
2 teaspoon vanilla extract

TOOLS:

Baking sheet
Rolling pin or skillet
Measuring spoons
Dry measuring cups
Large metal bowl
Saucepan
Flexible spatula
Small ice cream scoop or two teaspoons

❶ Line a rimmed baking sheet with parchment paper. Place the cornflakes in a large ziplock bag; seal the bag. Crush the cornflakes by beating the bag with a rolling pin or the bottom of a heavy skillet. Turn the bag over a few times to crush all the cornflakes.

❷ In a large metal bowl set over a saucepan of simmering water, combine the butterscotch chips and peanut butter. Allow them to melt, stirring occasionally with a flexible spatula (this will take about 5 to 7 minutes). When melted and smooth (except for the chopped peanuts if you're using crunchy peanut butter), remove the bowl from the heat. Add the vanilla and the crushed cornflakes and stir well, until all the ingredients are combined.

❸ Use a small ice cream scoop or two teaspoons to portion the bites and place them on the baking sheet. You can place them right next to each other; they won't expand or run. When all of the bites are portioned, place the sheet in the refrigerator and chill until firm, about 1 hour. Store them in an airtight container in the refrigerator. If you stack them, place a sheet of parchment or waxed paper between each layer.

Honeyed Fudge, Cranberry Cornmeal Cookies, and Peanut-Butterscotch Bites

CHOCOLATE RUM BALLS

Prep time: 1 hour ⏱ Chilling time: 30 to 60 minutes 🖐 Makes 36

I remember loving boozy chocolate rum balls even as a kid, and trying to pick them out among trays of sweets at family parties. Make these and wrap them in a pretty tin as a holiday gift.

INGREDIENTS:

23 Oreo cookies

½ cup (2 ounces) confectioners' sugar

2 tablespoons unsweetened cocoa powder

1 cup chopped walnuts or pecans

$1/8$ teaspoon salt

3 tablespoons honey

$1/3$ cup rum

Chocolate sprinkles

TOOLS:

Food processor (see "Good to know!" below)

Dry measuring cups

Liquid measuring cup

Medium bowl

Shallow bowl

Measuring spoons

Small ice cream scoop or melon baller

❶ In the bowl of a food processor fitted with a metal blade, combine the Oreos, confectioners' sugar, cocoa powder, chopped nuts, and salt. Turn the machine on and off quickly several times (this is called "pulsing"), until all of the ingredients are finely ground and well mixed. Add the honey and rum and pulse again until everything is blended together. Transfer the mixture to a medium bowl, cover with plastic wrap, and refrigerate for 30 to 60 minutes.

❷ Place the chocolate sprinkles in a shallow bowl. Use a small ice cream scoop or the larger end of a melon baller to divide the chilled chocolate dough into approximately 1-inch blobs, then roll each one between your palms to finish forming them into balls. (If the dough feels sticky, lightly moisten your hands with water as needed--that will keep the dough from sticking to your palms.) Roll each ball in chocolate sprinkles until lightly coated. Place the balls in a single layer in airtight containers in the refrigerator for 1 day to let the flavors develop.

Good to know! If you don't have a food processor, you can still make this recipe. To crush the Oreos, place them in a large ziplock bag and tightly seal the bag. Slam the bag with the bottom of a skillet, a rolling pin, a meat mallet, or any other heavy object until the cookies are crushed. Flip the bag over a few times to make sure all the cookies are finely crushed. Chop the nuts as finely as you can with a sharp chef's knife. Place the cookie crumbs and nuts in a medium bowl and stir in the confectioners' sugar, salt, honey, and rum with a wooden spoon or flexible spatula.

I used a small ice cream scoop for these and got 36. If you use the large end of a melon baller, the balls will turn out smaller and you'll get more of them (around 45). Use whichever one you like (or have handy).

From left: Mint Chocolate Truffles, Pumpkin-Chocolate Truffles, and Chocolate Rum Balls

MINT CHOCOLATE TRUFFLES

Prep time: 30 minutes ⊙ Chilling time: 4 hours ♨ Makes 50

I absolutely love to make truffles and give them as gifts or serve them after dinner, and you will too —they're yet another item that people think are so impressive, but are actually incredibly easy to make. Don't care for mint? Leave it out and stir in a teaspoon or two of vanilla extract instead. Roll the truffles in unsweetened cocoa powder or finely chopped nuts instead of the ground cookies.

INGREDIENTS:

1 pound semisweet chocolate
1½ cups heavy cream
6 tablespoons unsalted butter, at room temperature, cut into 6 pieces
Pinch of salt
1 tablespoon peppermint extract
1 7-ounce package Mint Milano cookies
2 tablespoons unsweetened cocoa powder

TOOLS:

Cutting board
Chef's knife
Saucepan
Liquid measuring cup
Flexible spatula or whisk
Measuring spoons
Large bowl
Small bowl
Food processor
Small ice cream scoop or teaspoon
Baking sheet

Good to know! When shopping for the extract, be sure to get peppermint. Sometimes extract labeled "mint" is spearmint, which, needless to say, would not make for good truffles.

❶ On a cutting board, using a sharp chef's knife, chop the chocolate (see page 187 for more on how to do this).

❷ In a saucepan, warm the cream to a simmer over medium heat, but don't quite let it boil (you should begin to see steam, and the top of the cream will form a light skin). Remove the saucepan from the heat and add the chopped chocolate, stirring with a flexible spatula or whisk until the chocolate has melted and the mixture is smooth. Add the butter, one piece at a time, stirring until it's melted and smooth. Stir in the salt and peppermint extract and mix well.

❸ Pour the chocolate mixture into a large bowl and cover the mixture with plastic wrap, lightly pressing the plastic directly onto the surface of the chocolate mixture. Refrigerate it for at least 4 hours, or overnight.

❹ Place all of the cookies and the cocoa in a food processor and process until finely ground. Transfer the crumbs to a small bowl. Line a baking sheet with parchment or foil.

❺ Uncover the chocolate mixture. Using a small ice cream scoop or a teaspoon, spoon out a bit of the chocolate mixture and form a ball in your hands (the ball should be about 1 inch in diameter, but don't worry about being exact). Repeat with the rest of the chocolate mixture, placing the balls on the baking sheet (you can place them right next to each other).

❻ When you have all the balls formed, toss each one, one at a time, in the cookie crumbs until each ball is lightly coated. Place them back on the baking sheet and refrigerate them until they're well chilled and firm, about 1 hour. Then transfer them to a plastic container with a tight-fitting lid (you may need a few containers). To stack the truffles, place a sheet of parchment or foil between each layer. Keep the truffles refrigerated.

(See photo, page 155)

PUMPKIN-CHOCOLATE TRUFFLES

Prep time: 40 minutes ⏱ Chilling time: 25 minutes ✋ Makes 20 truffles

Pie, cake, cookies—I've never met a pumpkin dessert I didn't love. Combine it with chocolate, and it's pure heaven. These truffles, with pumpkin and pumpkin pie spice in them, are a great fall treat.

INGREDIENTS:

20–24 gingersnaps (depending on size)
4 ounces semisweet chocolate
1 tablespoon unsalted butter
½ cup (2 ounces) confectioners' sugar
2 teaspoons pumpkin pie spice
Pinch of salt
¼ cup canned pumpkin puree

TOOLS:

Food processor (see "Good to know!"
    below)
Baking sheet
Cutting board
Chef's knife
Saucepan
Dry measuring cups
Measuring spoons
Flexible spatula
Large bowl
Medium bowl
Small bowl
Small ice cream scoop or two teaspoons

❶ Place the gingersnaps in the bowl of a food processor and turn the machine on and off quickly until the cookies are crushed (this is called "pulsing"). Transfer the crushed cookies to a medium bowl. You should have 1½ cups of gingersnap crumbs.

❷ Line a baking sheet with foil or parchment. On a cutting board, using a sharp chef's knife, chop the chocolate (see page 187 for more on how to chop chocolate). Place it in a saucepan with the butter and put it on the stove over the lowest heat setting. Warm the mixture, stirring constantly with a flexible spatula, until the chocolate and butter have just melted. Remove from the heat and scrape the mixture into a large bowl.

❸ Add ¾ cup gingersnap crumbs, the confectioner's sugar, pumpkin pie spice, salt, and pumpkin to the bowl, and stir with the flexible spatula until all the ingredients are well combined. Refrigerate the mixture for 10 minutes.

❹ Use an ice cream scoop or two teaspoons to form the truffles into 1-inch lumps. Roll the lumps between your palms to form balls. Refrigerate for another 15 minutes. Place the remaining ¾ cup gingersnaps in a small bowl. When you have formed all the balls, place them, one at a time, in the bowl of gingersnap crumbs. Toss each ball until it's coated, then place it on the lined baking sheet. (You can place them right next to each other.)

❺ When all the balls are coated, serve them, or place them in an airtight container in the refrigerator for up to 2 days. (If you layer them in a container, place a sheet of parchment or foil between each layer.)

(See photo, page 155)

Good to know! You can make the crumbs without a food processor. Place the cookies in a large ziplock bag, seal the bag tightly, and beat the cookies with a rolling pin or skillet until the cookies are crushed. Turn the bag over a few times so that you crush all of the cookies.

Sauces and Frostings

HOT FUDGE SAUCE 159

CARAMEL SAUCE 160

RASPBERRY SAUCE 162

BOOZY BUTTERSCOTCH SAUCE 164

BRANDIED CHERRIES 165

CRÈME ANGLAISE 166

CHOCOLATE FROSTING 167

CREAM CHEESE FROSTING 168

RICH CARAMEL FROSTING 169

GINGER-BOURBON PEACH SAUCE 170

HOT FUDGE SAUCE

Prep time: 15 minutes ⏱ Cooking time: 8 minutes ✋ Makes 2 cups

Who doesn't love a hot fudge sundae? Even just a scoop of vanilla ice cream doused with good hot fudge is so satisfying. Honey and a tiny bit of instant espresso powder give this sauce a nice depth. Enjoy it at home, or pour it into a pretty jar, label it, and give it as a hostess gift.

INGREDIENTS:

6 ounces semisweet chocolate

⅔ cup heavy cream

½ cup honey

¼ cup (2.1 ounces) packed dark brown sugar

¼ cup (0.73 ounce) unsweetened cocoa powder, sifted

¼ teaspoon salt

½ teaspoon instant espresso powder, or instant coffee granules

1½ teaspoons vanilla extract

2 tablespoons unsalted butter, at room temperature

TOOLS:

Dry measuring cups

Liquid measuring cup

Measuring spoons

Cutting board

Chef's knife

Saucepan

Flexible spatula

Small cup

Whisk

❶ On a cutting board, using a sharp chef's knife, chop the chocolate (see page 187 for more on how to do this).

❷ Place the cream, honey, brown sugar, cocoa, salt, and half of the chopped chocolate in a saucepan, set over medium heat, and cook, stirring with a flexible spatula, until the ingredients have melted together and the mixture begins to boil.

❸ Reduce the heat to low and let the mixture boil lightly for 5 minutes, stirring often. Dissolve the instant espresso in the vanilla extract in a small cup.

❹ Remove the chocolate mixture from the heat and stir in the remaining chopped chocolate, butter, and vanilla mixture. Stir with a whisk until melted and smooth. Let it cool slightly.

❺ Serve the sauce warm, or spoon it into a bowl, let it cool completely, cover, and refrigerate it to serve later. To rewarm it, place it in a saucepan over medium-low heat and stir until smooth.

(See photo, page 161)

CARAMEL SAUCE

Prep time: 5 minutes: ⏱ Cooking time: 13 to 14 minutes 🖐 Makes 1¾ cups

Caramel can be a little tricky—you want the sugar to melt and cook enough to get that caramel-y flavor, but if you cook it for too long, it can burn and get bitter. This is the simplest way I know of to make caramel sauce, and it's pretty foolproof. Just pay close attention to it, and you'll be fine. It's worth it! Homemade caramel sauce is worlds better than anything you'll get out of a squeeze bottle at the supermarket.

INGREDIENTS:

1½ cups (12.6 ounces) packed dark
    brown sugar
¾ cup heavy cream
8 tablespoons (1 stick) unsalted butter,
    at room temperature, cut into pieces
2 teaspoons vanilla extract
⅛ teaspoon salt

TOOLS:

Dry measuring cups
Liquid measuring cup
Measuring spoons
Saucepan
Whisk
Medium bowl

❶ Place the brown sugar, heavy cream, and butter in a saucepan. Cook over medium heat, whisking, until the butter is melted and the mixture is smooth and bubbling, about 5 minutes. Stop whisking and let the mixture bubble for 2 minutes. Turn the heat down to low and cook it 3 to 5 minutes longer, whisking occasionally.

❷ Remove the saucepan from the heat and whisk in the vanilla and salt (the mixture will bubble up a bit for a few seconds; that's okay). Pour the caramel sauce into a medium bowl. Gently press a sheet of plastic directly on the surface of the sauce (be very careful—the caramel will be extremely hot); set aside to cool.

❸ Serve the sauce warm, or refrigerate it for up to a week. Warm it in a saucepan over medium-low heat or in the microwave on low power before serving.

From top left: Ginger-Bourbon Peach Sauce, Boozy Butterscotch Sauce, Caramel Sauce, and Hot Fudge Sauce

RASPBERRY SAUCE

Prep time: 5 minutes ⏱ Cooking time: 10 to 12 minutes ✋ Makes 1½ cups

You don't have to wait for summer to enjoy this bright, sweet-tart sauce, because it's made with frozen berries. Be sure to buy unsweetened berries; the ones packed in syrup will be too sweet. Spoon this over Flourless Chocolate Cake (page 70), Creamy Vanilla Cheesecake (page 56), Molten Dark Chocolate Cakes (page 66), or Perfectly Simple Pound Cake (page 31).

INGREDIENTS:

½ cup (3.5 ounces) sugar
3 tablespoons lemon juice
1 tablespoon cornstarch
⅛ teaspoon salt
1 12-ounce bag frozen raspberries, thawed

TOOLS:

Dry measuring cups
Measuring spoons
Saucepan
Whisk
Wooden spoon
Flexible spatula
Medium bowl

❶ In a saucepan, combine the sugar, lemon juice, cornstarch, and salt; whisk until well mixed and there are no lumps of cornstarch. Using a wooden spoon or flexible spatula, stir in the raspberries and any liquid that has accumulated in the bag. The mixture will look a bit cloudy from the cornstarch.

❷ Place the pan over medium-low heat and cook, stirring gently, but constantly, with a flexible spatula, until the sauce begins to thicken and become clearer, and lightly bubbles, about 8 to 10 minutes. Reduce the heat to the lowest it will go, stop stirring, and let the sauce bubble for about 1½ minutes, then stir again.

❸ Remove the pan from the heat, pour the sauce into a medium bowl, and cover it with plastic wrap, pressing it directly onto the surface of the sauce, taking care to cover the whole surface. Serve the sauce warm, or let it cool to room temperature and refrigerate for up to 4 days. To reheat, warm the sauce gently in a saucepan over medium-low heat.

Good to know! I like this sauce with little bits of raspberry in it, but if you would prefer a smooth, seedless texture, run it through a fine-mesh sieve while the sauce is still hot. Place the sieve over a medium bowl, pour the sauce into it, and stir with a whisk or flexible spatula to force it through the mesh, getting as much liquid through as possible. Discard the remaining seeds and solids.

Creamy Vanilla Cheesecake with
Raspberry Sauce

BOOZY BUTTERSCOTCH SAUCE

Prep time: 10 minutes ⏱ Cooking time: 10 minutes 🖐 Makes 1¾ cups

This is a fun sauce to serve with ice cream or cake. If you prefer a more traditional butterscotch flavor (or you're serving this to kids), omit the scotch and add another teaspoon of vanilla extract.

INGREDIENTS:

⅔ cup (5.6 ounces) packed dark brown
    sugar
3 tablespoons all-purpose flour
¼ teaspoon salt
4 tablespoons (½ stick) unsalted butter
1 cup half-and-half
2 tablespoons scotch
2 teaspoons vanilla extract

TOOLS:

Small bowl
Dry measuring cups
Measuring spoons
Liquid measuring cup
Fork
Saucepan
Whisk
Medium bowl

❶ In a small bowl, combine the brown sugar, flour, and salt; stir with a fork to combine.

❷ Melt the butter in a saucepan over medium heat. Whisk the flour-sugar mixture into the melted butter until all of the ingredients are moistened. Whisk in the half-and-half, then cook, whisking often, for about 8 minutes, or until the sauce thickens, bubbles, and becomes smooth. Remove the sauce from the heat and whisk in the scotch and vanilla.

❸ Pour the sauce into a medium bowl and cover it with plastic wrap, gently pressing so that the plastic touches the surface of the sauce. Let the sauce cool to room temperature before refrigerating. (The sauce will firm up as it cools, but will thin again as it's reheated.)

(See photo, page 161)

Good to know! This sauce will keep for up to a week. If you've refrigerated it and then want to serve it warm, microwave it on low power or spoon it into a saucepan and gently warm it over medium-low heat, stirring frequently.

BRANDIED CHERRIES

Prep time: 10 minutes ⏲ Cooking time: 10 to 12 minutes ✋ Makes 1¾ cups

Try this spooned over ice cream, or over Flourless Chocolate Cake
(page 70) or Yogurt Panna Cotta (page 89). Or, put it in a Mason jar,
write a pretty label, and give as a hostess gift.

INGREDIENTS:

½ cup (3.5 ounces) sugar

½ cup brandy

2 tablespoons cornstarch

2 tablespoons freshly squeezed lemon
    juice (from 1 lemon)

⅛ teaspoon salt

1 12-ounce bag frozen sweet cherries,
    thawed

TOOLS:

Dry measuring cups

Measuring spoons

Liquid measuring cup

Saucepan

Whisk

Flexible spatula

Medium bowl

❶ In a saucepan, whisk together the sugar, brandy, cornstarch, lemon juice, and salt until the mixture is smooth and no lumps of cornstarch remain. Place over medium-low heat and cook, whisking, until the mixture is warm, about 2 minutes.

❷ Add the cherries and any liquid that's accumulated in the bag and cook the sauce, stirring often with a flexible spatula, for about 6 to 8 minutes, until it begins to thicken and bubble. (The sauce will start off with a cloudy appearance from the cornstarch and will become a darker, clearer red as it thickens and bubbles.)

❸ Stop stirring, reduce the heat to as low as it will go, and let the sauce simmer for 2 minutes. Stir it again, then remove the pan from the heat and pour the sauce into a medium bowl. Press a piece of plastic wrap gently on top of the sauce so that the plastic touches the whole surface. Set the bowl aside to let cool.

(See photo, page 67)

Good to know! This sauce can be served warm or cold. It can be refrigerated for up to 4 days. To reheat it, place it in a saucepan over medium-low heat and stir it to gently warm it through.

CRÈME ANGLAISE

Prep time: 10 minutes: ⏱ Cooking time: 8 to 10 minutes ✋ Makes 2 cups

This classic vanilla sauce tastes delicate and light. Don't be intimidated by the number of steps—it's really easy to make. It's delicious with so many different desserts, even just spooned over fresh berries. For a real treat, try it with Flourless Chocolate Cake (page 70) and fresh raspberries.

INGREDIENTS:
1½ cups half-and-half
⅓ cup (2.3 ounces) sugar
5 large egg yolks
Pinch of salt
1 tablespoon vanilla extract

TOOLS:
Liquid measuring cup
Dry measuring cups
Measuring spoons
Saucepan
Flexible spatula
Whisk
Medium bowl
Wooden spoon
Dish towel

❶ In a saucepan, warm the half-and-half over medium-low heat until just about to boil (you should see a bit of steam coming off it, but no large bubbles).

❷ While the half-and-half is heating, combine the sugar, egg yolks, and salt in a medium bowl and whisk until the mixture is pale yellow and slightly thickened, about 2 minutes.

❸ Take the pan with the half-and-half off the stove. While vigorously whisking the yolks with one hand, with the other hand pour a small amount of the hot half-and-half in a slow, steady stream into the yolk mixture. Keep whisking and pour slowly—this will allow the yolks to mix with the half-and-half without turning into scrambled eggs. (Place a damp dish towel under your bowl to hold it steady while you're whisking and pouring.)

❹ When you have the half-and-half fully incorporated with the yolk mixture, pour the mixture back into the saucepan (use a flexible spatula to scrape all of it out of the bowl). Place the pan back on the stove over medium-low heat and cook, stirring gently with the whisk, until the mixture has thickened and is just about to boil (don't let it boil, or it will curdle), about 4 to 6 minutes. To make sure it's done, stick a wooden spoon into the mixture, then pull it out. Run your finger down the middle of the back of the spoon—the path that your finger created should hold its shape.

❺ Pour the sauce into a bowl and stir in the vanilla extract. If you see tiny lumps in the sauce, whisk it vigorously or pour it into a food processor and process it for a few seconds until smooth. Let the sauce cool, stirring occasionally, then cover and refrigerate.

(See photo, page 73)

CHOCOLATE FROSTING

Prep time: 20 minutes ⏲ Cooking time: 5 minutes 🖐 Makes 2 1/2 cups

Try this yummy fudge frosting on Chocolate–Chocolate Chip Cupcakes (page 45), Orange Cream Cupcakes (page 42), or Banana Snack Cake (page 78). Or on a spoon . . .

INGREDIENTS:

6 ounces semisweet chocolate

8 tablespoons (1 stick) unsalted butter, softened

3¼ cups (13 ounces) confectioners' sugar

¾ cup (2.2 ounces) unsweetened cocoa powder

¼ teaspoon salt

2 teaspoons instant espresso powder

2 teaspoons vanilla extract

½ cup half-and-half, slightly warmed

TOOLS:

Cutting board

Chef's knife

Dry measuring cups

Measuring spoons

Liquid measuring cup

Saucepan

Flexible spatula

Fine-mesh sieve

Large bowl

Medium bowl

Small cup

Electric mixer

❶ On a cutting board, using a sharp chef's knife, chop the chocolate (see page 187 for more on how to do this). Place the chopped chocolate in a saucepan. On the same cutting board, cut the butter into 10 pieces and add to the saucepan. Place the pan on the stove over the very lowest heat setting to melt the chocolate and butter, about 7 minutes; stir very often with a flexible spatula to help the mixture melt and to prevent scorching. When the mixture is smooth, remove the pan from the heat, pour the mixture into a medium bowl, and set it aside.

❷ Place a fine-mesh sieve over a large bowl. Put the confectioners' sugar and cocoa in the sieve, hold the sieve over the bowl, and lightly tap the sides of the sieve with your fingers to sift the sugar and cocoa into the bowl (this will remove any lumps). When you get to the end of the mixture in the sieve, if there is a small pile left that won't go through the sieve, run the back of a spoon over the mixture to force it through. Add the salt. Dissolve the espresso powder in the vanilla in a small cup and add it to the bowl. Pour in the half-and-half, then scrape the chocolate mixture into the bowl.

❸ Beat the mixture with an electric mixer until it's smooth and thick, about 5 minutes. If it's too thick, add more half-and-half, a teaspoon at a time. If it's too thin, add more confectioners' sugar, a teaspoon at a time, until it reaches a smooth consistency that spreads easily but holds its shape. Scrape down the sides of the bowl to make sure all the dry ingredients are incorporated.

(See photo, page 192)

CREAM CHEESE FROSTING

Prep time: 10 minutes ⏱ Makes 2 cups

I prefer cream cheese frosting to buttercream, both to make and to eat. Cream cheese frosting has that bit of tang to cut the sweetness, and it's so much simpler to make. Try it on Carrot Cupcakes (page 37), Orange Cream Cupcakes (page 42), Chocolate–Chocolate Chip Cupcakes (page 45), or Banana Snack Cake (page 78).

INGREDIENTS:

8 ounces cream cheese, at room temperature

8 tablespoons (1 stick) unsalted butter, at room temperature

1 cup (4 ounces) confectioners' sugar

2 teaspoons vanilla extract

1/8 teaspoon salt

TOOLS:

Dry measuring cups

Measuring spoons

Large bowl

Electric mixer

Flexible spatula

❶ In a large bowl with an electric mixer (or wooden spoon), beat the cream cheese and butter together on medium speed until they're mixed well and smooth. Turn off the mixer, add the sugar, and mix on low speed until the sugar is incorporated (a higher speed will make the sugar fly out all over the place). Add the vanilla extract and salt, turn up the speed to medium, and mix until smooth. Scrape down the sides and bottom of the bowl with a flexible spatula and beat again.

❷ Taste the frosting. I prefer it on the less-sweet side, but you might feel differently. If so, beat in more confectioners' sugar a teaspoon at a time until you get the flavor you want.

(See photo, page 192)

RICH CARAMEL FROSTING

Prep time: 5 minutes ⏱ Cooking time: 9 to 12 minutes 🖐 Makes 1 cup

Try this very sweet frosting with Banana Snack Cake (page 78). Spread it on as soon as you make it, or it will firm up too much and become hard to spread. It's the kind of frosting that forms a little sugary crust, so be ready for that.

INGREDIENTS:

1½ cups (11.5 ounces) packed light
    brown sugar
⅓ cup heavy cream
5 tablespoons unsalted butter, cut into
    10 pieces
⅛ teaspoon salt
1 teaspoon vanilla extract

TOOLS:

Dry measuring cups
Liquid measuring cup
Measuring spoons
Saucepan
Whisk
Large bowl
Electric mixer

❶ Combine the brown sugar, cream, butter, and salt in a saucepan. Place over medium heat and cook, whisking often, until the butter has melted, the sugar is fully moistened, and the ingredients are combined, about 2 minutes. Continue to cook, whisking more frequently, until the caramel reaches a full boil (that is, even when you whisk it, it still boils). Once it reaches the full boiling stage, let it boil for 1 to 2 minutes, whisking vigorously and constantly. Remove it from the heat and whisk in the vanilla. (Be careful: The caramel might spatter a bit, and it is extremely hot.)

❷ Pour the hot caramel into a large bowl and beat with an electric mixer on medium-high speed until cooled to lukewarm, and frosting has thickened to a spreading consistency and lightened in color, about 6 to 8 minutes. Use the frosting right away.

(See photo, page 79)

GINGER-BOURBON PEACH SAUCE

Prep time: 5 minutes ⏱ Cooking time: 12 minutes 🖐 Makes 2 cups

Try this spicy-sweet sauce with Perfectly Simple Pound Cake (page 31), Creamy Vanilla Cheesecake (see page 56), or spooned over butter-pecan ice cream.

INGREDIENTS:

1 15-ounce can sliced peaches, in heavy syrup
¼ cup (1.75 ounces) sugar
2 tablespoons finely chopped crystallized ginger
2 teaspoons ground ginger
1 tablespoon cornstarch (mixed with 1 tablespoon water)
Pinch of salt
¼ cup bourbon

TOOLS:

Dry measuring cups
Measuring spoons
Liquid measuring cup
Saucepan
Whisk
Flexible spatula
Blender or food processor
Medium bowl

❶ Drain the peaches, pouring the syrup into a saucepan. Add the sugar and both gingers, and whisk to combine. Bring the mixture to a boil over medium-high heat, whisking frequently.

❷ Cook the boiling mixture, whisking often, until the liquid has reduced by about half, about 6 minutes. Whisk in the cornstarch-water mixture. Add the peaches, bourbon, and salt, and cook, whisking, until the mixture is very thick and syrupy, about 2 to 4 minutes. Turn the heat down to the lowest it will go and let the sauce simmer for 1 minute.

❸ Pour the sauce into a blender or food processor and puree. Transfer the sauce to a medium bowl and cover with plastic wrap, carefully pressing the plastic wrap directly onto the surface of the sauce. Refrigerate until cool.

(See photo, page 161)

Good to know! This sauce will keep for up to a week, covered and refrigerated. It's best a day or two after it was made, when the flavors have had a chance to develop. To reheat it, microwave it on low power for 30 seconds, stir, and microwave again if not yet warm. Or pour it into a saucepan and warm it over medium-low heat, stirring, until warmed through.

EMERGENCY DESSERTS (DON'T PANIC!)

Okay, so you are having people over, or going to someone else's house, and you need a dessert—but you only have an hour. Don't panic! Here are some ideas for very-very-very-last-minute treats.

CHEESE PLATE

A cheese plate can be an elegant and sophisticated way to end a meal. Choose a few cheeses that vary in flavor and texture. I also like to select cheeses made from different kinds of milk—one goat cheese, one sheep's milk cheese, one cow's milk cheese, etc. Arrange each guest's plate so that the cheeses go from mildest to strongest, and offer some good crusty bread or crackers (stick to plainer varieties, so they don't interfere with the flavors in the cheeses). Something sweet on the plate, such as fresh or dried fruit, thin slices of quince paste (many cheese shops sell it), or honey, rounds out the flavor.

The best way to create a cheese plate is to go to a cheese shop that you trust and work with a manager or experienced salesperson. Give him or her as many details as possible about what else you're serving, what cheeses you like, etc., and taste the cheeses he or she recommends. Be sure to get serving tips as well (for example, if you need to let any of the cheeses come to room temperature before you serve them).

CHOCOLATE TASTING

This is an unconventional but conversation-sparking dessert. Buy a range of chocolates, from the mildest (white chocolate) to the darkest bittersweet you can find (don't get unsweetened; no one wants to taste that!). If you feel adventurous, throw in a few flavored varieties, such as Green & Black's Maya Gold (it has orange, cinnamon, nutmeg, and other spices) or Dagoba Lavender-Blueberry. Allow for a few small pieces of each variety for each person. Offer a few palate cleansers along with the chocolates—unsalted plain crackers, chunks of baguette, or sliced green apples all work well. Guide everyone through the different chocolates, beginning with the mildest and working your way up to the most bittersweet, and give everyone a chance to discuss each one before trying the next one.

ANGEL FOOD CAKE WITH MACERATED STRAWBERRIES

Remove the hulls from 4 cups of strawberries and slice the berries. Place them in a bowl with 2 tablespoons sugar, a small pinch of salt, and 2 tablespoons Grand Marnier or other orange liqueur, or balsamic vinegar. Mix with a spoon until all the ingredients are well combined. Let the mixture sit at room temperature for 30 minutes (stir it every 10 minutes)—the berries will get very juicy but not mushy.

When you're ready to serve, slice a store-bought angel-food cake and lightly toast the slices in a toaster oven. Spoon the berries and a little bit of their liquid on top and serve. (You can also top this with freshly whipped cream or a small dollop of store-bought crème fraîche.)

PAIN AU CHOCOLAT

Sounds fancy, right? To serve 4 people (you can scale this up or down if you're serving more or fewer people), buy 2 large croissants. Preheat the oven to 400°F. Slice the croissants in half lengthwise, as if you were going to use them to make sandwiches. Place them cut-side up on a baking sheet. Bake them until toasted, about 3 minutes. Spread each cut side with 1 to 2 tablespoons Nutella chocolate-hazelnut spread. Put the croissants back together, then cut them crosswise into quarters. Serve hot (each person gets 2 pieces).

Cheese Plate

SUNDAE PARTY

Make Hot Fudge and either Caramel Sauce or Raspberry Sauce (see pages 160 and 162 for the sauce recipes). Buy two or three ice cream flavors, maraschino cherries, and the smallest, most elegant-looking sugar cookies you can find at the supermarket. Make fresh, lightly sweetened whipped cream (see page 190). Toast chopped walnuts or coconut (see pages 59, 87, and 190). Place everything (except the ice cream) in pretty bowls and set them out on the table. Bring out the ice cream when ready to serve. Let everyone dress up his or her own sundae.

THE TOOLS

We've all seen the cooking shows where the chefs have a fancy gadget for everything, knives that cost hundreds of dollars each, and pans in every size and shape. But in reality, most of us have neither the budget nor the space for a Wolf stove or a chocolate fountain. And you don't need them. You can make a whole host of fantastic desserts with just a few basics, none of which have to cost a fortune.

So, what do you really need?

To make absolutely everything in this book, you need only the items in this chapter. Looking at the list of bowls, pans, tools, and utensils, it may seem like a lot at first, but don't worry! You probably have some of them already, and the others you can get in one trip to Bed Bath & Beyond or Target. I've also found some great deals online at Amazon.com and Cooking.com.

MUST HAVES:

Electric mixer (hand mixer) You don't need a fancy, expensive stand mixer—buy yourself a good, strong handheld mixer, preferably one with a few speeds. Cuisinart makes good ones, as does KitchenAid. In theory you can bake without a mixer, but I include it under "must-haves" because not having one can make baking a chore. It's not a big investment of money or space, and if you're going to bake more than once, it's really worth it. Of course, if you already have a stand mixer, here's your chance to use it!

Measuring cups Baking is precise, and measuring properly can mean the difference between a show-stopping dessert and a heart-stopping panic attack. So get yourself separate liquid and dry measuring cups—trust me, this tiny investment will make your baking life 100 percent easier and more successful. A 2-cup liquid measure with a spout should do the job for you (be sure it has a notch for ¼ cup), though a 4-cup is even better. For dry measures, get a set with graduating sizes from ¼ cup up to 1 cup. It doesn't matter if they're metal or plastic, as long as the tops are level. Avoid the fancy silicone ones—I find them difficult to use because the tops are sometimes not level, making precise measurement more difficult than it should be.

Measuring spoons   I prefer the metal ones, but plastic is fine too. Get real measuring spoons—don't use the spoons in your silverware drawer; it's harder to measure accurately with them. It's much easier to measure with proper measuring spoons, and that will help your desserts to come out better and be more consistent.

Knives   Good knives will last for years and make any cooking endeavor easier, so spend as much as you can on them. If your budget is tight, don't worry—even if you buy inexpensive knives, just keep them sharp, and they'll serve you well. The most important things about knives are how they feel in your hand (test a few out and see what feels most comfortable for you) and sharp blades. A dull knife will make your work in the kitchen much harder; plus it's dangerous to use a dull blade because you have far less control, so you can actually get cut very easily. High-carbon stainless-steel blades are best because they're resistant to discoloration and you can sharpen them over and over again, so they'll last longer. But if that type is too pricey, regular stainless-steel knives are very good too.

You can buy knives in sets in places like Sears, Macys, and Target. Here are the three you really need:

Chef's knife: Use this for chopping chocolate and nuts (and if you cook, for chopping vegetables).

Paring knife: This versatile tool lets you remove the hull (that is, the stem and the white core) from strawberries, loosen cakes from the sides of pans, slice apples, and more.

Serrated knife: Use this to slice bread and delicate cakes.

Mixing bowls   I recommend having at least three mixing bowls: small, medium, and large. Stainless steel is durable and won't break when you drop it (trust me, I know from personal experience). A stainless-steel bowl also can be used as a double boiler when placed over a saucepan, which is handy. A set of three stainless-steel bowls is versatile, and you can get one at a great price at stores like Bed Bath & Beyond or Target.

Of course, you can't put a stainless-steel bowl in the microwave, so if you don't have a medium-sized bowl that's microwave-safe (glass or ceramic), it's a good idea to get one of those, too. Many of the recipes in this book call for small bowls for mixing ingredients together such as flour and baking powder—for that, you can use any bowl in your cabinet (I often grab one of my cereal bowls).

Baking pans   Opt for simple baking pans made from heavy-gauge aluminized steel. Personally, I stay away from nonstick—a little cooking spray, butter, or the occasional sheet of parchment paper or foil will keep your goods from sticking. Nonstick bakeware is dark in color, and darker pans cause food to cook faster because they conduct heat more. The recipes in this book were not developed with dark pans, so if you use nonstick pans, your baking times and temperatures are likely to be different from mine. I also don't love silicone bakeware. I've had mixed results with silicone, and the quality among the different brands varies wildly. Cakes and pies made in silicone pans tend to brown less on the outside and sometimes don't cook as well on the inside.

If you're stocking up on metal pans, get the following:

- 9 x 2-inch round pan
- 9 x 2-inch square pan
- 8 x 2-inch square pan
- 9 x 13 x 2-inch pan
- 5 x 9-inch loaf pan
- Standard-size 12-cup muffin tin

Also, if you're going to invest in a pie plate, I prefer glass, because I find that crusts bake up crisper in them, and you can see what's going on with the crust during baking. You can get a 9-inch Pyrex glass pie plate in most supermarkets for a few dollars.

You can also find many cake pans in disposable aluminum form at the supermarket—it's fine to start with those if you don't want to go out and buy a bunch of pans or you don't have the space to keep them. Some of the recipes in this book also call for an 8- or 9-inch springform pan, an 8 x 4-inch loaf pan, or a 10-inch tube or Bundt pan. These are great to have, and you can get good ones for not much money (look for deals and sales on Cooking.com)—but feel free to hold off on buying either until you're ready to make a recipe that calls for it.

Baking sheet

A 10 x 15-inch rimmed baking sheet is essential for baking cookies and other items, and also, when lined with foil, is useful for placing under pies to catch drips. (A 13 x 18-inch sheet pan is fine, too—just measure your oven before buying it to be sure the pan will fit.) Two is plenty. I recommend pans made out of aluminum, not nonstick—you can grease the pan or line it with parchment to prevent sticking.

Flexible spatula

These are often called rubber spatulas, but I recommend that you get silicone instead of rubber. You use this to stir ingredients together, to scrape down mixing bowls, to help incorporate ingredients, and to get every last bit of batter out of a bowl. Why silicone? It can withstand high heat, so it can be used for cooking as well as baking (they're great for stirring scrambled eggs, for example), but a rubber one will melt into your food if it gets too hot. I like to have a few in different sizes, but you can get away with having just one in a medium size. Also, silicone spatulas come in pretty colors—always a plus.

Wooden spoons

These are good for mixing the dry ingredients into cookie dough, and many other tasks. If you cook, buy yourself a separate wooden spoon for baking, as they can absorb flavors and odors over time.

Rasp grater (Microplane) or box grater

I prefer the rasp (Microplane is a brand name) for grating ginger and citrus zest (the fragrant, flavorful, colored part of orange, lemon, or lime peel—see page 191 to learn more about this). The rasp is easier to use, and it gets more of the zest off the fruit. You can also use it for hard cheeses such as Parmesan. But if you already have a box grater that has small teeth on at least one side, it will work fine.

Can opener

You don't need anything fancy, but avoid the plain metal ones they sell in the supermarket—they're hard to use and they rust easily. I like the one made by Oxo because it has a comfortable ergonomic handle. Be sure to wash your can opener after every use.

Wire whisk

Nowadays you can find these in many different sizes and shapes, with lots of features. But really, this is one of the simplest tools, and one that you'll use again and again in baking to beat ingredients together or to break up eggs. Get a medium-sized one, and avoid the super-wide balloon whisks and the flat whisks—these are better for certain tasks and not others, so they're not as versatile. Just get a plain old regular whisk. I find it really handy to have a small one as well, but that's optional.

Vegetable peeler Get yourself a good one (again, Oxo is a great choice). If you have a rusty metal one that you got at the supermarket, toss it. I mean it—put down the book right now, go into the kitchen, and throw it into the trash. A good peeler makes it easy to peel stuff, and the peels will come off more cleanly, so your dessert will look nicer. This is one of those things that costs so little, but makes all the difference.

Wire cooling rack These are essential because they let air circulate underneath your baked goods as they cool. I recommend getting 10 x 16-inch racks (get two—they don't take up much space, and having two allows you to cool large batches of cookies) with stable "feet" and a mesh or grid pattern, which won't let anything slip through.

Cutting boards There are different schools of thought on whether wood or plastic is better. Here's my take: Wood is more attractive, but you can stick a plastic one in the dishwasher. I have both, one of which I use only for baking. You definitely need more than one if you cook—you don't want to chop chocolate and onions on the same cutting board, for example, because chocolate can absorb odors and flavors from other foods that have been left behind on your cutting board. Also, be sure you have a cutting board large enough to accommodate your needs (11 x 14-inch is a standard size, but any size in that range should be fine).

Saucepan You only really need one, in a medium size (2- or 3-quart capacity), but nowadays you can get a set with several sizes of saucepans and skillets for relatively little money, so go for it if your budget and space allow. Check out Target, Marshalls, and department stores for good deals. Look for heavy-bottomed stainless-steel pans. (I have a set of saucepans and skillets by Wolfgang Puck that I got on the Home Shopping Network Web site on the recommendation of a chef at Canyon Ranch spa, and it works great.) Personally, I don't like nonstick—stainless steel cleans very easily, and it's more versatile.

Fine-mesh sieve I use a sieve to sift dry ingredients together, or to sift confectioners' sugar or cocoa on top of desserts. Sifting removes lumps from dry ingredients and incorporates air, which allows the dry ingredients to mix better with the moist ones. Don't worry about sifting unless a recipe calls for it. I use a sieve instead of a sifter because it does double duty—it can be used as a strainer as well, which a sifter can't, and my tiny kitchen can only accommodate so many toys. If you happen to have a sifter, though, feel free to use it.

Pastry cutter This is a half-moon-shaped contraption with a handle and rounded, thick blades. Use this to cut butter into things like streusel, fruit crisp toppings, and biscuits (see page 185 to find out more about "cutting in" butter). It's especially good to have if you don't have a food processor. They're very reasonably priced and don't take up much space, and I've had the same one for about ten years.

Get a firm one, not one with thin wires—the latter are flimsy and harder to use. I like the stainless-steel version that they sell for about $10 at Williams-Sonoma.

Pastry brush Use this for brushing butter or cream onto scones and greasing pans with melted butter, among other tasks. I recommend buying a brush with silicone bristles—they can withstand heat and won't shed.

GOOD-TO-HAVES (BUT YOU CAN GET BY WITHOUT THEM):

Food processor I've had the same 7-cup Braun food processor for about fourteen years, and I've never needed anything else. You can do without it, but they're not expensive and if you plan to bake and cook with any regularity, you'll use it. I'm lazy, and I'm less likely to do something if it's difficult or time-consuming. If you're like that too, get a food processor—you can find one online for less than $150.

Kitchen scale The recipes in this book list the weights for ingredients such as flour and sugar as well as the cup measures. Professional chefs often use weights when cooking and baking because it's more accurate, so you get more consistent results. I used weights in developing these recipes partially for that reason—but honestly, I also used them because, as I said, I'm lazy, and it's actually much easier and faster to weigh dry ingredients than to measure them. I have a tiny Salter digital scale, which I love—it's flat, so it barely takes up any space. It was around $50—but you can get a good digital kitchen scale for about half that price.

Melon baller I like to use this to take the cores out of apples and pears—it makes a clean-looking, uniform shape. Plus, you can use it to make pretty fruit salads.

Ice cream scoop Aside from the obvious, this is a great tool for making perfectly uniform, professional-looking cookies, and for evenly dividing muffin and cupcake batter into pans. Get one or two—one that holds about 1½ to 2 tablespoons' worth of dough/batter, and one that holds about 2 teaspoons' worth, which is great for truffles. Be sure your scoops have handles that releases the dough when you squeeze them.

Offset spatula This tool, which usually has a wooden handle and then a metal head that's partially bent at nearly a 90-degree angle, is great for spreading batter evenly in pans, icing cakes, and getting that first stubborn slice out of a pie neatly. If you have a small or medium-sized one, you'll use it, I promise.

Rolling pin This is last on the list for a reason. There's very little rolling out of dough in this book, and if you do have to roll something out, you can use a wine bottle (preferably full) or a can of cooking spray. A rolling pin also can be useful for crushing cookies for piecrusts if you don't have a food processor—but you could also use a heavy skillet for that. So a rolling pin is definitely not essential, but it can be useful, so grab one if you're stocking up on kitchen items.

THE INGREDIENTS

You don't have to be a novice baker to feel intimidated by supermarket shelves these days. With so many varieties of even the most basic ingredients, it's easy for even an experienced cook to get overwhelmed. This chapter is designed to take the mystery and guesswork out of grocery shopping, so you can sail in and out of the store with confidence and get right back to the fun part: baking.

All purpose flour   There are several types of flour sold at supermarkets—all-purpose, whole-wheat, cake flour, bread flour, self-rising—and they all serve different purposes (you can probably guess what bread flour is best for). The different types have varying amounts of protein (called gluten)—more in heavier flours used in bread, and less in lighter ones like cake flour, used in more delicate desserts. But you can use all-purpose flour for most things (hence the name).

I developed all of the recipes in this book with all-purpose flour—that is, all the recipes that contain flour. I prefer unbleached all-purpose flour. Companies bleach flour to whiten it, but the end result doesn't look any different, so I just don't see the point. But if all your local store has is bleached all-purpose flour, it will work fine too.

Store flour in an airtight container, or keep it tightly sealed in a zip-top plastic bag in the freezer (I recommend the latter if you use it infrequently).

Baking powder   This is a chemical leavening agent, which means it helps baked goods to rise. The way it works is really interesting, but I don't think you're here for a science lesson. Without getting too esoteric, baking powder reacts twice, first to moisture and then to heat (usually the cans of baking powder say "double-acting"; this is what that means).

Baking powder and baking soda are not interchangeable—use whichever one the recipe calls for (and if it calls for both, use both, and be sure to use the amounts of each that are listed in the recipe—that is, don't swap them). Also, baking powder can lose its leavening mojo if it sits around too long, so if you have a can for longer than six or eight months, it's a good idea to replace it. Store baking powder in a cool, dry place, such as a pantry or cabinet. Keep it away from the stove, and don't refrigerate it. Be sure that any measuring spoons you dip into the can of baking powder are perfectly dry.

Baking soda This is another leavening agent (its technical name is sodium bicarbonate), but it works differently than baking powder. Suffice it to say that because of the way baking soda works, you'll often find it in recipes that have an acid in them, such as buttermilk or lemon juice. Store baking soda in a cool, dry place, such as a pantry or cabinet. Remember, it is not interchangeable with baking powder; if a recipe calls for baking soda, you must use baking soda.

Butter Always use unsalted butter in sticks—never buy whipped butter or salted butter for baking. It may seem strange to use unsalted butter and then add salt to a recipe, but that way you have much more control over the amount of salt in your final product.

As for storing it, I keep butter in the freezer or refrigerator. It's in the freezer if I don't know when I'm going to use it; if I know I need it for a recipe, I'll move it into the fridge.

Many recipes in this book call for butter either at room temperature or cold. It's important that you stick to those instructions.

Butter at room temperature should be soft and pliable, but not mushy or melted. Press it with your finger; it should hold the indentation, but your finger shouldn't mush right through the butter. How long it will take to soften butter to this state after being in the fridge or freezer depends on how warm your kitchen is. But if you need to get butter to room temperature quickly, cut it into thin slices (about ¼-inch thick), separate the slices, and let it sit on the countertop (on the wrapper or on a piece of plastic wrap) for about 10 minutes. Using butter that is too soft can result in heavy or greasy cakes and cookies, because it won't get light and fluffy when you beat it with the sugar.

Usually butter needs to be cold when it's being mixed into streusel (the crumbly mixture on top of muffins or coffee cake), biscuits, or the topping for fruit crisps and crumbles. If you need cold butter cut into pieces and your kitchen is warm, cut it up and then stick it back in the fridge until you're ready to use it.

Chocolate There are hundreds of varieties and flavors of chocolate, but here are the basics:

Cacao: Sometimes chocolate bars specify the cacao content on the label (it's listed as a percentage: 60 percent, 75 percent, etc.). What you need to know about that number is that the higher it is, the more intense and less sweet the flavor will be. It has nothing to do with quality —it simply depends on your personal taste or what you're using the chocolate for. Also, the higher the number, the "darker" the chocolate, but the general term "dark chocolate" is subjective. Hershey's Special Dark is really semisweet, which I don't think is all that dark. But that's me—to someone else it might taste very dark.

Unsweetened: As the name implies, this has no added sugar, so it isn't sweet at all. Unsweetened chocolate is often used in brownies (along with lots of sugar). If you see a bar with 100 percent cacao, it's unsweetened. Don't eat it! Chop it up and use it for baking.

Bittersweet: This is one step up on the sweetness scale from unsweetened, but it still has a strong, bitter flavor. It falls into the dark chocolate family, along with semisweet, but it's darker and less sweet than semisweet.

Semisweet: This is still dark chocolate, but it's milder and sweeter than bittersweet. Chocolate chips are usually semisweet (unless the package specifies otherwise)—but don't use them in place of bar chocolate. Chocolate chips have less cocoa butter in them to help them keep their shape, so they don't melt as easily as bar chocolate and don't have as strong a chocolate flavor.

One thing that's good to know about bittersweet vs. semisweet is that you can swap them for each other. I call for one or the other in this book, but if you make a recipe with bittersweet chocolate and it's too intense or not sweet enough for you, try it with the same amount of semisweet next time.

Milk chocolate: This is the sweet chocolate found in most candy bars. In general, milk chocolate is better for snacking than for baking, because it's very sweet and its less-intense chocolate flavor can get lost when it's mixed with other ingredients. I sometimes combine it with darker chocolate such as semisweet in recipes to balance the flavor.

White chocolate: Some chocolate snobs would say that this isn't really chocolate because it doesn't have any cocoa solids in it. Personally, I don't care—I like it! It can make a nice addition to baked goods, especially to offset a tart ingredient like dried cherries or cranberries. For the best flavor, check the label to make sure the white chocolate you're buying is made with cocoa butter and not vegetable oil.

Cocoa powder: This is dry, unsweetened chocolate. There are two kinds, "Dutch process" and natural. Dutch process is generally milder in flavor. I developed the recipes for this book using Ghirardelli unsweetened cocoa—it's reasonably priced, available in supermarkets, and has really good flavor. I've also baked with Hershey's unsweetened cocoa, and it works fine too. No matter what brand you use, be sure to buy unsweetened cocoa powder and not hot chocolate mix, which is sweetened.

Buying chocolate: There are dozens of brands of chocolate that are readily available, and they can vary wildly in price and quality. Ghirardelli makes very good chocolate, and you can often find it in supermarkets. I also like Chocolove, Lindt, Scharffen Berger, and Green and Black's. You can certainly bake with really exceptional chocolate, like Valrhona, but it's very expensive and not necessary. Any of the brands I've mentioned will give you great results.

Storing chocolate: Store chocolate wrapped tightly at cool room temperature, between 60° and 75°F. It's best not to refrigerate it, because chocolate can absorb flavors and odors, and the last thing you want is your chocolate tasting like last night's Chinese takeout. Try to avoid subjecting chocolate to big temperature changes—that can cause the chocolate to "bloom." If you've ever seen chocolate with little white streaks in it, that means it has bloomed—that is, some of the cocoa butter has separated and risen to the top. It's still okay to eat, but it's best to avoid that if you can.

Condensed milk Also called sweetened condensed milk, this is a canned product that consists of a mix of milk and lots of sugar, and it has 60 percent of the water removed. What's left is a very sweet, thick, sticky mixture that's used often in baking to sweeten and thicken desserts. If you've ever had a Thai iced tea, it's usually made with sweetened condensed milk. It's shelf stable, but it does expire eventually, so buy it as you need it and keep an eye on the expiration date. Don't confuse it with evaporated milk—it's similar in that it's a canned milk product that has 60 percent of the water removed, but evaporated milk is not sweetened, so it's not a good substitute for sweetened condensed milk. They're often placed right next to each other on supermarket shelves, so read the labels carefully.

Cornmeal   Cornmeal is available either finely ground or coarse, though coarse is not as widely sold. For baking purposes, buy finely ground. Whether it's yellow or white doesn't matter, but blue cornmeal will turn your baked goods blue or blue-ish or gray. Keep cornmeal tightly sealed in the refrigerator.

Cornstarch   This is a thickener used often in sauces and puddings. It's best to first dissolve it in a bit of cold liquid to remove the lumps, then add it to the rest of the recipe. It will thicken up when it's warmed, but don't cook it too long or make it too hot, or the thickness will break down. Keep it in a cool, dry place, and be sure that any spoons dipped into the box are perfectly dry.

Crystalized ginger   Also known as candied ginger, this is made with pieces of fresh ginger, which are cooked in a sugar syrup until the sugar crystallizes. It has a strong spicy-sweet flavor, and it's delicious chopped up and added to muffins, cakes, and cookies.

Eggs   Always use large eggs for recipes in this book. Don't swap in extra-large or jumbo eggs—the difference in volume can change your end result. Whether you choose brown or white makes no difference—shell color is determined by the hen's breed and does not affect flavor or quality. Store eggs in their container in the refrigerator, and not on the door—the door tends to be exposed to more outside air and is therefore not as cold as the shelves. Also, the container has the expiration date stamped on it, and you don't want to lose that.

Recipes for cakes often call for eggs at room temperature. It's very important that you fol-

low this instruction, because cold eggs added to cake batter can hurt the cake's texture and keep it from rising properly. To bring eggs to room temperature, simply leave them on a countertop for about 30 minutes, in their shells. If you forget to do that, put them in a bowl (in the shells) and cover them with very warm tap water for 10 minutes. Gently dry them with a kitchen towel before cracking them.

If you need to separate eggs, it's easiest to do so when they're cold, so separate them right out of the fridge if you can. Then leave the whites out for 20 to 30 minutes to warm to room temperature before beating. (See "Separating Eggs" in The How-Tos chapter, page 189, for more details.) When whipping egg whites, be sure your bowl and beaters are perfectly clean and dry. Any residue in the bowl or on the beaters can keep your egg whites from whipping up. Whip egg whites in a metal bowl for best results.

Gelatin   I use gelatin to thicken some items, such as panna cotta (see page 89)—and what I'm referring to is unflavored, granulated gelatin (Knox, in the orange and white box, is the most common supermarket brand), not the flavored Jell-O stuff. Unflavored gelatin is also available in sheets, but I call for packets of granulated gelatin because I think it's the most commonly available. One packet is equivalent to ¼ ounce or 1 tablespoon. Keep gelatin in a cool, dry place, such as your pantry.

Half-and-half   True to its name, this is half milk and half cream, and it has between 11 and 18 percent fat. It's too light to whip, but I often use it to make puddings and custards, because it gives them a really nice richness without going overboard. Don't buy fat-free half-and-half—it's full of chemicals and tastes terrible.

Heavy cream Also called heavy whipping cream, it has at least 36 percent fat. If you're using it to make whipped cream, be sure to buy heavy cream or heavy whipping cream, not light cream, half-and-half, or anything else. Well-chilled heavy cream is easier to whip.

Honey This thick liquid sweetener literally comes in hundreds of flavors. Keep in mind when buying honey that the lighter its color, usually the milder its flavor. Orange blossom and clover are two of the most common varieties; both are mild. Buckwheat honey has a stronger flavor. Keep honey tightly covered in a cool, dark place. If it crystallizes, uncover the jar and place it in a saucepan of water that reaches a few inches up the sides of the jar. Warm the water over medium heat until simmering; the crystals will dissolve pretty quickly.

Milk Use whole milk, unless low-fat or nonfat is specified. If you're watching your calories, it's better to have a smaller portion than to try to make a pudding or another dessert with nonfat milk, which will hurt its texture and flavor considerably. Make it with the full-fat stuff, enjoy a little bit of it, and go for a walk or a jog later.

Molasses This is a thick, dark, syrupy liquid sweetener with a distinctive, deep flavor. You'll find it in recipes for strongly flavored goodies like gingerbread. Use unsulfured dark molasses, not light, and avoid any with labels that say "robust," "extra strong," or anything similar—they're too strong in flavor and are likely to overpower your end result. Also, don't use blackstrap molasses— it's too strong and not sweet. Store molasses in a cool, dry place, like your pantry.

Salt A little bit of salt in baked goods helps brighten and balance their flavor. Use regular table salt, not a coarse salt such as kosher salt, which may not dissolve enough and can leave you with pockets of salty bits in your baked goods. It doesn't matter whether you choose iodized salt or sea salt, as long as it's finely ground. Many sea salts are coarse, so check the label carefully.

Spices Spices such as cinnamon and nutmeg are essential to baking. Their flavor is intense, but it does diminish over time, so don't buy them in huge quantities unless you know you're going to use them up. Ground spices usually last about two to three years before losing significant flavor. If you need just a little bit of a lesser-used spice (such as mace or allspice), try to find it in a bulk bin at a health food store or a Whole Foods and just buy a little bit, instead of purchasing a whole bottle. Don't open the bottle and shake the spice into a steaming pot on the stove—this allows moisture into the bottle, which can cause the spices to clump and lose flavor. Make sure any measuring spoons you dip into a spice jar are perfectly dry, and replace the cap as soon as you're finished measuring. Keep spices in a cool, dry place, away from sunlight (that means, not the top of your stove!).

Sugar

Granulated: This is the common white sugar you're used to. At the supermarket, look for granulated white cane sugar. Avoid beet sugar, as it doesn't always work as well in baking. Store it in an airtight container in a cool, dry place.

Confectioners': Also referred to as 10X or icing sugar, this is the fine, powdered variety used in frostings and glazes. You sometimes also see it sprinkled on top of baked goods. Confectioners' sugar tends to form tiny lumps, so it often has to be sifted before use.

Light brown: Brown sugar is granulated sugar that has molasses mixed in. Light brown has less molasses than dark, and is milder in flavor.

Dark brown: I often call for dark brown sugar in recipes because I prefer its rich, caramel-y flavor. If you find that the flavor is too strong for your taste, feel free to swap in the same amount of light brown sugar. (When I say the same amount, I mean by measure, not weight. Dark brown sugar weighs more than light brown. See below for a list of what various ingredients weigh.) Store either type of brown sugar tightly closed in the refrigerator.

If your brown sugar has hardened, place it in a bowl, cover it with a slightly damp paper towel, cover with plastic wrap, and microwave for 20 seconds. Check to see if it has softened. If it has, use it right away, or it will soon harden up on you again. If it hasn't, replace the paper towel and plastic and microwave again at 20-second intervals until it has softened.

Tapioca Instant tapioca is a good thickener for fruit fillings for pies, crisps, and cobblers. It's readily available in the supermarket (Minute brand is the one I find most often). Be sure to buy instant tapioca or tapioca starch, not regular tapioca—the end result with regular tapioca is likely to be lumpier. Mix the tapioca with the other ingredients and let it sit at room temperature for 5 to 10 minutes. If you're making a fruit crisp, for example, make the filling first and let it stand while you make the topping. Store tapioca covered (or wrapped) in a cool, dry place.

Vanilla extract There are many flavored extracts out there, but vanilla is the most common in baked goods. It's made from vanilla beans that have been steeped in alcohol. Always, always, always use pure vanilla extract—stay away from the imitation stuff. Pure vanilla extract costs a little bit more, but the flavor is vastly better. (The same holds true if you ever need to buy mint or almond extract or any other flavor—spring for the real stuff.) You may see some vanilla extracts that specify where the vanilla is from (Madagascar or Tahiti, for example), but don't worry about that.

WEIGHTS OF OFTEN-USED INGREDIENTS

I list the weights as well as the measurements for most dry ingredients because I find it easier, quicker, and more accurate to weigh them. Measuring is what most home cooks do, and it works fine—but if you're just starting out, let me encourage you to get in the good habit of weighing. Here is a basic cheat sheet of weights for different commonly used ingredients (each figure is for 1 cup). For reference, I use the measurements in Rose Levy Beranbaum's *Cake Bible*. She's an accomplished food scientist as well as a master baker, and every time I've turned to her book for recipes or with questions about ingredients, she's always steered me well.

Per 1 cup:
All-purpose flour: 4.25 ounces
Unsweetened cocoa: 2.9 ounces
Sugar: 7 ounces
Confectioners' sugar: 4 ounces
Light brown sugar (packed): 7.66 ounces
Dark brown sugar (packed): 8.4 ounces

THE LINGO

Here are the definitions of a few basic baking terms. I've tried not to use any jargon in the recipes themselves without explaining what it means, but you may find it useful to have all of these terms in one place. Plus, you can use this as a reference if you ever get stumped using another cookbook.

Baste: To spoon or pour liquid over something as it cooks. This adds flavor and helps keep the item moist.

Beat: To mix something quickly and add air to it, usually using an electric mixer or a whisk.

Blind-bake: To prebake a pie or tart shell before adding the filling. This is done with pies where the filling isn't baked at all or is only baked for a short time, not long enough for the crust to fully bake. In blind-baking, usually the crust is lined with parchment or foil and filled with a faux filling such as uncooked rice, dried beans, or ceramic pie weights to keep it in place as it bakes. After an initial baking time, the lining and faux filling are removed and the crust is baked a bit longer, until it turns golden brown.

Cream: (as a verb, e.g., "Cream the butter and sugar . . . "): To beat butter or another fat on its own or with sugar, until it is well softened and free of lumps. The softened texture allows the mixture to be combined with other ingredients (such as flour) more easily.

Cut in: To combine a fat such as butter or short-ening with another ingredient, such as flour, so that the fat is broken down into small pieces, but not actually mixed into the other ingredient—in other words, there will still be tiny lumps of fat after it has been cut in. Usually recipes will instruct as to what the final texture should be, as in "cut in until the mixture resembles coarse sand," or "cut in until pea-sized pieces of butter remain." This is best done with cold ingredients, to keep the fat from melting. Cutting in creates flaky biscuits and piecrusts. It's done with a pastry cutter (see page 177 for more information on this), by pressing the fat and flour together with your fingers, or by using short on-and-off turns in a food processor.

Fold: To mix ingredients together by scraping the bottom ingredient up and over the top ones gently but thoroughly, using as few strokes as possible, to get them combined without deflating or overmixing them. Whipped egg whites or whipped cream are two ingredients that are often folded in, and chocolate chips and nuts are often folded into cake batter or cookie dough. A flexible spatula is the most common tool for this, sometimes aided by a whisk. When working with whipped egg whites or cream, often recipes will instruct you to fold in some of it to lighten the mixture, then fold in the rest.

Pulse: To mix ingredients in a food processor or blender by using quick on-and-off turns. This keeps the item from being completely pureed. When cutting fat into dry ingredients (see "Cut in," page 185), pulsing allows the fat to be cut up without incorporating it completely, which would hurt the texture of the end result. Pulsing is also useful when making fruit sauces, when you don't want the sauce to be completely smooth.

Puree: To mix something in a food processor or blender (or by hand) until it's completely broken down into a thick liquid. Puree is also a noun, referring to the final product (e.g., "Drizzle raspberry puree over the brownies").

Reduce: To boil a liquid so that some of the liquid evaporates to concentrate the flavor and thicken the texture.

Room temperature: This refers to a temperature between 65° and 75°F.

Scald: To heat milk or cream to a temperature just below the boiling point, to where tiny bubbles form at the edge of the pan, steam just begins to show, and a very thin skin forms on top.

Score: To cut the surface of a food, but not slice all the way through. This is often done with warm shortbread, because it helps in cutting the cooled cookies without crumbling them.

Sift: To remove tiny lumps from and incorporate air into a dry ingredient such as flour or confectioners' sugar by moving it through a fine mesh, such as a sieve or sifter. Don't sift unless it's called for specifically in a recipe, because flour is usually pre-sifted now, and sifting again can affect the texture of your product.

Simmer: To cook something at just below the boiling point. Usually the liquid is brought to a boil at a higher temperature, then the heat is turned down to low to allow it to simmer.

Steep: To soak something in a hot liquid to soften it or extract its flavor, such as a tea bag in hot water.

Water bath: Also called bain-marie, this is a pan of hot water into which a baking pan or ramekins is placed during baking. This is often done with custards, cheesecakes, and pots de crème to protect them from the dry heat of the oven and allow them to cook gently, so they don't crack.

Zest: The colorful, fragrant outer part of citrus peel. The zest of citrus fruits is packed with flavor, and I call for it a lot in this book. The word "zest" is sometimes used in recipes as a verb, e.g., "Zest the orange," meaning remove the zest of the orange. (For more on zesting fruit, see page 191.)

THE HOW-TOS

Here are a few easy steps you can take to avoid many of the pitfalls bakers run across. Hopefully these will answer any questions that may arise, and generally make the whole process simpler.

Chopping chocolate Place the chocolate on a cutting board. If you're chopping more than one bar, chop them one at a time. Turn the bar so that it's at an angle, and use a chef's knife to chop the corners. Keep turning the bar so that it's always on an angle—this will keep the chocolate from flying off the board. The power in your knife is in the heel, the wider part of the blade that's closest to the handle, so concentrate on chopping with that part. Use the fingers of your left hand to gently hold the tip of the knife on the board, and use your right hand to raise and lower the heel of the knife onto the chocolate. Push the blade down but also forward in a sweeping motion. (Reverse the hands for these instructions if you're left-handed.)

Melting chocolate I almost always call for melting chocolate with something else, such as butter. Chocolate is unstable and can seize into a lumpy, grainy mess that can't be saved. This happens when melting chocolate comes into contact with moisture, such as a few drops of water. Melting it with butter protects it from seizing. Chocolate also can burn easily, so be sure to use a very low temperature on the stove. If using a double boiler, make sure the water is simmering, not boiling, and that the bottom of the bowl doesn't touch the water.

Chopping nuts See "Chopping chocolate" for instructions on how to use a chef's knife. When measuring, pay attention to how the recipe is worded. If it says, "1 cup pecans, chopped," then measure the nuts first, before chopping. If it says, "1 cup chopped pecans," chop before measuring. Also, don't overload your cutting board; chop in stages if you need to, and transfer the chopped nuts to a bowl before beginning to chop another portion.

Crushing cookies The easiest way to do this is with a food processor. But if you don't have one, put the cookies in a large ziplock bag. Seal the bag completely, squeezing out any excess air. Place the bag on a solid countertop and smack it with a heavy skillet, rolling pin, meat mallet—any hard, unbreakable object. Be aggressive—you want those cookies crushed. Turn the bag over a few times to get at all of the cookies.

Greasing and flouring pans

You can use butter, oil, or cooking spray to grease pans. Butter lends a bit of flavor and gives cakes a crisper crust, so I sometimes call for it specifically instead of cooking spray. To grease a pan with butter, it's best to start with room-temperature butter. Place some on your fingertips or a piece of plastic wrap and rub the inside of the pan (be sure to get the inside tube if it's a Bundt or tube pan), taking care to cover every corner with a light film of butter. Another way to do it is to actually melt the butter and use a pastry brush to brush it on. That's what I do—though I admit it's a fussier method.

To coat the pan with flour, spoon a few tablespoons of flour into the already-greased pan and swirl or shake the pan until every bit of the surface is coated with a light layer of flour. If you see a spot that's not covered, that means you missed it with the butter or cooking spray. Gently dab some on the spot and then swirl the flour over it again. Tap the excess flour out and discard it.

To mist a pan with cooking spray, simply hold up the pan with one hand and use the other to press down on the nozzle of the spray. Take care to cover every bit of the surface. A light mist is plenty—avoid spraying so much that it pools at the bottom of the pan. If that happens, dab some of it out with a paper towel.

There are products in supermarkets that have cooking spray and flour in one can, so all you do is mist it on, no need to add additional flour (Baker's Joy is one common brand). This works very well, but there's no need to buy it specifically if you're already buying butter and flour.

Lining pans

With foil: To line a baking pan with foil, turn the pan upside down. Tear out a sheet of foil that's about 6 inches longer than the long side of the pan. Place the sheet of foil on top of the pan and gently press it down so that it forms to the outside of the pan. Carefully remove the foil, leaving its shape intact. Turn the pan over and place the foil inside. Gently push the corners of the foil into the corners of the pan, taking care not to tear the foil and leaving a 2-inch overhang on two sides. I find that doing it this way leads to fewer tears in the foil. Mist the foil with cooking spray if the recipe calls for it. You're going to use the foil overhang to pull the finished baked item out of the pan.

With parchment: Parchment paper is useful for lining pans for cookies and cakes. It's made to withstand high heat, and one sheet can be used a few times to bake multiple sheets of cookies. It's sold in supermarkets, in the same aisle as foil and plastic wrap. It's not interchangeable with waxed paper. To line a sheet pan, simply tear out a sheet of parchment and place it on top of the sheet pan; trim it to fit, if necessary. To line a cake pan, tear out a sheet of parchment. Place the cake pan on top, and use a pen or pencil to trace the bottom of the pan. Cut the parchment along your tracing lines. Grease the pan as instructed, place the parchment cut-out on the bottom of the pan, pressing it down, then grease the parchment if the recipe calls for it.

Measuring dry ingredients

Measuring accurately is extremely important in baking, because the ratio of dry to wet ingredients determines the texture of your end result.

Always level off cups and spoons to get the right amount by running a flat item (such as the flat side of a butter knife) over the top of the spoon or cup.

The most accurate way to measure is to weigh the dry ingredients—that is, set a bowl on your scale and set it to 0 (so that the weight of the bowl isn't included in your measurements). Spoon the flour or other ingredient into the bowl until you reach the desired amount (for a chart with the weights of various dry ingredients, see page 184). This is most important with ¼ cup or more—with tablespoons and teaspoons, and fractions of them, it's fine to scoop the ingredient out with a measuring spoon.

If you don't have a scale, then the best way to measure is to spoon the flour or other dry ingredient into the dry measuring cup until the ingredient is heaping out of the cup, then level it off. Don't pack the ingredient into the dry measuring cup or tap it on the counter to settle it—spoon it in gently.

I don't recommend dipping your cup into the flour and scooping it out (this is known as the "dip and sweep" method), because you end up with a lot more of the ingredient in your dry measuring cup than by weighing or spooning it in, and your end result can be heavier and/or drier.

Separating eggs   Recipes often call for either the yolks or whites of eggs, or need both but use them separately. To separate eggs, have two bowls ready. Make sure the one for the whites is completely clean and dry (any grease or water in the bowl may prevent the whites from whipping well). Cold eggs separate more easily than warm ones, so if you need separated eggs at room temperature, separate them right out of the fridge and then let them sit on the counter until they reach room temperature. Keep in mind that a little bit of egg white in the yolk won't hurt the yolk, but a bit of yolk in the white will keep it from whipping well.

To separate an egg, crack it on the side of the bowl that you plan to put the yolk in. Try to break the egg so that you'll have two even halves of shell. Move the cracked egg over the bowl you have for the whites. Carefully pour the yolk into one half of the shell, allowing some of the white to drip off into the bowl. Pour the egg yolk into the other half, allowing more white to drip into the bowl. Keep doing this until the white and yolk are separated, then drop the yolk into its bowl.

Sometimes you'll find a firm white strand attached to the egg—this is called the chalaza. It's not a defect—in fact, it's often found in fresh eggs. It's okay to leave it in with the yolks, but if you can remove it, especially when making puddings or pots de crème, it's better to do so. Let it cling to the yolk while separating. Then, when the yolk is in the bowl, gently remove the chalaza with a spoon. Don't worry about it when using whole eggs in cakes or cookies.

Sifting   Sifting removes tiny lumps from dry ingredients such as flour and confectioner's sugar, and adds air to lighten the texture of your end result. Most flour is presifted nowadays, so there's no need to sift it. I call for it very occasionally in recipes—but if I don't, there's no need to do it. To sift, place a sifter or fine-meshed sieve over a bowl. Add the dry ingredient(s) to the sifter or sieve and, if using a sifter, turn the crank until all of the ingredients are through it and in the bowl. If using a sieve, lightly tap the side of the sieve with your fingers to force the dry ingredients through it and into the bowl. With either method, if you have little lumps left over, rub them with the back of a spoon to force them through.

Toasting nuts   Preheat the oven to 375°F. Spread chopped nuts out on an ungreased, unlined baking sheet, so they lie in a single layer. Bake for about 5 to 10 minutes, until they're fragrant and turn light golden brown. Stir the nuts on the baking sheet with a large spoon or flexible spatula every 2 to 3 minutes. When stirring, be sure to bring the nuts on the edges into the center and vice versa for even toasting.

If you're toasting whole nuts, it will take a few minutes longer, and sliced almonds will toast more quickly—be sure to watch carefully. It's better to have lightly toasted nuts than overdone ones, because once they're burned, they turn bitter and can't be used.

Whipping cream   Whipped cream can be a garnish or an element within a dessert. It's so delicious, I don't understand how anyone can use Cool Whip or other fake whipped cream. Promise me you won't—especially after you've put in the effort to make a dessert from scratch!

First, the basics: Always use heavy cream, whipping cream, or heavy whipping cream (those three are basically the same). Don't use half-and-half or light cream—they won't whip. Make sure the cream is very cold, and for best results, place the bowl and beaters in the fridge or freezer for a few minutes just before whipping. Pour the chilled cream into the cold bowl and beat, beginning on low speed, until bubbles form, about 30 seconds to 1 minute (starting on low speed and moving up gradually will keep the cream from splattering). Raise the speed to medium and beat for another 30 seconds to 1 minute, until the cream is slightly thickened, then raise the speed to high and beat until the cream is thick and billowy and has doubled in volume. You also want either soft or firm peaks to form, depending on the recipe.

Soft peaks: When you lift the beaters out of the cream (turn off the mixer first!), the cream should form a peak, but it will kind of droop down over itself, not stand straight up. If it doesn't hold its shape at all, keep beating it a little longer.

Stiff or firm peaks: When you lift the beaters out of the cream, the cream should form a peak and stand straight up. Be careful when beating to this stage—if you overbeat the cream, you'll end up with clumps. Once it gets to that stage, you can't save it, and you'll have to start over.

Sometimes I call for "medium-firm peaks" in recipes. This means I want you to whip the cream just past the soft peaks stage but not quite to firm peaks. Don't stress about this— do it once or twice, and it will become clear.

I always specify in this book how much cream to use (unless I'm suggesting whipped cream as a garnish, then it's up to you to decide how much you want), but in other recipes elsewhere, watch out for the wording. If a recipe says, "1 cup heavy cream, whipped," then start with 1 cup of cream and whip it. If it says, "2 cups whipped cream," then whip 1 cup of cream—remember, it will double in volume when whipped.

To sweeten whipped cream, simply add sugar. When you've turned your mixer up to high speed and the cream is beginning to get slightly fluffy, gradually pour in the sugar, 1 spoonful at a time. Add 1 to 2 tablespoons of sugar per cup of cream. You can add more, but it will start to get very sweet. You can also flavor whipped cream with vanilla extract; add up to 2 teaspoons per cup of cream, at the same time that you add the sugar.

Whipping egg whites   See "Separating eggs" for more information about getting the whites.

For best results whipping egg whites:
- Be sure the bowl and the beaters of your mixer (or your whisk, if beating by hand) are completely clean and dry.
- Make sure there are no traces of yolk in your whites.
- Bring the whites to room temperature.
- A little bit of acid will help to stabilize the whites and get them to beat up to a fuller volume, so add ⅛ teaspoon cream of tartar or ¼ teaspoon freshly squeezed lemon juice per 1 to 2 large egg whites. To do this, beat the egg whites until they get foamy, then add the acid, then continue beating.
- If you need to add sugar to your egg whites (this makes meringue), slowly spoon in the sugar when the whites have become frothy.

See "Whipping cream" for more information about soft and firm peaks—it's the same for egg whites.

As for speed, start with your mixer on medium-low. When the whites are frothy and you've added any acid or sugar, raise the speed to medium-high until the egg whites have formed soft peaks. If the recipe calls for soft peaks, stop here. If you're going for firm peaks, raise the mixer speed to high. Watch carefully—if you overwhip, the egg whites will break down again. Use beaten egg whites within 5 minutes, or they'll start to deflate.

Zesting citrus fruit   Zest is the colorful, fragrant outer part of citrus peel. It's very easy to remove. Before you start, be sure to remove any stickers from the fruit and scrub it well under warm water. Pat dry with a kitchen towel. If you're using a rasp or Microplane grater (see page 176 to learn more about these), which I recommend, gently run your finger over the grater to see which way the blades go. Hold the grater in one hand and the fruit in the other. Set the grater over a bowl, plate, or piece of plastic wrap—you'll need something below it to catch the zest. Press and move the fruit over the grater so that the blades scrape the zest off the fruit. Keep moving the fruit around so that you're always scraping a piece that still has zest on it (don't run a section of fruit over the grater that you've already zested—you only want the colorful part of the peel, not the bitter white pith). Be sure to scrape down the underside of the grater after you've finished, to get any bits of zest that have clung to it.

You can also zest with the fine cutters of a box grater, though I don't think it works as well. Follow the same procedure as for the rasp grater.

ACKNOWLEDGMENTS

First of all, a big thanks to Sarah Burningham, who looked at me across the table on our first lunch date and said, "Are you thinking about writing a cookbook? Because you should write a cookbook!" Without your support and invaluable advice (and your recipe-testing skills!), this book would not have happened.

Major thanks to the truly wonderful Denise and Charlie Schiller for so generously allowing us to use your studio and teaching both Mark and me so much.

To my agent, Renee Zuckerbrot, a million thank yous and trays of brownies whenever you want them for always, always believing in this project, answering all of my silly questions so patiently, reading everything with your eagle eye, and being so honest.

To Heather Carreiro, Jenn Taber, and the whole team at Globe Pequot for all of your hard work in creating a book more beautiful than I could have imagined.

To Clare McHugh, the best boss ever, thank you for being so excited about this project and so encouraging, and for opening up the *All You* prop closet to me.

To Jayna Maleri and Elizabeth Blake, a big thanks for selecting the lovely props so carefully and lending your considerable talents to help create the look of this book—not to mention your unending kindness and friendship.

To Andrea Steinberg, I can't thank you enough for all of your hard work doing the food styling, always with a smile and a laugh. You made the food look beautiful and the photo shoots fun.

To Brenda Angelilli and Lynn Bradley, thank you for lending your eyes.

To Molly Rundberg, Karen Ferries, and Loren Cunniff, thank you for testing the recipes so thoroughly. Thanks also to so many friends who also tested recipes and offered such valuable feedback—I'm sorry I can't name you all here, but I am so grateful to you.

To Jacqui LeBow, thank you for a great title!

Last but certainly not least, to Mom—how can I ever thank you for being the kindest, most loving, most supportive person in my life, for always being there, for laughing with me and always being honest with me. And for your Mexican wedding cookie recipe, which I think is the best in the world!

Opposite page, from top: Carrot Cupcake with Cream Cheese Frosting, Chocolate–Chocolate Chip Cupcake with Chocolate Frosting, and Cheesecake Cupcake

Dottie's Deluxe Noodle Pudding

METRIC
CONVERSION TABLES

Approximate U.S. Metric Equivalents

LIQUID INGREDIENTS

U.S. MEASURES	METRIC	U.S. MEASURES	METRIC
¼ TSP.	1.23 ML	2 TBSP.	29.57 ML
½ TSP.	2.36 ML	3 TBSP.	44.36 ML
¾ TSP.	3.70 ML	¼ CUP	59.15 ML
1 TSP.	4.93 ML	½ CUP	118.30 ML
1¼ TSP.	6.16 ML	1 CUP	236.59 ML
1½ TSP.	7.39 ML	2 CUPS OR 1 PT.	473.18 ML
1¾ TSP.	8.63 ML	3 CUPS	709.77 ML
2 TSP.	9.86 ML	4 CUPS OR 1 QT.	946.36 ML
1 TBSP.	14.79 ML	4 QTS. OR 1 GAL.	3.79 LT

DRY INGREDIENTS

U.S. MEASURES		METRIC	U.S. MEASURES	METRIC
17⅗ OZ.	1 LIVRE	500 G	2 OZ.	60 (56.6) G
16 OZ.	1 LB.	454 G	1¾ OZ.	50 G
8⅞ OZ.		250 G	1 OZ.	30 (28.3) G
5¼ OZ.		150 G	⅞ OZ.	25 G
4½ OZ.		125 G	¾ OZ.	21 (21.3) G
4 OZ.		115 (113.2) G	½ OZ.	15 (14.2) G
3½ OZ.		100 G	¼ OZ.	7 (7.1) G
3 OZ.		85 (84.9) G	⅛ OZ.	3½ (3.5) G
2⅘ OZ.		80 G	1⁄16 OZ.	2 (1.8) G

RECIPE INDEX

A

almonds
    "Almond Joy" Cheesecake, 58–59, 60
    Almond-Raspberry Cake, 74, 75
    Cranberry Cornmeal Cookies, 27, 153
    Raspberry Jam Bars, 15, 16
Angel Food Cake with Macerated
    Strawberries, 173
apples
    Apple Crumble, 128, 129
    Baked Apples, 117, 147
    Double Apple Streusel Coffee Cake, 34,
        38–39
    Elegant Apple Tartlets, 129, 130–31

B

Baked Apples, 117, 147
bananas
    Banana-Nutella Wontons, 138, 139
    Banana Snack Cake, 78, 79
    Caramelized Banana Bread Pudding, 91,
        92–93
    Peanut Butter and Banana Bread, 23, 80
bars. See also cookies
    Coffee–Chocolate Chip Blondies, 3, 5
    Cookies-and-Cream Cheesecake
        Bars, 3, 6

Fudge Brownies, 1, 3
Hello Dollies, 8, 9
Peanut Butter and Jelly Bars, 22, 23
Pecan Pie Bars, 11, 12
Pistachio-Cranberry Bars, 25, 26
Raspberry Jam Bars, 15, 16
Salty-Sweet Caramel Nut Bars, 12, 13
S'mores Bars, 2, 3
Toblerone Brownies, 4, 25
berries. See also cherries; cranberries;
    raspberries; strawberries
    Blackberry Cobbler, 135, 136
    Cheesecake Cupcakes, 43, 44
    Cherry-Berry Stovetop Cobbler, 1
        42, 143
    Cool Blueberry Soup, 126, 127
    Fresh Berry Shortcakes, 111, 112–13
    Lemon-Berry Semifreddo, 123, 124–25
    Nectarine-Blueberry Crisp, 114, 115
biscotti
    Cappucino Biscotti, 18, 19
    Rosemary Biscotti, 19, 20
Black-and-White Trifles, 88, 94–95
Blackberry Cobbler, 135, 136
blueberries. See berries
Boozy Butterscotch Sauce, 161, 164
Brandied Cherries, 67, 165

bread puddings
    Caramelized Banana Bread Pudding,
        91, 92–93
    Double Chocolate Croissant Bread
        Pudding, 90, 91
breads. *See also* cakes
    Peanut Butter and Banana Bread,
        23, 80
    Pumpkin Bread, 32, 33
    Zucchini Bread, 33, 81
Brownie Ice Cream Torte, 68, 69
brownies. *See* bars
buckle. *See also* cakes, 36
Buttermilk Pie, 106, 107
butterscotch
    Boozy Butterscotch Sauce, 161, 164
    Butterscotch Pudding, 84, 85
    Peanut-Butterscotch Bites, 152, 153

C

cakes. *See also* cupcakes, 30–81
    "Almond Joy" Cheesecake, 58–59, 60
    Almond-Raspberry Cake, 74, 75
    Banana Snack Cake, 78, 79
    Brownie Ice Cream Torte, 68, 69
    Creamy Vanilla Cheesecake, 56, 57
    Currant-Cranberry Spice Cake, 72, 76–77
    Double Apple Streusel Coffee Cake, 34,
        38–39
    Flourless Chocolate Cake, 70–71, 73
    Fresh Berry Shortcakes, 111, 112–13
    Geraldine's Chocolate-Date Cake, 48, 49
    Great Big Coconut Cake, 50, 51
    Lime-Glazed Citrus Tea Cakes, 46, 47
    Molten Dark Chocolate Cakes, 66, 67
    Peanut Butter and Banana Bread, 23, 80
    Perfectly Simple Pound Cake, 31, 33
    Pineapple Upside-Down Cake, 54, 55
    Pumpkin Bread, 32, 33
    Raspberry Buckle, 34, 36

Sour Cream Coffee Cake, 34, 35
Susan's Zucchini Bread, 33, 81
Tiramisu, 64, 65
Tres Leches Cake, 61, 62–63
Warm Gingerbread Pudding Cake,
    96, 97
candies, 150–57
    Chocolate Rum Balls, 154, 155
    Honeyed Fudge, 151, 153
    Mint Chocolate Truffles, 155, 156
    Peanut-Butterscotch Bites, 152, 153
    Pumpkin-Chocolate Truffles, 155, 157
Cappuccino Biscotti, 18, 19
caramel
    Caramel Sauce, 160, 161
    Rich Caramel Frosting, 79, 169
    Salty-Sweet Caramel Nut Bars, 12, 13
Caramelized Banana Bread Pudding, 91,
    92–93
Carrot Cupcakes, 37, 192
Chai Pots De Crème, 101, 102–3
cheese plate, 171, 172
cheesecakes
    "Almond Joy" Cheesecake, 58–59, 60
    Cheesecake Cupcakes, 43, 44
    Cookies-and-Cream Cheesecake
      Bars, 3, 6
    Creamy Vanilla Cheesecake, 56, 57
cherries
    Brandied Cherries, 67, 165
    Cherry Clafouti, 140, 141
    Cherry-Berry Stovetop Cobbler,
      142, 143
    Pear–Tart Cherry Crisp, 129, 132
chocolate
    Banana-Nutella Wontons, 138, 139
    Black-and-White Trifles, 88, 94–95
    Brownie Ice Cream Torte, 68, 69
    Chocolate–Chocolate Chip Cupcakes,
      43, 45

Chocolate Frosting, 43, 167
Chocolate-Peanut Butter Pie, 108–9, 110
Chocolate Rum Balls, 154, 155
chocolate tasting, 171
Coffee–Chocolate Chip Blondies, 3, 5
Dark Chocolate Pudding, 83, 85
Double Chocolate Croissant Bread
    Pudding, 90, 91
Flourless Chocolate Cake, 70–71, 73
Fudge Brownies, 1, 3
Geraldine's Chocolate-Date Cake, 48, 49
Honeyed Fudge, 151, 153
Hot Fudge Sauce, 159, 161
Mint Chocolate Truffles, 155, 156
Mocha Cream Pie, 120–21, 122
Molten Dark Chocolate Cakes, 66, 67
Orange-Scented Chocolate Chip
    Cookies, 8, 10
Pain au Chocolat, 173
Pumpkin-Chocolate Truffles, 155, 157
Silky Chocolate Nutella Mousse, 98, 101
S'mores Bars, 2, 3
Toblerone Brownies, 4, 25
Cinnamon-Hazelnut Shortbread, 24, 25
clafouti. *See also* pies, 140
Classic Rice Pudding, 85, 86
cobblers. *See also* fruit desserts
    Blackberry Cobbler, 135, 136
    Cherry-Berry Stovetop Cobbler, 142, 143
coconut
    "Almond Joy" Cheesecake, 58–59, 60
    Coconut Rice Pudding, 87, 88
    Great Big Coconut Cake, 50, 51
    Hello Dollies, 8, 9
coffee cakes. *See also* cakes
    Double Apple Streusel Coffee Cake, 34,
        38–39
    Sour Cream Coffee Cake, 34, 35
Coffee–Chocolate Chip Blondies, 3, 5
coffee flavored. *See also* espresso powder

Chocolate–Chocolate Chip Cupcakes,
    43, 45
Tiramisu, 64, 65
cookies. *See also* bars, 1
    Cappuccino Biscotti, 18, 19
    Cinnamon-Hazelnut Shortbread, 24, 25
    Cranberry Cornmeal Cookies, 27, 153
    Currant Scones, 28, 192
    Gingersnaps, 7, 8
    "Kitchen Sink" Oatmeal Cookies, 8, 29
    Mom's Mexican Wedding Cookies, 14, 15
    Orange-Scented Chocolate Chip
        Cookies, 8, 10
    Peanut Butter Cookies, 21, 23
    Rosemary Biscotti, 19, 20
    Sesame-Oat-Pecan Cookies, 15, 17
Cookies-and-Cream Cheesecake Bars, 3, 6
Cool Blueberry Soup, 126, 127
cranberries
    Cranberry Cornmeal Cookies, 27, 153
    Currant-Cranberry Spice Cake, 72,
        76–77
    Pistachio-Cranberry Bars, 25, 26
cream cheese. *See also* cheesecakes
    Cream Cheese Frosting, 43, 168
    Dottie's Deluxe Noodle Pudding, 99, 194
    Tiramisu, 64, 65
Creamy Vanilla Cheesecake, 56, 57
Crème Anglaise, 73, 166
crisps. *See also* fruit desserts
    Nectarine-Blueberry Crisp, 114, 115
    Pear–Tart Cherry Crisp, 129, 132
crumbles. *See also* fruit desserts, 128
cupcakes. *See also* cakes
    Carrot Cupcakes, 37, 192
    Cheesecake Cupcakes, 43, 44
    Chocolate–Chocolate Chip Cupcakes,
        43, 45
    Orange Cream Cupcakes, 42, 43
    Strawberry Ice Cream Cupcakes, 52, 53

White Chocolate–Strawberry Cupcakes, 40–41, 192

currants

Currant-Cranberry Spice Cake, 72, 76–77

Currant Scones, 28, 192

custards. *See* puddings

D

Dark Chocolate Pudding, 83, 85

dates. *See* Geraldine's Chocolate-Date Cake

Dottie's Deluxe Noodle Pudding, 99, 194

Double Apple Streusel Coffee Cake, 34, 38–39

Double Chocolate Croissant Bread Pudding, 90, 91

Drunken Pears Stuffed with Cookie Crumble, 146, 147

E

Elegant Apple Tartlets, 129, 130–31

espresso powder. *See also* coffee flavored

Cappuccino Biscotti, 18, 19

Coffee–Chocolate Chip Blondies, 3, 5

Hot Fudge Sauce, 159, 161

Mocha Cream Pie, 120–21, 122

F

Flourless Chocolate Cake, 70–71, 73

Fresh Berry Shortcakes, 111, 112–13

frostings, 158

Chocolate Frosting, 43, 167

Cream Cheese Frosting, 43, 168

Rich Caramel Frosting, 79, 169

fruit desserts, 104

Apple Crumble, 128, 129

Baked Apples, 117, 147

Banana-Nutella Wontons, 138, 139

Blackberry Cobbler, 135, 136

Cherry-Berry Stovetop Cobbler, 142, 143

Cool Blueberry Soup, 126, 127

Drunken Pears Stuffed with Cookie Crumble, 146, 147

Elegant Apple Tartlets, 129, 130–31

Fresh Berry Shortcakes, 111, 112–13

Grapefruit Granita, 118, 119

Lemon-Berry Semifreddo, 123, 124–25

Nectarine-Blueberry Crisp, 114, 115

Pear–Tart Cherry Crisp, 129, 132

Rustic Plum Gallette, 115, 116

Wine-Poached Peaches, 127, 148

Fudge Brownies, 1, 3

G

gallette. *See* Rustic Plum Gallette

Geraldine's Chocolate-Date Cake, 48, 49

ginger

Ginger-Bourbon Peach Sauce, 161, 170

Gingersnaps, 7, 8

Warm Gingerbread Pudding Cake, 96, 97

graham crackers

"Almond Joy" Cheesecake, 58–59, 60

Cappuccino Biscotti, 18, 19

Chocolate-Peanut Butter Pie, 108–9, 110

Creamy Vanilla Cheesecake, 56, 57

Hello Dollies, 8, 9

S'Mores Bars, 2, 3

Tipsy Key Lime Pie, 105, 106

Grapefruit Granita, 118, 119

Great Big Coconut Cake, 50, 51

H

hazelnuts. *See* Cinnamon-Hazelnut Shortbread; Nutella

Hello Dollies, 8, 9

Honeyed Fudge, 151, 153

Hot Fudge Sauce, 159, 161

K

Key limes. *See* Tipsy Key Lime Pie

"Kitchen Sink" Oatmeal Cookies, 8, 29

L

lemons
    Lemon-Berry Semifreddo, 123, 124–25
    "New Wave" Lemon Meringue Pie, 88,
        144–45
Lime-Glazed Citrus Tea Cakes, 46, 47

M

Maple Walnut Pie, 133, 134
mascarpone. *See* Tiramisu
Mint Chocolate Truffles, 155, 156
Mocha Cream Pie, 120–21, 122
Molten Dark Chocolate Cakes, 66, 67
Mom's Mexican Wedding Cookies, 14, 15
mousses. *See also* puddings
    Pumpkin Mousse, 100, 101
    Silky Chocolate Nutella Mousse, 98, 101

N

Nectarine-Blueberry Crisp, 114, 115
"New Wave" Lemon Meringue Pie, 88,
    144–45
no-bake desserts. *See also* candies
    Angel Food Cake with Macerated
        Strawberries, 173
    Black-and-White Trifles, 88, 94–95
    Brownie Ice Cream Torte, 68, 69
    Butterscotch Pudding, 84, 85
    cheese plate, 171, 172
    Cherry-Berry Stovetop Cobbler, 142, 143
    chocolate tasting, 171
    Classic Rice Pudding, 85, 86
    Cool Blueberry Soup, 126, 127
    Dark Chocolate Pudding, 83, 85
    Grapefruit Granita, 118, 119
    Lemon-Berry Semifreddo, 123, 124–25
    Pumpkin Mousse, 100, 101
    Silky Chocolate Nutella Mousse, 98, 194
sundaes, 173

Tiramisu, 64, 65
Wine-Poached Peaches, 127, 148
Yogurt Panna Cotta, 85, 89
Nutella
    Banana-Nutella Wontons, 138, 139
    Pain au Chocolat, 173
    Silky Chocolate Nutella Mousse, 98, 101
nuts. *See also* almonds; peanut butter;
    walnuts
    Banana Snack Cake, 78, 79
    Chocolate Rum Balls, 154, 155
    Cinnamon-Hazelnut Shortbread, 24, 25
    Mom's Mexican Wedding Cookies, 14, 15
    Orange-Scented Chocolate Chip
        Cookies, 8, 10
    Pecan Pie Bars, 11, 12
    Pistachio-Cranberry Bars, 25, 26
    Salty-Sweet Caramel Nut Bars, 12, 13
    Sesame-Oat-Pecan Cookies, 15, 17
    Sweet Potato Pie with Streusel
        Topping, 134, 137

O

oats
    Apple Crumble, 128, 129
    Baked Apples, 117, 147
    "Kitchen Sink" Oatmeal Cookies, 8, 29
    Peanut Butter and Jelly Bars, 22, 23
    Raspberry Jam Bars, 15, 16
    Sesame-Oat-Pecan Cookies, 15, 17
oranges
    Lime-Glazed Citrus Tea Cakes, 46, 47
    Orange Cream Cupcakes, 42, 43
    Orange-Scented Chocolate Chip
        Cookies, 8, 10
Oreos
    Chocolate Rum Balls, 154, 155
    Cookies-and-Cream Cheesecake Bars, 3, 6
    Mocha Cream Pie, 120–21, 122

P

Pain au Chocolat, 173

panna cotta. *See* puddings

peaches

 Ginger-Bourbon Peach Sauce, 161, 170

 Wine-Poached Peaches, 127, 148

peanut butter

 Chocolate–Peanut Butter Pie, 108–9, 110

 Peanut Butter and Banana Bread, 23, 80

 Peanut Butter and Jelly Bars, 22, 23

 Peanut Butter Cookies, 21, 23

 Peanut-Butterscotch Bites, 152, 153

pears

 Drunken Pears Stuffed with Cookie Crumble, 146, 147

 Pear–Tart Cherry Crisp, 132, 139

pecans

 Pecan Pie Bars, 11, 12

 Sesame-Oat-Pecan Cookies, 15, 17

Perfectly Simple Pound Cake, 31, 33

pies, 104, 105–11

 Buttermilk Pie, 106, 107

 Cherry Clafouti, 140, 141

 Chocolate–Peanut Butter Pie, 108–9, 110

 Maple Walnut Pie, 133, 134

 Mocha Cream Pie, 120–21, 122

 "New Wave" Lemon Meringue Pie, 88, 144–45

 Sweet Potato Pie with Streusel Topping, 134, 137

 Tipsy Key Lime Pie, 105, 106

pineapples

 Carrot Cupcakes, 37, 192

 Pineapple Upside-Down Cake, 54, 55

Pistachio-Cranberry Bars, 25, 26

plums. *See* Rustic Plum Gallette

pound cake. *See* cakes

puddings, 82–102

 Black-and-White Trifles, 88, 94–95

 Butterscotch Pudding, 84, 85

 Caramelized Banana Bread Pudding, 91, 92–93

 Chai Pots De Crème, 101, 102–3

 Classic Rice Pudding, 85, 86

 Coconut Rice Pudding, 87, 88

 Dark Chocolate Pudding, 83, 85

 Dottie's Deluxe Noodle Pudding, 99, 194

 Double Chocolate Croissant Bread Pudding, 90, 91

 Pumpkin Mousse, 100, 101

 Silky Chocolate Nutella Mousse, 98, 101

 Warm Gingerbread Pudding Cake, 96, 97

 Yogurt Panna Cotta, 85, 89

puff pastry. *See* Elegant Apple Tartlets

pumpkin

 Pumpkin Bread, 32, 33

 Pumpkin Mousse, 100, 101

 Pumpkin-Chocolate Truffles, 155, 157

R

raspberries

 Almond-Raspberry Cake, 74, 75

 Raspberry Buckle, 34, 36

 Raspberry Jam Bars, 15, 16

 Raspberry Sauce, 57, 162, 163

rice pudding

 Classic Rice Pudding, 85, 86

 Coconut Rice Pudding, 87, 88

Rich Caramel Frosting, 79, 169

Rosemary Biscotti, 19, 20

Rustic Plum Gallette, 115, 116

S

Salty-Sweet Caramel Nut Bars, 12, 13

sauces, 158

 Boozy Butterscotch Sauce, 161, 164

 Brandied Cherries, 67, 165

 Caramel Sauce, 160, 161

Crème Anglaise, 73, 166
Ginger-Bourbon Peach Sauce, 161, 170
Hot Fudge Sauce, 159, 161
Raspberry Sauce, 162, 163
scones. *See* currants
Sesame-Oat-Pecan Cookies, 15, 17
shortbread. *See* Cinnamon-Hazelnut
    Shortbread
shortcakes. *See* Fresh Berry Shortcakes
Silky Chocolate Nutella Mousse, 98, 101
Sour Cream Coffee Cake, 34, 35
strawberries
    Angel Food Cake with Macerated
        Strawberries, 173
    Black-and-White Trifles, 88, 94–95
    Fresh Berry Shortcakes, 111, 112–13
    Strawberry Ice Cream Cupcakes, 52, 53
    White Chocolate–Strawberry Cupcakes,
        40–41, 192
sundaes, 173
Susan's Zucchini Bread, 33, 81
Sweet Potato Pie with Streusel Topping,
    134, 137

T
tahini. *See* Sesame-Oat-Pecan Cookies
Tipsy Key Lime Pie, 105, 106
Tiramisu, 64, 65
Toblerone Brownies, 4, 25
Tres Leches Cake, 61, 62–63
trifles. *See* Black-and-White Trifles

truffles. *See also* candies
    Mint Chocolate Truffles, 155, 156
    Pumpkin-Chocolate Truffles, 155, 157

W
walnuts
    Carrot Cupcakes, 37, 192
    Coffee–Chocolate Chip Blondies, 3, 5
    Currant-Cranberry Spice Cake, 72, 76–77
    Fudge Brownies, 1, 3
    Hello Dollies, 8, 9
    Honeyed Fudge, 151, 153
    "Kitchen Sink" Oatmeal Cookies, 8, 29
    Maple Walnut Pie, 133, 134
    S'Mores Bars, 2, 3
    Toblerone Brownies, 4, 25
Warm Gingerbread Pudding Cake, 96, 97
white chocolate
    Cranberry Cornmeal Cookies, 27, 153
    White Chocolate–Strawberry Cupcakes,
        40–41, 192
Wine-Poached Peaches, 127, 148

Y
yogurt
    Cool Blueberry Soup, 126, 127
    Yogurt Panna Cotta, 85, 89

Z
zucchini. *See* Susan's Zucchini Bread

GENERAL INDEX

B

baking pans, 175–76
  greasing and flouring,
    188
  lining, 188
baking powder, 179
baking sheet, 176
baking soda, 180
baking terms, 185–86
baste, 185
beat, 185
Beranbaum, Rose Levy, 184
blender. *See* food
  processor
blind-bake, 185
bowls, mixing, 175
box grater, 176
butter, 180

C

cacao. *See* chocolate
Cake Bible (Beranbaum),
  184
candied ginger. *See*
  crystalized ginger
can opener, 176
chef's knife, 175

chocolate, 180–81
  chopping and melting, 187
  types of, 180–81
cinnamon, 183
citrus fruit, zesting, 191
cocoa powder. *See also*
  chocolate
  weight per cup, 184
condensed milk, 181–82
cookies, crushing, 187–88
cornmeal, 182
cornstarch, 182
cream, 183
  half-and-half, 182
  scalding, 186
  whipping, 190
cream (baking term), 185
crystalized ginger, 182
cups, measuring, 174–75
cut in, 185
cutting boards, 177

D

dry ingredients. *See also*
  specific ingredients
  measuring, 188–89
  sifting, 189

E

eggs, 182
  separating, 189
  whipping whites, 191
electric mixer, 174

F

flour, 179
  weight per cup, 184
foil, lining pan with, 188
fold, 185–86
food processor, 178
  crushing cookies,
    187–88
  pulse and puree, 186

G

gelatin, 182
ginger, crystalized, 182
grater, 176

H

heavy cream. *See* cream
honey, 183

I

ice cream scoop, 17, 178

ingredients. *See also* specific
    ingredients, 179–84
    chocolate, 180–81
    measuring dry, 188–89
    sugar, 183–84
    weights of, 184

K

kitchen scale, 178
knives, 175

M

measuring cups, 174–75
measuring spoons, 175
    measuring dry ingredi-
        ents, 188–89
melon baller, 178
Microplane grater, 176
milk, 183
    condensed, 181–82
    half-and-half, 182
    scald, 186
mixer, 174
mixing bowls, 175
molasses, 183

N

nutmeg, 183
nuts
    chopping, 187
    toasting, 190

P

pans
    baking, 175–76
    greasing and flouring, 188
    lining, 188
    saucepan, 177
parchment, lining pan
    with, 188
paring knife, 175
pastry brush, 178
pastry cutter, 177–78
pulse, 186
puree, 186

R

racks, cooling, 177
rasp grater, 176
reduce, 186
rolling pin, 178
room temperature, 186

S

salt, 183
saucepan, 177
scald, 186
scale, kitchen, 178
score, 186
serrated knife, 175
sieve, fine-mesh, 177
sift, 186, 189
simmer, 186

spatula
    flexible, 176
    offset, 178
spices, 183
spoons
    measuring, 175
    wooden, 176
steep, 186
sugar, 183–84
    weight per cup, 184

T

tapioca, 184
tools, baking, 174–78

V

vanilla extract, 184
vegetable peeler, 177

W

water bath, 186
whipping cream, 183
wire cooling rack, 177
wire whisk, 176–77
wooden spoons, 176

Z

zest, 186, 191